The
RICH HERITAGE
of
Panama City
Beach
and
Communities of
BAY COUNTY

By MARLENE WOMACK

Business Biographies by
PAUL COX

Reflections and Recollections by
JACK MASHBURN

(From Left to Right)

Denise Mass, Office Assistant

Don Oliver, Information Specialist

Bertie Reynolds, V.P. Hospitality & Sales

Joyce Kidd, Receptionist/Information Specialist

Martha Gorsline, Information Specialist

Debi Parish Knight, President

Norma Molloy, V.P. of Sales & Marketing

Tom Mixon, V.P. Membership Services

Chamber Breakfast Seminar

Business Expo-98, Salute to Hollywood

Hospitality Appreciation Party-2000

P. C. 15—Sun Bathing, Long Beach Resort, Panama City, Fla.

Foreword

On behalf of the Panama City Beaches Chamber of Commerce, I am pleased to present to you The Rich Heritage of Panama City Beaches and Communities of Bay County. What better title could describe a rich heritage founded in tourism that has made us one of the leading destinations in the country.

Today, Bay County continues to weave its future through expansions of existing manufacturers, attracting new industry, and encouraging the entrepreneurial spirit of a strong work force. Panama City Beach, the second auto destination in the State of Florida is playing a leading role in the rapid expansion of one of the fastest growth areas in the United States.

From beautiful crystal emerald water, to soft snow-white beaches, Bay County beckons those who have the pioneer spirit seeking new opportunities to build a better tomorrow for their families.

The Panama City Beaches Chamber of Commerce is pleased to sponsor this book with Gordon Sorrell and Community Heritage Publications. We know that it will provide a glimpse at what makes our community unique for those who live, work and visit here. Our unique tapestry will continue to be woven by the people of Bay County, to whom we dedicate this book.

Debi Parish Knight
President

Debi Parish Knight

By 1917 women had shed the skirts and bloomers from their bathing suits, along with the customary stockings, revealing their bare legs. Men and women donned similar styled suits, made of lighter, thinner fabrics. When some of the old-timers complained and stared, as this woman seems to do, they were informed, "This is the age of equality!"

Preface

*H*ere is the first book on Panama City Beach!

Through these pages you'll read stories about the way Panama City Beach went from a pristine unknown location of glistening white beaches, clear emerald-green water and towering sand dunes to a thriving metropolis and year-round vacation land over the course of the last 75 years.

You'll follow the Indians who were the beaches' first tourists and learn about pirates who buried treasure. You'll experience salt making on the desolate bay and lakeshores during the Civil War.

You'll explore the early settlements on the fringes of the beaches at the turn of the century.

You'll read about early fishing and the discovery of an Old Spanish galleon buried deep in the sand.

You'll travel to the bottom of the Gulf to Florida's 6th underwater archaeological preserve, the steamship Tarpon.

Some of the beaches, such as Sunnyside and Long Beach, evolved from 80 to 160 acre homesteads in the 1920s at a cost of $1.25 an acre. Other homesteaders on the beaches were Manning Vickers, J.T. Harper, Harry Calley, Emory and John Hobbs and Wallace Laird. But until that time most land from Hathaway Bridge to Phillips Inlet was simply known as "the Beaches."

Then many began enjoying Brown's Beach on the Gulf, south of Grand Lagoon. Hubert Brown and W.W. Sharpless developed Long Beach. In 1936 Gid Thomas and Claudia and Angus Pledger opened tiny Panama City Beach while M.E. McCorquodale promoted Sunnyside.

Several other communities such as Edgewater Gulf Beach, Laguna Beach and West Panama City Beach followed. The Panama City Beach that we know of today did not come into being until 1970 when several of the old communities merged to form the new City of Panama City Beach.

The actual "bridge to bridge" dream of early developers has not yet come to pass. When people cross Phillips Inlet heading east or Hathaway Bridge traveling west, they believe they're in Panama City Beach. But they are really in "the County."

The city itself extends only about eight miles from near DeLuna Place on the west to about Joan Avenue on the east. The Panama City Beach Parkway (Back Beach Road) and Hutchison Boulevard (Middle Beach Road) serve as boundaries to the north, although some properties and subdivisions above these roads are included in the city.

But Panama City Beach is growing and annexations occur almost every month.

Marlene Womack

THE RICH HERITAGE OF PANAMA CITY BEACH AND COMMUNITIES OF BAY COUNTY

Published By:
Community Heritage Publications
8608 Harvest Ridge Drive
Montgomery, Alabama 36116
(334) 244-1085

Publisher:
Gordon Sorrell

Published with the Cooperation and Assistance of the Panama City Beaches Chamber of Commerce

Executive Editor:
Donnie Sorrell

Written By:
Marlene Womack

Book and Dust Jacket Layout and Design By:
Scott C. Andrews
Creative Director

Special Photography By:
Tom Mason

Reflections and Recollections By:
Jack Mashburn

Business Biographies By:
Paul Cox

Marketing Associates:
Craig Barrows, Bernie Barbuti, Jack Mashburn

A Limited Edition Printing of the Heritage Book Series
By Gordon Sorrell and Community Heritage Publications

THE HERITAGE BOOK DEDICATION

This book is respectfully dedicated to the memory of the late Hank Swicord II, long-time Panama City Beach businessman, civic and community leader. Hank was born in Samoset, Florida and grew up in Georgia. He was educated in Georgia and South Carolina, served his country in World War II and the Korean War and was decorated for his service. Moving to Panama City Beach in 1959, Hank established himself in business as owner and operator of Flagala Hardware and Flagala Construction for many years. Although recognized as an astute businessman, Hank's community involvement on the Beach was legendary. Those who knew him best say his quiet work behind the scenes encouraging and guiding young people, as well as his humanitarian traits, showed the real depth of his personality and dedication to the community.

Hank was a charter member of the Beach Optimist Club and was instrumental in the founding of the Panama City Beaches Chamber of Commerce, serving as that organization's first president and continuing his support for the Chamber as an active member. The Chamber honored him in July 2000 with its Pioneer Award for community service. Through Flagala Hardware, Swicord sponsored youth baseball teams and he was also an active supporter of the Boy Scouts.

Hank worked tirelessly for the betterment and advancement of his community, not afraid to speak his mind on issues he believed in, not afraid to offer a helping hand to those who needed one. Thank you Hank, for being such a big part of the rich heritage of Panama City Beach.

The writers, the Panama City Beaches Chamber of Commerce and the Publisher gratefully acknowledge the assitance of Bronwen DuKate and Robert W. Stewart as proofreaders. Their timely assistance is appreciated.

Table of Contents

OSCEOLA

Osceola, a famous leader of the Seminole Indians, was born about 1803 on the Tallapoosa River in the Creek country of what is now Georgia. His name, "Asi-Yahola," was derived from the Indians' well-known black drink made from the leaves of the yaupon plant.

He daringly fought the United States, determined to keep the Seminoles a free people able to retain possession of their land.

Osceola became the most heroic figure in the Indian Wars when he was captured under an American flag of truce and imprisoned by Gen. T.S. Jesup. He died in 1838 at Ft. Moultrie, Charleston, S.C.

THE LEGEND OF SHELL POINT

When the first white settlers came to this area in the early 1800s, huge piles of oyster shells stood at several locations around St. Andrew Bay. But Shell Point, at the entrance to West Bay, seemed to attract the most attention.

Here, a great pile of oyster shells extended far into the water. These shells dated back hundreds of years to the days when the Indians came to the bay to hunt and fish, as the area's first tourists. During meetings and feasts they roasted their favorite mollusks over fires, then tossed the shells on the tall heap. Legend has it that long after the red men were driven from Florida, one settler became so fascinated with this commanding location that he built a home on the top of the oyster shells at the point.

But the white man was never happy living at this location because the spirits of dead Indian braves haunted him during the night with sounds like the beating of drums.

Finally, the settler abandoned the property; unable to tolerate the "thump, thump" noises any longer. The house fell into ruins, and the county excavated the pile of oysters to build many of the early roads.

Today, Shell Point remains an isolated site frequented by the occasional boater and fisherman. Some who have camped here say they can still hear faint drum-like sounds deep in the night.

PART I

THE PAST, PRESENT AND FUTURE OF PANAMA CITY BEACH

and Communities of Bay County

We all have a vested interest in remembering the past, celebrating the present and inspiring the future. The past asks only to be remembered, the present seeks only to be enjoyed. The future, however, requires dedicated planning with an inspired vision.

—Jack Mashburn

THE EARLY YEARS

For hundreds of years the location we know as Panama City Beach remained a wild stretch of wind, surf and sand. Since no towns existed along its shores, the entire Bay County area of today was called St. Andrew Bay, a name given by 16th century Spanish explorers.

Panfilo de Narvaez, Cabeca de Vaca, Hernando de Soto and Francisco Maldonado visited Northwest Florida during the Spanish conquest years, along with several other explorers. Although some may have come ashore in this area, no proof exists with many of their reports sketchy at best.

The Spanish did give St. Andrew Bay its name as "St. Andre" and "St. Andreas." They also named locations such as St. Joseph, St. Vincent Island, St. George Island and St. Marks. But overall their efforts were concentrated more on St. Marks and Pensacola, the older settlements of the Northern Gulf Coast.

Sea captains plying the Gulf noticed the narrow entrance channel to St. Andrew Bay, now known as Old Pass or East Pass. But they believed it led to a river of little importance and sailed by.

During the 1700s, France, England and Spain all fought for possession of Florida. Spanish schooners fished off what is now Panama City Beach. They cured their catch aboard ship then transported this dried fish to Havana.

In 1717, the French established a fort, named Crevecoeur, in the vicinity of Mexico Beach. But after the Spanish discovered this small outpost, the French abandoned the fort rather than risk a confrontation with their enemies.

Indians and Runaway Slaves

In the early 1800s, large numbers of Creek and Seminole Indians fled the hatred of the white men in Georgia and Alabama. They made their way into Florida where the English and Spanish provided them supplies and protection. Many slaves also escaped from these states for the freedom of the deep, undisturbed forests.

After making a name for himself in the Creek War, at Pensacola and New Orleans, General Andrew Jackson stormed into Florida in 1818 determined to bring an end to the coddling of these two races.

Territorial Days & Statehood

In 1821 after American Secretary of State John Q. Adams and Spanish Minister Luis de Onis reached an agreement and signed the Adams-Onis treaty, Florida became a United States territory, with Jackson its first territorial governor.

Communities were established at Econfina, Bay Head, Austerlitz (Parker) and St. Andrews during this era.

In the 1830s, the St. Andrews Bay Land Co., organized by Jackson County businessmen, took on the promotion of St. Andrews, located then along what is now Beach Drive, between Lake Caroline and Frankford Avenue.

Florida became a state on March 3, 1845.

During the antebellum days, Old Town, St. Andrews was popular as a seaside resort frequented in summer by families from Jackson County, Alabama and Georgia. Swimming and strolling along the beach were two favorite pastimes. After their maids scared the crabs away, the girls and women bathed along what is now Beach Drive, while the boys and men swam separately farther west at Buena Vista Point.

At Old Town, a long wooden dock extended out into the bay where visitors promenaded in their fancy clothes and listened to music played in the evenings.

The Civil War

The Civil War affected all of the state as it did everyone living above and below the Mason Dixon line. Early in the war, President Abraham Lincoln imposed a blockade of all Southern ports, which ended the importation of salt desperately needed in soldiers' diets and to preserve food since they had no refrigeration.

St. Andrew Bay became one of the most well known locations in Florida for its salt makers who received exemption from conscription into the Confederacy if they produced 20 bushels of salt per day. Federal troops established their headquarters on Hurricane Island, which existed then in the Old Pass. Besides destroying hundreds of salt making camps, the Union men attempted to catch supply ships running the blockade.

After being warned not to venture ashore, a group of Yankees made the fatal mistake of trying to obtain water from the Tavern Spring at Old Town on March 20, 1863. In the skirmish that ensued, Confederates killed two Yankees and mortally wounded four others. But the Yankees retaliated in December 1863 by torching all 32 homes that existed in Old Town.

After the war a fledgling fishing industry began to develop around the bay during the spring and fall months of the year. The fishermen used drag seines. Spanish mackerel, mullet, pompano, trout, redfish, sheepshead and bluefish were the main fish caught. Since ice was not manufactured around St. Andrew Bay until the early 1900s, all fish had to be consumed fresh or salted soon after they were caught.

RECOLLECTIONS & MEMORIES BY JACK MASHBURN

Oldest Family Reunion in the United States The Mashburn Family

"MY ROOTS EXTEND BACK TO THE FIRST MASHBURNS, JAMES MANON AND CLARA REBECCA SEALY, WHO CAME FROM GADSDEN COUNTY TO THE ECONFINA AREA AROUND 1850. THEY SETTLED ON 200 ACRES OF RICH FARM LAND.

"MY GREAT-GRANDFATHER MASHBURN RAISED LARGE CROPS OF TOBACCO, CORN AND COTTON WITH THE HELP OF HIS CHILDREN AND SLAVES. HE TRANSPORTED THESE CROPS BY WAGON DOWN TO THE CEDAR CREEK AND BEAR CREEK LANDINGS WHERE THEY WERE SHIPPED TO PORTS ALONG THE GULF COAST.

"JAMES MANON DIED IN 1859 AT THE AGE OF 38 FROM A STROKE WHILE ROOFING A HOUSE. HE WAS BURIED ON HIS PLANTATION, WHICH WAS THE CUSTOM THEN, LEAVING MY GREAT-GRANDMOTHER WITH 9 CHILDREN AND 6 MONTHS PREGNANT ALONE IN THESE NEW LANDS. HIS BURIAL PLACE BECAME PART OF THE MASHBURN CEMETERY OFF MASHBURN ROAD.

"TWO OF THE MASHBURNS FOUGHT ON OPPOSITE SIDES DURING THE CIVIL WAR, AND THEY WERE BROTHERS. RICHARD, JAMES MANON'S OLDEST SON, JOINED THE CONFEDERATE FORCES AT APALACHICOLA. BUT STEPHEN, A TEEN ABOUT 18 WHO SOME SAY FEARED CONSCRIPTION INTO THE CONFEDERACY, SLIPPED OFF TO BAY HEAD, A FEW MILES DOWN THE CREEK. HE BORROWED A SMALL BOAT AND ROWED AROUND ST. ANDREWS BAY TO HURRICANE ISLAND, WHICH WAS THE HEADQUARTERS OF THE YANKEES. HE WAVED A WHITE FLAG, THEN THEY TOOK HIM TO KEY WEST WHERE HE JOINED AND SERVED WITH THE 2ND CALVARY OF THE UNION ARMY FROM FLORIDA.

"STEPHEN WAS DISCHARGED AT THE END OF THE WAR. AFTER HE CAME HOME TO ECONFINA ONLY HIS MOTHER AND FEW OTHERS TALKED TO HIM, BUT WITHIN A YEAR HE WAS ACCEPTED BACK INTO THE FAMILY, STEPHEN MASHBURN WAS MY GRANDFATHER.

"BUT NO ONE KNEW ANYTHING ABOUT RICHARD. HE HAD BEEN CAPTURED ON MAY 28, 1864 NEAR DALLAS, GA. AND HELD A PRISONER AT ROCK ISLAND PRISON CAMP IN ILLINOIS. IT TOOK RICHARD A WHOLE YEAR TO GET HOME, AND HE WALKED MOST OF THE WAY. HE REACHED HOME ON MAY 28, 1866, ONE YEAR TO THE DAY OF HIS RELEASE FROM ROCK ISLAND PRISON IN ILLINOIS.

"WHEN HE GOT HOME HIS FAMILY HELD A BIG CELEBRATION. THAT WAS THE BEGINNING OF THE MASHBURN'S ANNUAL REUNION. EVERY FOURTH SATURDAY IN MAY WE HAVE RICHARD B. MASHBURN MEMORIAL PICNIC AND THE ANNUAL FAMILY REUNION. THIS REUNION IS ONE OF THE OLDEST CONTINUOUS REUNIONS IN THE UNITED STATES. MAY 27, 2000 MARKED THE 135TH CONTINUOUS FAMILY REUNION."

—J.M.

The St. Andrews Bay Railroad, Land & Mining Co., headquartered in Cincinnati, Ohio, undertook a nationwide advertising campaign to sell 20,000 acres in and around St. Andrew Bay.

The colorful advertisements, which depicted lovely women plucking succulent oranges in groves, did attract many families who remained in St. Andrews. Others struck out for different sections of the bay, taking up homesteads and forming their own communities.

The development company planned to construct a railroad to the bay that connected with the L&N. But the company's financial difficulties caused the railroad and the St. Andrews project to fail. With the St. Andrew Bay area protected by century-old forests at that time, newcomers could actually grow citrus trees and a variety of vegetables then. But when the severe freezes came in the mid-1890s the citrus industry all but died in North Florida and moved farther south.

The Late 1800s

When adventurer Nathaniel H. Bishop made his way east across the Northwest Florida Coast in 1876, he met two families living at the community of West Bay. One man told Bishop about seeing 16 deer that morning and offered him half a hindquarter from the deer he killed.

As late as 1880, the government owned 99% of the land in Florida.

In 1883, the completion of the Louisville & Nashville Railroad, which began as the Pensacola & Atlantic, opened this vast area for development.

In 1907, the first bank in this entire area opened at the corner of 10th St. and Beck Avenue in St. Andrews. J.H. Drummond served as the bank's president and F. Bullock as cashier. St. Andrews was experiencing a rebirth at that time. Drummond intended to make St. Andrews a thriving seaport. Numerous stores and businesses lined the streets. In the 1930s, a second story was added to the bank building. Today the old bank is the site of a police substation.

THE SPELLING OF ST. ANDREWS

Over the past 200 years, three different spellings have been used for "St. Andrews." St. Andrews as now printed, St. Andrew's and St. Andrew. Early visitors knew the location as St. Andrews, but the Post Office listed the town as St. Andrew's, and then in 1902 changed the spelling to "St. Andrew."

The bay was called St. Andrews until 1930, when it became "St. Andrew Bay."

Although residents slowly converted to spelling their town and bay without the "s," most businesses and organizations founded after 1900 continued to incorporate "St. Andrews" as part of their name. And now with the revitalization of St. Andrew, many people have returned to calling the town its original name – "St. Andrews."

Other New Communities

As a result of the Cincinnati Company's advertisement of this area, many new communities were established around the bay. Some of these were Farmdale, Belle Isle, Auburn, San Blas, Cromanton, Redfish Point and Beacon Beach on what is now Tyndall Air Force Base. Then along North Bay stood Tompkins, High Point, Bay Head, Gay, and Southport to name some of the communities.

Development of Millville, Panama City and St. Andrews

In the late 1880s, early homesteaders Samuel J. Erwin, G.B. Thompson, Clark B. Slade, C.J. Demorest and G.W. Jenks

attempted to promote "Floriopolis," "Park Resort" and "Harrison," all early names for the town that would become Panama City.

With visions of making old Harrison the main shipping port to the Panama Canal, which was under construction at that time, A.B. Steele began building his Atlanta & St. Andrews Bay Railway to the bay in 1905. In the company of G.M. West, a developer of the town, and others, Steele suggested "Panama City" as the new name for Harrison to call attention to it and the canal.

In the late 1890s, French Canadian Henry Bovis with lumber interests in Bagdad, Florida built a sawmill at the head of Watson Bayou and called it the St. Andrews Lumber Co. Millville, founded by W.W. Holmes, flourished as mill workers flooded into town for job openings. A German syndicate purchased the mill about 1902 and renamed it the German American Lumber Co. By then Millville was well on its way to becoming the largest town in this area.

J.H. Drummond, a banker and developer, took over the rebirth and promotion of St. Andrews and became its first mayor. Steele finally brought his A. & St. A.B. R.W. into Panama City in June 1908, putting Panama City on the map.

W.H. Lynn, a developer from New York, established a colony for Northern veterans of the Civil War at Lynn Haven in 1911. At the same time, workmen completed the second railway to the bay, known as the Birmingham, Columbus & St. Andrews Bay Railroad, from Chipley to Southport.

Creation of Bay County

All this time, Bay County was part of Washington County and the location known as the East Peninsula, now Tyndall AFB, belonged to Calhoun County. Those wishing to trans-

act courthouse business were forced to make the long two or three-day journey to either Vernon or Blountstown, the county seats.

After discussing the need for years, R.L. McKenzie, a Panama City mayor and past legislator, and Representative L.H. Howell decided the time was right to carve out a new county. Hundreds celebrated the creation of Bay County on July 1, 1913. After a hotly contested vote, Panama City became the new county seat in 1914.

During World War I, Millville received a contract to build government barges, and

When the train belonging to the Atlanta & St. Andrews Bay Railway, now the Bay Line, reached Panama City from Dothan, passengers could walk to town or ride a launch to St. Andrews, Lynn Haven or Millville. In the photo, this wooden walkway leads to the Pines Hotel, which stood near the depot at Sixth Street and Beach Drive.

51 soldiers were brought in to protect the important Millville Shipyard. The government seized the German American Lumber Co. under the Trading With the Enemy Act during the war and operated it as the American Lumber Co.

Once the fighting ended, sawmill owner W.C. Sherman and the "banana king," Minor C. Keith, of the United Fruit Co. purchased the American Lumber Co. and renamed it the St. Andrews Bay Lumber Co. This concern became one of this area's largest employers in the 1920s. It also furnished electricity to Panama City and other communities.

Panama City's Beach Drive looked much different in the early 1900s than it does today with its shaded roadway and long line of fine homes running along the bay. Hurricanes sometimes washed away or changed the shoreline on this section between Panama City and St. Andrews. After the railroad spur closed in St. Andrews, a lot of trucks used this road to carry fresh fish from St. Andrews to the railroad depot in Panama City.

Minor C. Keith, owner of the Bay Line Railroad for several years, built the Lynn Haven Hotel in 1919 to attract more tourists to Lynn Haven. The hotel stood along the beach, west of the Lynn Haven-Southport Bridge. From the hotel, guests could swim in the bay or enjoy fishing, oystering or boating on North Bay.

When the Bay County Courthouse was completed in 1914, it sported a dome and clock. But a fire in December 1920 destroyed all but its outside walls. The courthouse was rebuilt. In 1963, the Bay County Courthouse was the site of the landmark Clarence Earl Gideon case after the U.S. Supreme Court granted every man the right to have a lawyer represent him in court. Fred Turner of Panama City served as Gideon's attorney.

Women in long white dresses and men in black suits gathered in what is now McKenzie Park to celebrate the creation of Bay County on July 1, 1913. Spanish moss swayed in the gentle breeze and a clear, cold spring bubbled up from the ground at the edge of the park. At noon, the crowd dined on beeves roasted over hot coals, fried mullet, sliced tomatoes, lemonade, coffee, along with an assortment of salads and desserts.

The Panama City Beach Hotel typified the two-story wooden structures popular until after WWII. Visitors either rented rooms in the hotel or cottages along the beach. Gulf breezes cooled both places. Guests delighted in opening their windows and listening to the breaking waves at night. After the war, when Panama City Beach began to grow, the name "motel" made its way east from California to the Northern Gulf Coast. Photo circa 1950.

Bathing Beaches

Then, as now, people were drawn to this area's magnificent beaches. Places popular for bathing at the turn of the century were Cromanton, across the bay from Parker; Millville; Parker; St. Andrews; and Lynn Haven. At that time all these beaches contained beautiful white sand and the clear water was free from any forms of pollution. In Millville young boys dove down deep to retrieve silver and gold coins tossed overboard for them by passengers on the Tarpon and other vessels.

In the early 1900s, Panama City boasted several fine two-story wooden hotels where tourists came to spend a few days or weeks. The pavilion at Lands End (eastern end of Shell Island) attracted large crowds of excursioners from Dothan for a day of sun and fun.

Those few daring enough to venture to Panama City Beach either crossed by ferry where Hathaway Bridge now stands or took the long way round through the town of West Bay. The only beach with any type development at all was Brown's Beach, which stood somewhat east of where Thomas Drive curves west to run along the Gulf. Those going to that location were advised to arrive early or they would have a very long walk to reach the Gulf. The beach contained no concession stands but still the crowds came. When they left, many faced the task of digging their vehicles out of the sand.

Building Boom of the 1920s

Bay County, like all of Florida, boomed during the real estate fever that raged all over the state in the mid-1920s. Sherman constructed his ten-story Dixie Sherman Hotel, the county's first high-rise, with a "roof garden" on top; and the Panama Country Club golf course near Lynn Haven. H.L. Sudduth, developer of the Cove, built the Cove Hotel, which touted a beautiful bayside beach along with a kiddies' pool.

Bay High, the first county high school opened in 1926; Evangelist Bob Jones established his first college at College Point in 1927; and Seminole Hills, a 35,000 acre plantation offered investors a chance to grow pecans, Satsuma oranges, grapes and blueberries.

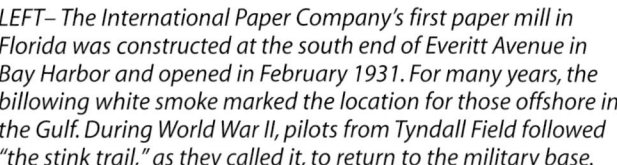

LEFT– The International Paper Company's first paper mill in Florida was constructed at the south end of Everitt Avenue in Bay Harbor and opened in February 1931. For many years, the billowing white smoke marked the location for those offshore in the Gulf. During World War II, pilots from Tyndall Field followed "the stink trail," as they called it, to return to the military base.

James Manon Mashburn and others built this log school in 1857 at Sulfur Springs, Econfina Creek. The school was used until the early 1900s, then burnt in 1929. Johnny Cox, appears in this photo.

LEFT– In April 1970, many gathered to watch the implosion of the Dixie Sherman Hotel, which stood at the northeast corner of Fifth Street and Jenks Avenue. The Dixie Sherman, built in 1925-1926, was this area's first high rise. During WWII, the hotel's roof garden attracted many soldiers and their sweethearts. From this vantage point, they could scan the Gulf and the horizon and the war seemed far away. The downtown Panama City Post Office and the Panama City News Herald building can be seen on opposite street corners.

Bay High School is shown under construction in 1926, the same year it opened on sand and clay covered Harrison Avenue. The site was considered far from town, which was concentrated more on lower Harrison Avenue at that time. Flooding proved to be a problem east of the school. The water rose so high in periods of heavy rain that residents traversed this location in boats.

RECOLLECTIONS & MEMORIES BY JACK MASHBURN

The Early Years

"MY FATHER, MANSEL MASHBURN, ALWAYS TOLD ME IF YOU DON'T DO SOMETHING FOR OTHERS YOU REALLY DON'T JUSTIFY THE TIME AND SPACE YOU TAKE UP ON THIS EARTH. MY PERSONAL PHILOSOPHY IS THAT SERVICE TO OTHERS IS THE PRICE WE PAY FOR MEMBERSHIP TO THE HUMAN RACE ON THIS WONDERFUL PLANET WE CALL MOTHER EARTH.

"MY FATHER RAISED NINE OF US ON A 40-ACRE PEA PATCH ON CAMP FLOWERS ROAD THAT HE LOVINGLY REFERRED TO AS A FARM.

"THE NINE CHILDREN IN MY FAMILY WERE PRETTY WELL SPACED OUT AND THERE ARE ONLY TWO SURVIVORS AT THIS TIME, MYSELF AND A HALF-SISTER WHO LIVES WITH ME ON THE FARM, ABOUT FIVE MILES OFF HIGHWAY 231.

"MY OLDER BROTHER, M.M. MASHBURN, DIED IN 1989 WHEN HE RAN HIS PICKUP TRUCK INTO A TRACTOR TRAILER NEAR HIS HOME.

"YES, I WAS BORN AND RAISED HERE. I OFTEN SAY I CHOSE THE RIGHT FATHER WHEN I WAS BORN. HE WAS 59 YEARS OLD WHEN I GOT HERE, AND I WAS FORTUNATE ENOUGH TO BE BORN WITH MY RIGHT HAND OFF.

"IN THOSE DAYS WE PICKED PEAS IN BASKETS, AND I TRIED TO GET OUT OF WORK BECAUSE I DIDN'T HAVE A RIGHT HAND. BUT MY FATHER ASSIGNED ME THE SAME NUMBER OF BASKETS THAT EVERYBODY ELSE HAD, AND I PICKED TWICE AS FAST WITH THE ONE HAND TO MAKE UP THE DIFFERENCE.

"I GREW UP BELIEVING I COULD DO ANYTHING. I LEARNED TO SHOOT A GUN WHEN I WAS ABOUT SIX YEARS OLD, AND I KILLED MY FIRST WILD TURKEY WHEN I WAS NINE. I RAISED BLACK AND TAN COON HOUNDS, AND I CAUGHT LIVE ALLIGATORS AND WILD HOGS. I WOULD DO JUST ABOUT ANYTHING TO RAISE A DOLLAR.

"DURING MY CHILDHOOD I TOUGHENED THE NUB OF MY RIGHT HAND BY POUNDING IN A SAND BOX. MY MOTHER WOULD HAVE TURNED ME INTO A CRIPPLE IF MY DAD HAD LET HER. WHEN I TOLD HER I WAS GOING TO PLAY FOOTBALL AT BAY HIGH, MY DAD TOLD HER I COULD DO ANYTHING THAT I WANTED TO.

"I PLAYED LINE BACKER AND CENTER FOR BAY. LATER I PLAYED IN A SEMI-PRO LEAGUE IN PANAMA CITY.

FOR TWO YEARS. THAT WAS BETWEEN 1950-1951. I ALSO PLAYED BASEBALL AND PITCHED FOR A SEMI-PRO TEAM CALLED THE "SEAHAWKS."

—J.M.

ABOVE –These children ride in the decorated wagon of J.T. Sapp. They are part of the parade that supported state prohibition laws, a hot item in the early 1900s. Herbert Sapp, at the front of the wagon, holds the sign.

First Bridges

After the opening of the Old Spanish Trail, U.S. 90, in the 1920s, the county pushed for a north-south connection to this new highway that crossed Florida near the Alabama line. The first wooden span between Lynn Haven and Southport was completed in 1925 and became known as the North Bay Bridge. It extended from Wisconsin Avenue in Lynn Haven to Grassy Point in Southport.

Panama City, St. Andrews and Millville continued as serparate towns. Then in a surprise move to attract more businesses to the area, legislators incorporated St. Andrews and Millville into Panama City in 1926, while irate residents grumbled over the loss of their towns' identities.

Talk of "bridging the east and west bays" began after World War I. The Pensacola Journal's F.L. Mayes championed the construction of the Coastal Highway, now US 98, which would run along the Gulf and pass over these spans. Through his brother-in-law, Ed Ball, A.I. Dupont acquired vast acreage in Northwest Florida. Dupont knew it would take roads and bridges to open this section. He served as president of the Gulf Coast Highway Association. Sections of the Coastal Highway were completed with the help of mules in 1929, along with DuPont Bridge,

The two Hathaway bridges extend side by side in this photo shot from the west. The new bridge on the left opened in 1959, the old bridge in 1929. Workmen cut the center span from the old bridge and it served as a popular fishing place for decades. When it became too great a liability for the county, it was removed in the 1980s.

which opened in April 1929, and Hathaway Bridge, in May 1929. Other sections of the roadway opened slowly in the early 1930s.

To cross either of these bridges the toll was 50 cents plus 10 cents for each additional passenger. Many hid in the trunks of the vehicles rather than pay the dime fee.

Then Panama City Beach began attracting the beachgoers and bathers, most of whom until that time either went to the Pavilion on the Gulf Beach or the beaches in Panama City.

RECOLLECTIONS *&* MEMORIES BY JACK MASHBURN

Old Hathaway Bridge

"WHEN A SHIP CAME TOWARD THE OLD BRIDGE IT HAD TO SWING OUT, NOT UP. OCCASIONALLY IT WOULD LOCK IN AN OPEN POSITION AND PEOPLE HAD TO WAIT A LONG TIME UNTIL IT WAS FIXED. I HAVE MANY BAD MEMORIES OF WAITING FOR THAT THING TO CLOSE.

"BEFORE THE BRIDGE STARTED TO SWING OUT THEY HAD A RED LIGHT UP BUT NOT AT THE END, SO TRAFFIC COULD NOT SEE THE LIGHT UNTIL THEY WERE NEAR THE CENTER.

"SOMEBODY APPROACHING FROM EACH END REALLY DIDN'T KNOW IF THE BRIDGE WAS OPEN OR CLOSED. ONE TIME A FRIEND OF MINE WAS SITTING THERE WAITING FOR THE BRIDGE WITH HIS CAR LIGHTS OFF BECAUSE HE KNEW HE'D BE THERE AWHILE. WELL, THE NEXT CAR DIDN'T SEE HIM AND KNOCKED HIM INTO THE WATER AND KILLED HIM. SO I GOT ON THE STATE DEPARTMENT OF TRANSPORTATION AND HAD THEM PUT A FLASHING RED LIGHT ON EITHER END OF THE BRIDGE AND RUN ELECTRIC LINES ALONG IT. THIS, AT LEAST, WARNED PEOPLE SO THEY COULD SEE FROM THE DISTANCE IF THE BRIDGE WAS OPENED OR CLOSED.

"I WAS THE LEGISLATOR WHO SPONSORED THE BILL IN 1953 THAT BUILT THE REPLACEMENT HATHAWAY AND DUPONT BRIDGES IN THE LATE 1950s. I SERVED ONLY ONE TERM IN THE STATE LEGISLATURE BEFORE I WAS DEFEATED BY DEMPSEY BARRON IN 1954. I GUESS BUILDING A PARK FOR BLACK PEOPLE PROBABLY HAD A LOT TO DO WITH LOSING THE RACE. DEMPSEY LATER OBTAINED THE FUNDING FOR THE NEW BRIDGES AND THEY FINISHED THEM ABOUT 1959.

"BEFORE HATHAWAY BRIDGE WAS OPENED FOR TRAFFIC SOMETHING HAPPENED TO THE OLD BRIDGE SO SCHOOL BUSES HAD TO GO AROUND SOUTHPORT AND WEST BAY TO THE BEACH. WELL, DEMPSEY GOT OUT ON THE APPROACH TO THE NEW BRIDGE AND TOOK THE BARRIERS DOWN HIMSELF AND STARTED DRIVING OVER IT. HE WAS A SENATOR, AND PEOPLE DIDN'T MESS WITH SENATORS, NOT EVEN THE DEPARTMENT OF TRANSPORTATION."

—J.M.

The "Worthless White Sand"

Many laughed at those who homesteaded or purchased land on Panama City Beach, saying the worthless white sand would never be as valuable as dirt. But gradually some decided to take a chance on the sand.

In 1931, the International Paper Co. opened its first mill in Florida, east of Millville at Bay Harbor. This mill provided work for many during the Depression and used waste products of the cutover forests to make paper.

The Corps of Engineers cut the New Pass, about eight miles west of the Old Pass in 1934, dividing the long projectile of land known as the West Peninsula. With its many shells, the eastern section of the old peninsula became known as Shell Island.

Panama City's tranquil seaside existence came to an end during World War II with the establishment of Tyndall Field in 1941; the Wainwright Shipyard in 1942; and the Navy Countermeasures Station that same year.

Thousands discovered the beaches during that time. The "worthless white sand" soon became "white gold".

THE INDIANS

Early settlers were amazed by the large number of Indian mounds they found in this area. During the 19th century, treasure seekers repeatedly vandalized these great links to the past expecting to find large amounts of gold.

In some they discovered skeletons in perfect preservation. In others they came across items such as chipped stone projectiles, bird and animal effigies, decorated and engraved pottery, vases and urns, smoothing stones and shell beads.

But the perfect beautiful pieces of pottery they unearthed with holes mystified them. They could not understand why the Indians ruined them in that way. These vessels were found over the skulls of dead Indians, while others were buried in caches.

Later they learned it was an early custom of the Indians to puncture a hole in the bottom of a vase or urn used for burial. These "kill holes" were made so the soul could escape and join that of the deceased.

Archaeologists and anthropologists divide the Indian culture in Northwest Florida into the following periods: Paleo Indian Period - 10,500 B.C. - 6,000 B.C.; Archaic Period — 8,000 B.C.- 1,000 B.C.; Orange Culture - 1,700 B.C. - 1,200 B.C.; Deptford Culture - 400 B.C. - 100 A.D.; Santa Rosa Swift Creek - 100 A.D. -500 A.D.; Weeden Island I - 500 A.D. - 800 A.D.; Weeden Island II - 800 A.D.- 1,200 A.D.; and Fort Walton - 1,200 A.D. - 1.650 A.D.

Some of the early Indian groups in this area were the Chatots, Okchais, Pawoktis and the Yuchis. They were followed by the Creeks and Seminoles.

Excavation of the Indian Mounds

In the 1890s, archaeologist Clarence B. Moore financed and oversaw investigations of many of the shell mounds in Florida. Moore discovered that a large number of these mounds had already been robbed of their treasures, but others remained untouched in hard to reach locations.

Moore engaged J.S. Raybon, Captain of the flat-bottomed steamer "Gopher," to locate all known mounds and obtain permission for digging. In 1902 Raybon began transporting Moore to 50 or more of these sites. Dirt from these mounds was lifted aboard the Gopher where workers sifted through the debris for artifacts.

Although Moore's methods were extremely crude compared to the meticulous excavation methods employed today, he did list all his findings and the location of the mounds he visited in his book "Certain Aboriginal Remains of Northwest Florida Coast." He also sent his artifact collection to the Academy of Natural Sciences in Philadelphia.

Moore collected hundreds of skulls, bones and vessels, but he admitted that he found far less of the implements and artifacts than he expected from this section.

In the vicinity of Panama City Beach, Moore excavated mounds at Alligator Bayou, near Bear Point; West Bay; and at Phillips Inlet. The artifacts unearthed in these mounds dated from the Santa Rosa Swift Creek, Ft. Walton and Weeden Island periods.

After ruthless digging and grave desecration at many of these sites the State of Florida finally passed statutes in the 1980s making it a felony to disturb the contents of graves and tombs.

THE ENGLISH TOWN OF WELLS

Besides stories of the Spanish, legend also told of the town of Wells that supposedly existed in the late 1700s around Dyers Point near Hathaway Bridge or in the vicinity of Courtney Point, where old tabby foundations were discovered years ago. But no evidence verifying the existence of this town has been found.

Those who researched this village depicted on Melish's map of the early 1800s believe the "wells" shown was nothing more than an old "well" where travelers could obtain water. It was most probably picked up by cartographers in err as a town.

BURIED TREASURE

Tales of pirates, shipwrecks and buried treasure are common along the Gulf Coast. With more than 600 miles of waterfront, Bay County has had its share of these stories through the years.

From the 1600s to the 1800s, St. Andrew Bay witnessed the activity of freebooters who preyed upon the richly laden vessels plying the sea between Mexico and Spain. In this sequestered waterway, they found the perfect hideout from their enemies.

These sea rovers camped on some of the heavily wooded points of land or in scattered, moss-draped clearings. Spanish coins dating back hundreds of years have been found at old Beacon Beach, along North Bay at College Point and at Grassy Point.

Smack Bayou, near Redfish Point on today's Tyndall AFB, was one of the main places that pirates sought shelter. They took advantage of the deep water near the shore to turn over their vessels, scraping bottoms and making necessary repairs.

Joe Massalina, the first black settler on the bay, often told the story of the pirate ship that ducked into this scenic inlet to escape a Spanish ship. When a few men on lookout reported sails in the Gulf near the pass, the pirate captain quickly ordered eight men ashore to carry the heavy iron

chest that held their loot.

After covering the men's faces with cloths so they would not be able to see where they were going, the captain led them through the deep pine forest to a place where three huge live oaks stood in a triangle.

They buried their treasure and marked the spot by driving copper pins deep into three trees. Although many have sought this pirate cache, no one ever reported finding the treasure.

The sheltered body of water, known as Spanish Shanty Cove on the north side of what is now Shell Island, was another well known mooring location along the Gulf Coast. Here, according to an old legend, the Spanish established a small outpost that offered a commanding view of the pass and Gulf.

Sometime, during the pirate years, a Spanish ship took refuge at the cove hoping to outwit a pursuing English ship. The Spanish thought they were safe until they saw the English vessel bearing down on them.

The captain ordered his crew to heave the ship's treasure overboard with a rope attached so they could later retrieve it. But, during the battle, the rope broke loose from the boat and floated away.

After the English vessel sailed on, the crew dove into 12 feet of water to search for the chest, but it was nowhere to be found. The Spanish ship then

continued west. But off Phillips Inlet some of the crew jumped ship and made their way east along the coast. When they reached Spanish Shanty Cove, they dove and dove until they found the gold.

Then, unable to carry the heavy load with them, they buried most of the treasure in a nearby tall sand dune. Months later, they returned to recover the horde, but found a hurricane had transformed the spot. They could not locate the sand dune.

According to legend the gold still remains on Shell Island.

THE MASSACRE
AT PHILLIPS INLET

During the holiday season of December 1843, Captain Henry Nunes of Pensacola faced the difficult task of towing the barge Emperor from what is now Destin to Apalachicola. The lighter barge was destined for service on the Apalachicola River.

Accompanying Nunes were Edward Hale, Richard Larrymore, Robert Sayres, Sam, a young boy and Rose, a young slave woman.

As they sailed east, a winter storm struck with high winds and crashing waves, forcing most of them to seek shelter below deck in the frigid cold. Off Phillips Inlet on December 31, Nunes' schooner and barge ran aground.

The captain was well aware of the danger from Indians if his party sought shelter on the beach. But with their wrecked vessels and the icy weather, they had no choice. They recovered some of their supplies, stumbled ashore and built a fire to dry their clothes and keep warm. They then waited for the weather to clear, so they could repair the vessels.

Hale and Sayres spent some of their time hunting and fishing. One day they spotted an Indian canoe filled with skins and pots down the beach. Next day, a few Indians, a squaw and a child appeared at their camp. They seemed hungry, so Nunes fed them some food.

A few days later, more Indians approached, seeking food. Nunes fed them again, but this time the Indians who seemed friendly were reluctant to leave.

Nunes and the others remained around camp for awhile, and then Hale and Sam left to go fishing. Nunes told them he'd join them in a few minutes.

The captain had walked only a couple hundred yards from camp when he heard screams. The startled Nunes turned and saw Rose, Larrymore and Sayres scrambling to get away from the pursuing Indians, wielding guns and knives.

When he saw they were outnumbered, Nunes quickly ran to Hale and Sam. The three fled to the Tucker House, the nearest settlement, on Choctawhatchee Bay.

The next day Nunes returned with a party of ten men. He found all his property at the camp had been damaged or carried off. Down the beach they came across the body of Rose and buried her in a shallow grave. But they found no sign of Larrymore or Sayres. Eventually Larrymore made his way to Tucker's. Sayres' body was never found.

Once residents of Northwest Florida heard about the massacre, they demanded an end to these outrages. The Army ordered Lt. A. Montgomery of the 7th Infantry at Barrancas, Pensacola to capture these renegades.

Montgomery and his men rode the U.S. Sloop Caroline east to Phillips Inlet. Once on shore they combed the woods around the lake where they found several deserted old Indian camps, cornfields and numerous trails. Later, they sailed to St. Andrews to find out where they might find the Indians.

Over the course of the next several days, the soldiers followed more trails that led from Phillips Inlet to West Bay and others which crossed Crooked, Burnt Mill and Econfina creeks. They passed several more old Indian camps and even spotted a few Indians one day. But at the end of three weeks, they had to give up. The Indians remained elusive and always one-step ahead of them. They were never caught.

Some say that on dark nights, the restless spirit of Rose stalks the sand dunes near Phillips Inlet. If it is a quiet night, they say one can still hear the cries from this lost soul.

SALT WORKS

Salt Works – *Salt-making camps in Northwest Florida ranged from small, one-man kettle operations to huge government salt works, employing hundreds of people. A crew from the U.S. Bark Kingfisher raided this salt factory on September 15, 1862, depriving the Confederacy of desperately needed salt for preserving food and in soldiers' diets.*

Although the Yankees did everything possible to destroy the thousands of salt works around St. Andrew Bay, the salt makers had their boilers up and running in a few days.

At the beginning of the Civil War, the federal blockade of Southern ports halted the importation of salt necessary in soldiers' diets and for preserving meat, fish and animal hides. With the South accustomed to consuming 6 million bushels per year, people were forced to produce their own salt from seawater. A long drought made St. Andrew Bay especially salty and excellent for making salt.

As word got around, thousands flocked to the bay to enter this industry. They stayed in flapping white tents, canvas-covered wagons or crude log houses while they boiled sea water in big containers such as syrup kettles, vats and even cut-down locomotive engines.

When all the water evaporated they spread the wet mass that remained on boards to bleach in the sun or hung it in cloth bags to dry a darker color for a preserving salt.

Salt making started as a simple job but quickly became a patriotic mission. Any man producing 20 bushels of salt or more per day was exempted from conscription into the Confederate Army. As the war advanced salt making became a dangerous occupation, mixed with much profiteering.

Federal troops fired warning cannons before destroying hundreds of these camps around the bay during the war. They took those making salt prisoners only if they refused to pledge allegiance to the U.S. Most took the pledge but in a few days always seemed to be back at work, making more salt.

One of the largest raids took place at the beginning of December 1863. Approximately 50 officers and their men from the steamer Bloomer, sloop Caroline and steamer Restless attacked the huge Confederate government salt works seven miles up West Bay.

The salt making camp stretched over almost a mile and consisted of 27 buildings, 22 large boilers and some 200 kettles, averaging 200 gallons each, all of which were destroyed along with 2,000 bushels of salt.

Following this raid, the Union troops demolished almost 200 more salt works as they made their way out of West Bay. The entire damage to the Confederacy was estimated at $3 million.

Huge stacks of pine logs, used as fuel for the never-ending fires beneath the kettles, stood as landmarks at all camps and sites. Some of these piles remained in the early 1900s, more than 40 years after the war.

Salt kettles, such as this one displayed on lower Harrison Avenue, were held in place by bricks and used to boil salt water during the Civil War. When cooked down, the seawater produced salt, vital for preserving food and in soldiers' diets. This salt kettle was presented to the City of Panama City in 1960 by the United Daughters of the Confederacy.

Mr. And Mrs. P. Hutchison appear happy and contented as they enjoy a few minutes of rest with their dog in front of the hotel that they operated in West Bay. Circa early 1900s.

COMMUNITIES ON THE FRINGE OF PANAMA CITY BEACH

During the 1800s and early 1900s, Panama City Beach remained an isolated section, all but ignored by early inhabitants of the area. Some travelers occasionally tromped along the hardened sand at the water's edge to reach distant locations such as Apalachicola and Pensacola.

Others rode wagons over the deep sand rut trails to communities in Walton and Washington counties. During the "spring and fall runs," some fishermen spent their nights in camps on the lakes, and an occasional family enjoyed a few days near the surf in its covered wagon so the children could frolic in the Gulf.

Overall, Panama City Beach attracted little attention. But settlements grew up on the fringes of the beaches.

West Bay

Legend told of an old mission located in West Bay during the 1700s. Buccaneers and Indians harassed the people staying there. These people attempted to move the building in several sections to a safer location across the bay. But in crossing the wide expanse of water they encountered the unexpected squalls of a storm. The vessels all sank and the people drowned.

West Bay had its beginnings in the mid-1800s when it became a junction for three old roads. One, known now as the Side Camp Road, wove its way west from West Bay to Point Washington, the site of large sawmills before and after the Civil War.

Another boggy trail led north to Vernon. The third was nothing more than an old Indian trail that crossed Crooked and Burnt Mill creeks on logs then wound its way to Anderson, now Southport.

During the Civil War, the body of water known as West Bay had a high salinity content caused by droughts of several years. Salt making flourished around West Bay.

Early families in West Bay included such names as Sowell, Hutchison, Laird, Knowles, Thompson, Churchwell, Merritt, Pope, Smith, Rodgers, Ward and Buchanan.

The Pensacola & Atlantic Railroad, which began construction of an east-west line across Northwest Florida in the early 1880s, reportedly owned most of the property around the community of West Bay. Several families purchased their land from this railroad.

The P & A operated a logging railroad through the forest to carry out timber to the depot at the edge of West Bay. From that location this lumber was barged to the West Bay Mill on Dyers Point, St. Andrews.

About the turn of the century, Perry Hutchison operated a hotel and store in West Bay. John Rodgers ran another large store. The town boasted a sawmill, commissary, school, cafe and turpentine still, owned by the John Henry Laird family and operated by C.A. Buchanan.

Industries included logging, turpentining, fishing, oystering and keeping beehives for honey.

Several men ran boats from West Bay to St. Andrews and Panama City to deliver supplies or to transport families that needed to go to town.

In the 1920s, the huge Seminole Plantation, a vast horticultural company, began offering 100-acre lots and small farms to investors who wished to grow Satsuma oranges, paper shell pecans, cluster blueberries and Carmen grapes. The 35,000-acre plantation stretched from West Bay to Pine Log Creek.

But the plantation became a victim of the Depression. Several homes from its town of Seminole Hills were moved to West Bay and its famed "Jelly House" closed. Pine Log State Forest now covers some of this land.

Over the years several bridges were constructed over West Bay Creek, now the Intracoastal Waterway. The new bridge, erected in the early 1990s, bears the name of the B.V. Buchanan, a county commissioner who did a lot for the area.

Bear Point, the Lagoon and Botheration Bayou

Bear Point and the Lagoon are both easily identifiable on the west side of St. Andrew Bay, south of the Navy Base. Botheration Bayou lies on the south shore of West Bay.

When the Cincinnati Company promoted the mail-order purchase of land in and around the town of St. Andrews in the 1880s, Bear Point served as the crossing point for newcomers making the difficult trek east in wagons across what's now Panama City Beach.

At Bear Point they rode a ferry-barge across the bay to St. Andrews. Many spent most of their money on the trip. When they saw the land they purchased some were disappointed. They returned to the Bear Point area and took up 80 or 160-acre homesteads available for $1.25 per acre.

A few of them settled along Grand Lagoon, which was said to be spectacular then with its towering dunes and springs that bubbled up from the ground. In 1907, children attended classes at the "Lagoon School," which stood on Jesse Sowell's property.

Others living in the greater Bear Point-Grand Lagoon area then were Dan Sowell, J.R. Holley, schoolteacher Josephus Lipes, E.I. Mathews and for a time C.S. Anderson and J.H. Drummond.

For many years, the Lagoon section remained a quiet paradise where couples came on moonlight picnics by the dunes. A few of the old "claim houses," crude buildings where people spent 14 months out of five years to obtain homesteads, could be found at different locations.

Desolate Botheration Bayou, north of these settlements had been a big salt making spot during the Civil War. In the early 1900s, this place attracted several turpentining families when Will Tiller erected a still on the bayou.

Hubert Brown later purchased the still and moved it near "new pines" on property now belonging to the Navy Base by Hathaway Bridge.

Inlet Beach

Families by the names of Taylor, Miller, Marshall, Cain, Gainous, Ogburn, Melvin and Collins settled on or near Lake Powell in the late 1800s and early 1900s. Fishing served as their main means of livelihood.

Access to the lake was by the old wagon road that zigzagged its way from West Bay to Point Washington. This road was used to carry the mail and served as the main thoroughfare for western Bay County until the Coastal Highway was completed over Lake Powell in 1935.

Those living at the Inlet purchased groceries and supplies at West Bay. They ordered their clothing and other items

Inlet Beach – *All appeared peaceful across Lake Powell where waves built a bar at the entrance to the Gulf at Phillips Inlet in 1928. The photographer snapped this photo near the Inlet Beach Hotel, which became part of the past many years ago.*
With no bridge across Lake Powell until 1935, travelers headed east or west made their way over the old wagon road that wound around the north shore of the lake.

from Sears, Roebuck & Co. Families from Alabama journeyed to Inlet Beach during the fall months to trade produce for salted fish.

A school was established at Inlet Beach in the late 1800s. Ira Hutchison, who went on to become a circuit judge in Bay County, taught in this school while he was still a teenager. Anna Paget Wells of Vernon was another teacher at this school.

By 1920, Inlet Beach drew visitors to its two hotels. One, built by the Laird family, stood on the north shore of the lake.

The other, constructed by McCaskill Investment Co., the promoter of Inlet Beach, was located on the bluff overlooking the lake, a short distance from the Gulf.

In the Inlet Beach advertisements, the McCaskill Co. described its cottages, lighting plant, waterworks, bathhouses and boardwalks, along with its planned streets and parks, all on the southwest side of the lake.

Travelers from the north and west reached "this beauty spot" by crossing the

Choctawhatchee River at the Cowford Ferry near what today is Ebro. The hard times of the 1930s doomed the Inlet Beach venture. But many of the long-time residents remained in the area.

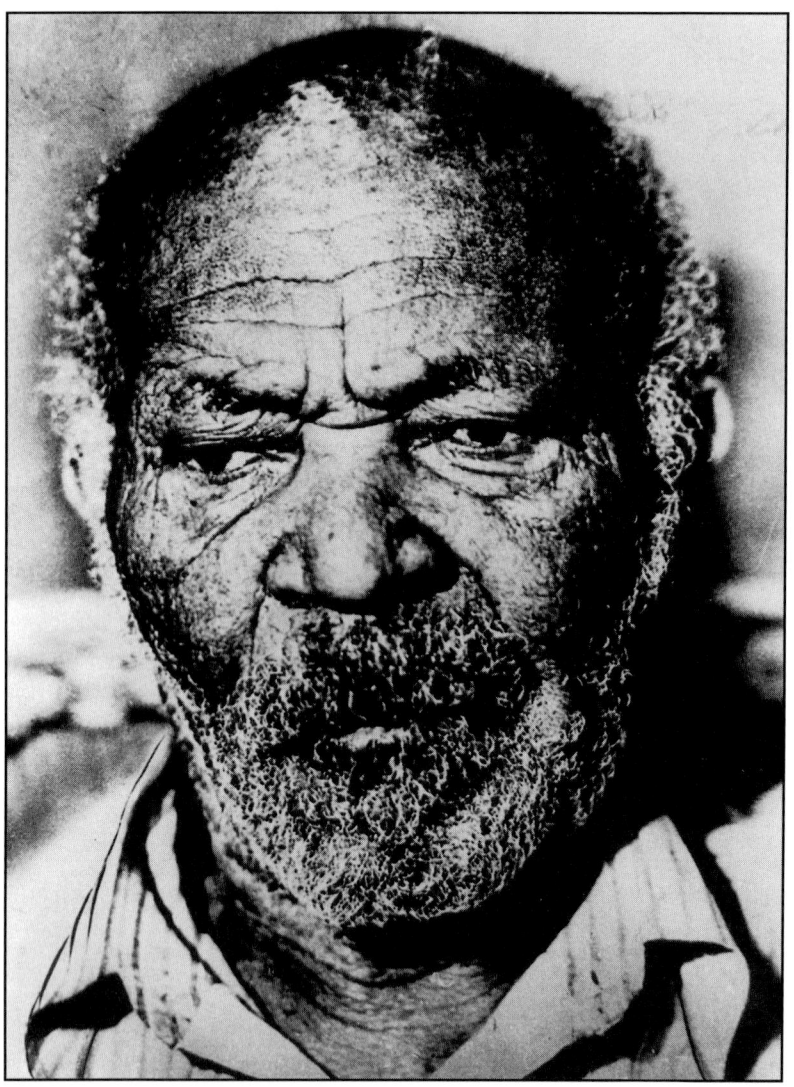

Narcisco Hawk Massalina, the son of free Spanish trader Jose Massalina, was born on St. Andrew Bay in 1840 while Florida was still a territory. He was five when Florida became a State. Hawk joined the Union Navy for service on St. Andrew Bay when Florida became a Confederate State between 1861-1865. His long life included periods of this country's past – the Spanish American War, 1898; World War I, 1914-1918; and World War II, 1941-1945. Before he passed away in 1948 at the age of 108, Massalina's wish was to be buried with his father and first wife, Belle, on Redfish Point. But all burials on Tyndall Field ceased after the government took possession of the property in 1941. Hawk was buried in Redwood Cemetery in Panama City, off 7th Street. In 1999, the City of Panama City erected a monument on his grave which read: "African-American Pioneer; Civil War veteran of the Union Navy; Massalina Bayou, Massalina Drive and Panama City Housing Authority's Massalina Homes were named in his honor."

NARCISCO HAWK MASSALINA

*I*n the early days before Bay County had much development, those traveling to St. Andrew Bay to fish or hunt sought a guide familiar with area waters. One of the best was Narcisco Massalina, better known as "Uncle Hawk." Massalina was the youngest son of Jose Massalina, a free Spanish black who came to this vicinity in 1830 and remained for the rest of his life.

During the years that Hawk served as a guide, he took visitors on 3-day fishing or hunting trips for $4 per outing. Favorite places were Crooked Island Sound and Watson Bayou.

In the early 1900s, Uncle Hawk began holding huge "Freedom Day" celebrations at his home on Massalina Point, now Davis Point. For the May 20 occasion Hawk raised a big American flag early in the morning before the arrival of family members and friends from Redfish Point, Econfina and other locations in the area.

This date marked the first time news reached Florida of the Emancipation Proclamation. It also honored the Homestead Act that granted 160 acres of government land to anyone 21 years of age or older who was a citizen of the United States.

As he grew older, Hawk enjoyed reminiscing. He told of seeing the first balls fired by Yankees on Confederates making salt for many of their troops. Hawk enlisted on one of the blockading vessels and led Union forces to other salt making locations around St. Andrew Bay.

Both Hawk and Jose were remarkable men. Jose had several other children some of whom were named Chrispina, Spenosa, Joseph and Betsy. Hawk had no children with Belle, his wife of 50 years, who was three-fourths Cherokee Indian. She died in 1911. He married again while he was in his 70s and his second wife bore him eight children.

Jose died at the age of 111 in 1902 and was buried on what is now Tyndall AFB. Hawk passed away at the age of 108 in 1948 and was interred in Redwood Cemetery in Panama City.

RECOLLECTIONS & MEMORIES BY JACK MASHBURN

Hawk Massalina

"HAWK MASSALINA WAS A PERSONAL FRIEND OF MY FATHER. HAWK'S FATHER, JOSE, CAME FROM CUBA. HE WAS NEVER A SLAVE. HE LIVED AT REDFISH POINT.

"DURING THE CIVIL WAR, HAWK HELPED GUIDE SHIPS IN HERE. HIS BIRTHDAY WAS APRIL 15, AND HE LIVED TO BE 108. ON HIS BIRTHDAY MY FATHER AND I ALWAYS TOOK HIM A JUG OF HONEY. AND EVERY FOURTH OF JULY WE TOOK HIM A WATERMELON BECAUSE HE WAS THAT CLOSE OF A FRIEND.

"IN HIS HOUSE HE HAD ONE ROOM FOR WHITES IF THEY WANTED TO SPEND THE NIGHT. A LOT OF PEOPLE DIDN'T KNOW THAT HE WAS A GRACIOUS MAN!

"MOST WHITE PEOPLE WOULD NOT GO OUT FISHING AT NIGHT BECAUSE THEY DIDN'T CATCH MANY FISH. HAWK WOULD GO OUT AND COME IN AT SUNRISE WITH HIS BOAT FILLED WITH FISH. HE TAUGHT WHITE MEN HOW TO FISH FOR MACKERAL AT NIGHT. HE DIDN'T MIND SHARING HIS SECRET. THE PEOPLE HE TAUGHT GUARDED THEIR SECRET CAREFULLY."

J.M.

Fishermen aboard the smack Princess set sail on a warm December morning in 1917. By then, ice had been manufactured almost 10 years in this area. The ice allowed fishermen to cool their catch immediately instead of having to salt the fish in the old way. The many piers and docks of St. Andrews appear in the background.

THE FISHING INDUSTRY

The fishing industry began long before the Civil War when planters and farmers journeyed to the bay each autumn to catch and salt mullet for their families and slaves.

Most times the fishermen used drag seines measuring 300 to 600 feet in length and six to twelve feet in depth. These nets were built with a pocket in the middle where the seine attained its greated depth. They were made from hand-woven cotton cord and water-proofed in oil. Fish caught included mackerel, pompano, trout, redfish, sheepshead, blue-fish and mullet.

Since ice was not available in the St. Andrew Bay area until the early 1900s, fishermen either sold their catch fresh or preserved the fish with salt. This process involved gutting and cleaning the fish, then salting them and packing the fish in 200-pound wooden barrels. Each of these barrels was guaranteed to be "good for a year."

Fishermen from around the bay sold this salted fish, which people shortened to "salt fish." Southport ranked as the center of this industry in the late 1800's. Besides those coming to the bay to trade produce and other goods for salted fish, peddlers departed in their covered wagons, which some referred to as "bay schooners," to sell salt fish and sacks of oysters as far north as lower Alabama and Georgia.

Schools of mullet three miles long and 500 yards wide were common in the Gulf at that time. Record catches of these fish were made. In 1918, the Fay brothers and the Raffield family of East Bay caught 50,000 pounds of mullet on one trip and cleaned enough to fill 125 barrels.

Those involved in the snapper and grouper fishing industry had to be strong and rugged. At the snapper banks they checked to see if fish were on the bottom by tossing a 4 to 8-pound lead weight filled with octagon soap over the side. If the weight came up with shells or rocks on it they knew they'd catch fish in that location. But if the weight bore nothing it meant they were over sand or mud and had to move elsewhere to catch fish.

During that time, they fished the old-fashioned way without poles using only drop lines with three or four hooks. When they felt bites, they pulled them up using "rubber nippers," glove-like mitts, on their hands until the expensive electric reels were finally installed on the boats.

Their old fishing boats contained centers where wells held water to keep the fish alive until they reached port. Snapper sold for 8 cents a pound then; Spanish mackerel cost $8 per barrel; mullet, $5; and pompano, $10.

The opening of the Atlanta & St. Andrews Bay Railway, better known as the Bay Line, in 1908 revolutionized the fishing industry. Fish on board these vessels were iced and shipped to large cities of the South. In fact, sometimes so many fish were ready for shipment; the railroad ran out of cars.

Oystering became another big industry in the early days. Those living along beaches purchased oysters then kept them fresh in the salt water by their docks. Shucked oysters sold for 15 cents per quart; oysters in the shell, $1 per 1,000.

In the 1830s and 1840s, oysters from St. Andrew Bay were touted as the best and sweetest along the Northern Gulf Coast.

Shrimp did not gain popularity until the early 1900s. When fishermen caught them in their nets, they customarily tossed them back into the water by the handfuls. But gradually people learned that shrimp tasted quite good when fried or boiled.

Scallops, which littered the bay floor by the millions, elicited little interest like shrimp. Fishermen considered them food eaten only by the poor in other parts of the world. Eventually people from this area realized the great treasure they had in all types of seafood from the bay and Gulf.

RECOLLECTIONS & MEMORIES BY JACK MASHBURN

Fishing

"THERE USED TO BE HUGE, LONG BOATS THAT CAME IN HERE. THEY WERE 70-90 FOOT BOATS JUST FOR SNAPPER FISHING FROM PENSACOLA AND SOUTH FLORIDA. THIS WHOLE PLACE 100 MILES FROM PENSACOLA WAS AN EXCELLENT PLACE TO FISH WITH SNAPPER BEDS OFF SHORE.

"MY FATHER WAS A COMMERCIAL FISHERMAN FOR A NUMBER OF YEARS. HE FISHED FOR SNAPPER AND MULLET. HE ALSO DOVE FOR SPONGES WITH THE GREEKS AT TARPON SPRINGS."

J.M.

Andersons

"I REMEMBER WHEN CAPT. WALTER, MAX AND VIRGIL ANDERSON WERE MOVING TO THE BOON DOCKS OF GRAND LAGOON. I SAW THEM DRIVING ALL THOSE PILINGS OUT HERE AND I SAID, 'WHAT ARE YOU DOING, BUILDING A NEW PLACE?' THEY SAID, 'NO, WE'RE GOING TO MOVE OUT HERE.' I SAID 'PEOPLE AREN'T GOING TO DRIVE OUT THIS FAR TO GO FISHING.' THE ANDERSONS SAID 'WE THINK THEY WILL.' IT WAS A GOOD MOVE. IF THEY'D STAYED DOWNTOWN THEY'D BE TIED UP WITH ALL THAT TRAFFIC."

J.M.

Fish were plentiful decades ago when boats often came in loaded with grouper and snapper. The Anderson family has a long legacy in this area. Thomas Anderson and his sons supplied Confederate troops with fish. Captain S. Walter Anderson can be seen on the left of this photo. Circa 1950.

Fishermen are seen departing on the Captain Anderson III when the Anderson fleet docked downtown near the foot of Harrison Avenue. Boat owners charged $2.50 to take a fisherman out for the day. That price remained in effect until the late 1950s, when prices increased. In the background, on the left, is the old USO Building from World War II. Circa of photo 1950.

Edwin Peters (L) and Bert Gwaltney (R) sit beside a huge 506-pound jewfish. These fish, a member of the grouper family, are of excellent food value and a challenge to bring into the boat.

THE INTRACOASTAL WATERWAY

During fair weather, tugs, barges and other vessels glide with ease over West Bay, St. Andrew Bay and East Bay. Through the drone of their engines, they call attention to the Intracoastal Waterway, often referred to as "the lifeline of marine trade."

It seems hard to believe in such a perfect setting that construction of this canal came about only after decades of proposals and hundreds of letters written in support of this important waterway.

The idea of building a canal to avoid the treacherous capes and straights of the coast actually dates back to the 1700s and the English in Florida. Once Florida became a territory in 1821, Congressional delegate J.M. White sought financial assistance from the federal government for such a project when he heard of the great success of the Erie Canal in New York.

With the continual problems of storms and pirates along the Gulf Coast, White and his constituents saw an intercoastal canal as a solution to east-west travel across the sparsely populated territory.

The first positive step in the inland waterway began with the construction of a channel between Mobile Bay and the Mississippi Sound in 1828. Even though Florida's territorial government passed an act to incorporate the Chipola Canal Company connecting the east-

ern arm of St. Andrew Bay with the Chipola and Apalachicola Rivers, the panic of 1837 and the proposed construction of a canal to St. Joseph ended all prospects for this company.

Few realized this waterway would become a reality only through a slow, tedious "link by link" process over the next hundred years.

The East Bay Canal

In the 1880s, several area leaders formed the East Bay Canal, Railroad and Land Company. They proposed constructing a six-mile canal from the East Prong of St. Andrew Bay to the waters of Lake Chipola and the Apalachicola River. But those in government showed little interest in this section of Northwest Florida.

During the early 1890s, talk of an inland waterway once again became popular. Several businessmen came forward with another plan for a canal for East Bay.

Lillian Carlisle, whose family owned extensive real estate holdings around the Callaway area, backed the project and wrote several articles for the Panama City Pilot concerning the proposed canal.

On June 25, 1910, Congress finally passed a bill allocating $100,000 for the waterway, with additional funds to be forthcoming as needed.

Between 1911-1915, hundreds of workers labored

through thick swamps fighting swarms of biting mosquitoes and dog flies. Bears, panthers, alligators and poisonous snakes also inhabited this section of land.

The "Blackwater" performed most of the dredge work, cutting the canal 100 feet wide and nine-feet deep. The waters between St. Andrew Bay and the Apalachicola River finally met "in the great ditch" on April 15, 1915, a year after completion of the link between Mobile and New Orleans.

The East Bay Canal opened just in time to provide protected shipping to vessels during World War I.

The West Bay Canal

During the 1920s, proposals to build the West Bay Canal connecting West Bay and Choctawatchee Bay were discussed several times. J.H. Drummond of St. Andrews agreed to serve as Vice President of the Chattahoochee Valley and Gulf Association, formed to secure the completion of the Intracoastal Canal.

Drummond, a personal friend of former President W.H. Taft, made several trips to Washington, soliciting support for this waterway. He also spent his own time and money in Boston and other northern cities obtaining title to land along the proposed canal.

By then, the links between Corpus Christi and New

Orleans were either under construction or completed. The stretches between Pensacola Bay and Choctawhatchee Bay and Apalachicola and

Carrabelle were connected by water and needed no work.

Several routes were proposed for this last important link in the waterway. The first

took the canal from Choctawhatchee Bay east through Peach Creek, then across Phillips Inlet, entering West Bay about two miles south of West Bay Creek.

Engineers finally settled on the route through West Bay Creek to Choctawhatchee Bay. Though construction was approved in 1932, work on the 25-mile or so canal that would become known as "the Drummond Cut" did not begin until late 1936.

On July 6, 1938, a huge celebration commemorating the completion of this link in the canal was held at the Valparaiso Inn and Tower Beach of Okaloosa County.

The next morning, a mile-long "cruisercade" of yachts and other vessels began the inaugural ride through the new cut from Choctawhatchee Bay to West Bay. The 60-mile trip included a stop at the town of West Bay where a huge fish fry was held to celebrate the canal's opening.

The ceremonies concluded in Bay Front Park at the foot of Harrison Avenue in Panama City. Speakers lauded Drummond and P.N. Hutchison of West Bay for the 25 years or so both spent making this link in the canal a reality.

The last section of the canal was finished just prior to World War II when the inland waterway protected oil shipments from enemy submarines prowling the Gulf.

When completed the Intracoastal Waterway extended 1,200 miles, connecting Apalachicola with Corpus Christi, Texas.

J.H. Drummond, St. Andrews first mayor appears with his son and a long catch of cleaned fish. Drummond was a big landowner and developer. He and P.N. Hutchison are credited with bringing about the construction of the West Bay Canal, now part of the Intracoastal Waterway. This section opened in 1938.

***West Bay Bridge** – The old "vertical lift bridge" at West Bay was one of several spans in this location during the early 1900s. This bridge, erected just after World War II, opened for boat and barge traffic on the Intracoastal Waterway. It was used for almost 50 years. Travelers on Highway 79 often had to wait several minutes for the bridge to close.*

But fishermen loved the low bridge where many speckled trout, flounder and sheepshead were caught through the years. This old bridge was replaced by the new high-rise span in the 1990s, which offers uninterrupted traffic flow in case of hurricane evacuation.

Two known burial places exist on greater Panama City Beach.

COLLINS CEMETERY

This graveyard, along the north shore of Lake Powell, takes its name from the Ben Collins family who moved to the sparsely populated location from Geneva, Alabama in the early 1900s.

Known burials in this cemetery are B.E. and Jessie May Collins, Mary Ann Palmer and a Vernon woman, with the unusual name of Queen Green, who died on a camping trip to the lake. Most of the people buried here died in the first half of the 1900s. In 1979, Mrs. Bennye Rohmiller, a Collins descendant, dedicated this two-acre plot so it would always be preserved.

THE SOWELL GRAVE

On Navy Base property southeast of the U.S. Coast Guard Station stands the solitary grave of a young woman named Christine (some say Christian) Sowell. She was born in 1877 and lived near the bay with her brother, Dan Sowell, and his family.

Descendants recall that she died from diphtheria (a highly contagious throat infection) about 1895. A protective chain-link fence surrounds this grave.

On May 4, 1937, Bill and Jean Holloway opened the Sea Breeze Hotel near the "Y" on Panama City Beach. Their property included several hundred feet on the Gulf. During WWII, the military occupied the hotel because it was the only spot where the water was deep enough to allow access by the enemy's largest submarine. Besides its location, the Sea Breeze offered guests "hot and cold water," a rarity at that time.

THE HOLLOWAYS

When Jean and Bill Holloway homesteaded at Phillips Inlet in 1921, they recognized the beauty and the potential of the area. Five years later in 1926 they operated a 40-room hotel along Lake Powell. That year visitors gathered at the hotel to name the proposed coastal highway that became U.S. 98.

The group chose the name "Gulf Coast Riviera." But after a mixture of tar and sand was used to cover the road, vehicles became stuck in the soft mixture whenever they attempted to park on it. Those interested in the highway renamed it "the Loopin' Trail" for a native flower of the area. But blight killed the loopins in 1944 and the designation was never used again.

At their hotel at Phillips Inlet, the Holloways charged $2.50 per night. In May 1937 they opened a new business called "Uncle Bill & Aunt Jean's Seabreeze Hotel" on 8-acres near what is now the end of Highway 79.

World War II brought the "horse soldiers" with their animals, stabled a short distance from the hotel. The federal government commandeered the hotel for officer housing, then returned it prior to the end of the war.

SUNNYSIDE

In 1925 M.E. McCorquodale, a Gadsden county native, happened to visit the desolate west end of Panama City beach while on a trip to Chipley, demonstrating shade tobacco. The lack of any type development "on the prettiest beaches in the world" amazed him.

When he heard the property was available through homesteading, he wasted no time motoring to Gainesville and filing a claim for 160 acres of waterfront property at the west end of the beach. Homestead rules required him to make improvements, cultivate some of the land and live on the acreage 14 months over the next five years. The usual cost for the land amounted to $1.25 an acre.

McCorquodale built a home west of the present Fourth Street near what is now Front Beach Road. Then he moved his wife, Mary Emma, and their children, Grace, Corky, Ruth Ellen and Mary to the beach. He and his family named the location "Sunnyside."

"Mr. Mac," as he came to be known, proved up the homestead and grew corn, peanuts, potatoes, watermelons and other crops in the sand, which were no easy tasks. The children's job became toting water to the plants. But when his money ran out and work on building the Coastal Highway (Front Beach Road) was postponed, the McCorquodales were forced to move to Panama City and take jobs.

In 1933 when construction of the highway resumed, the family returned to Sunnyside. Mr. Mac built rental cottages, a windmill and a water tower. He subdivided his property into lots. The children made the long trip each day to school in Panama City but were often delayed when Hathaway Bridge was out of service.

A few years later in 1937 when 50-foot lots at Sunnyside began selling for $25-$50, McCorquodale erected wooden walkways over the sand to protect the dunes. He also dedicated the south side of the highway so homeowners would always have an unobstructed beach for enjoyment.

As conditions improved, Mr. Mac built a store and gas station onto the front of their home. He had a phone installed so vacationers could receive and make calls. Mac's business became headquarters for that section of beach during World War II. In their retirement years, the McCorquodales returned to Gadsden County. He died in 1953; Mrs. Mac in 1960.

M.E. McCorquodale and his wife, Mary Emma, homesteaded Sunnyside Beach in the 1920s. After he platted the subdivision and sold 50-feet beach lots for $25–$50, he dedicated the strip of the beach south of Front Beach Road to lot owners so the beach would always be preserved.

The McCorquodales' home with a store, post office and gas pumps out front, became a gathering place for the community in the 1930s and the World War II era.

After the new pass into St. Andrew Bay opened in 1934, the jetties needed strengthening and lengthening to control erosion. A narrow gauge railroad was constructed from a pier on Grand Lagoon to the west jetty to carry supplies. A gasoline-powered engine pulled the cars across what is now St. Andrews State Recreational Area. Work on the improvement of the jetties continued through 1937. Additional dredging has been necessary over the years to maintain the channel's depth and width.

CUTTING THE NEW PASS INTO ST. ANDREW BAY

During the 1800s and early 1900s, the Old Pass, sometimes referred to as East Pass, served as the only entrance in and out of St. Andrew Bay. All experienced boat captains knew to be wary of this unstable channel where sands often shifted and winds blew out the range lights.

Hurricane Island stood at the entrance to the bay with larger East Pass and smaller West Pass running on each side of this two-mile strip of land. East Pass remained the main channel while storms continually altered the depth and course of West Pass.

In 1886 and 1906 hurricanes also cut passes through Spanish Shanty Cove then sealed them closed.

As shipping increased in the early 1900s, the need for improvements to the entrance channel became apparent. The loss of several fishing schooners trying to navigate the treacherous channel drew additional attention to the situation.

Developers G. M. West, J.H. Drummond and W.H. Lynn all pushed for harbor improvements, deepening the main channel from 11 feet to 22 feet and widening the pass to 200 feet.

Through connections with the Harbors and Rivers Board, Lynn succeeded in obtaining funds for dredging the pass in 1914. This coincided with the opening of the East Bay Canal (now part of the Intracoastal Waterway) in 1915. With the deeper pass, vessels could safely enter St. Andrew Bay and connect with the inland canal, which extended to the

Apalachicola River.

Additional dredging took place in the 1920s, which increased the depth to 30 feet and width to 300 feet. But with no jetties in place, boats could enter the channel only during daylight hours. Tugboats still had to guide vessels through the dangerous channel.

Then after more shipwrecks, increased shipping due to the area's growth and larger exports from Southern Kraft Paper Mill, the Corps of Engineers recommended the dredging of a new pass, eight miles west of the old pass.

Work commenced on this huge project in 1933. At the selected site, engineers took advantage of a large freshwater lake on the West Peninsula and cut through this body of water to create the new pass.

Funding for the project came from the Works Progress Administration, an agency created during the Great Depression. The new entrance channel was to measure 29 feet deep and 450 feet wide. The Techefuncta and its 50-man crew performed dredging. To stimulate the troubled marble industry, the government ordered large symmetrical blocks of this type rock, giving St. Andrew Bay the only marble channel in the world.

On Aug. 4, 1934, area dignitaries watched from boats as the bay and Gulf waters converged for the first time. Captain Charlie Anderson sailed his "Miss Panama" through the new entrance to St. Andrew Bay.

But the formal opening of this important waterway did not take place until November 1934 after dredging was complete and the lighthouse department had erected all of its markers.

Captain Reed decided he wanted his vessel to be the first to sail through the pass. Once Harbor Pilot Graydon York climbed on board to navigate the "Maiden Creek" through the old channel, Reed ordered him to sail west, up the coast and to enter through the new channel. Although they both suffered the ire of officials, they swiftly made it through the pass to receive the recognition.

This new pass was not without its problems, however. The east-west movement of the Gulf waters necessitated the dredging of this channel every few years.

THE FIRST
PANAMA CITY BEACH

Jackson County's Gideon Thomas always had a mind for trying new things. Some of his investments included a water mill, turpentine business, then a deer ranch.

Thomas knew the popularity of Sherman's Pavilion on the Gulf Beach, now Shell Island. In the 1920s he enjoyed visiting the Pavilion but really delighted in bringing his makeshift trailer, which he called his "covered wagon," across the ferry to camp on the deserted beach along the Gulf.

Once Hathaway Bridge opened in 1929, he followed W.W. Sharpless' plans for the successful development of Long Beach, until the promoter's untimely death.

A few years later Thomas decided the time was right. He purchased 104 acres at the edge of the Gulf, east of Long Beach,

with his daughter and son-in-law, Claudia and Angus Pledger. His friends from Jackson County told him he was crazy, investing in worthless sand instead of all-important dirt for growing crops.

Then in 1935, Thomas began building a two-story hotel, cottages, a windmill with a water tower and a 1,000-foot wooden pier on his property, covered today by the Sunbird Condominiums and Pineapple Willy's. One of Thomas' first improvements came with the entranceway. He ordered several loads of oyster shells from Apalachicola to make the deep sand road more accessible.

His complex, the original Panama City Beach, held its formal opening on May 2, 1936. Wallace Caswell, the local "Tarzan of the Deep," served as one of the attractions, riding

Gideon Marion Thomas was born October 8, 1871 and raised in the Cottondale, Florida area. He married Benia Everitt on May 5, 1895.
After several business ventures, the couple left their Bear Creek ranch in 1935 to start building their Panama City Beach Resort. Thomas died May 13, 1937, his wife in 1956. Both were buried in the Methodist Church's cemetery at Cottondale. Thomas Drive bears his name.

Thomas' daughter, Claudia Thomas Pledger, served as the first mayor of Panama City Beach.

porpoises and big sea turtles.

But Thomas did not live long enough to see the popularity of his resort. He died in May 1937. His family continued to operate the business, however, where many guests came to fish, bathe, rest and relax. The Pledgers erected a beautiful entrance arch, emblazoned with "PANAMA CITY BEACH" across it.

Druggist John M. McElvey moved from Albany, Georgia to Panama City Beach in 1939, intent on retirement. But when he found all the leisure time not to his liking, he opened the first drug store on the beach near this location.

In 1953, Panama City Beach was incorporated and Claudia Pledger became the city's first mayor. That same year, state officials honored the early developer by naming "Thomas Drive" for him.

Visitors to the pavilion on the Gulf Beach wore the latest in fashions for bathing. Those identified are: Marjorie Douglas, Francis Orr, Florrie Williams, Curtis McCall, Janie Huttin, Helen Ellis and David Davidson. Circa 1920s

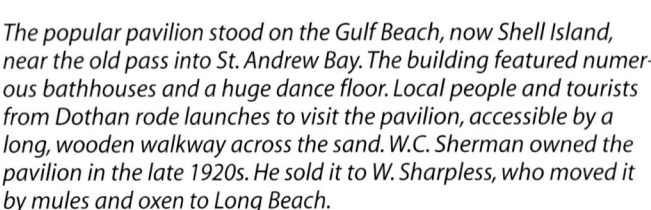

The popular pavilion stood on the Gulf Beach, now Shell Island, near the old pass into St. Andrew Bay. The building featured numerous bathhouses and a huge dance floor. Local people and tourists from Dothan rode launches to visit the pavilion, accessible by a long, wooden walkway across the sand. W.C. Sherman owned the pavilion in the late 1920s. He sold it to W. Sharpless, who moved it by mules and oxen to Long Beach.

RECOLLECTIONS & MEMORIES BY JACK MASHBURN

Mr. Gideon Thomas

"WHEN I WAS A SMALL CHILD ABOUT 5 OR 6 YEARS OLD, MR. GIDEON THOMAS OWNED A PLACE IN EXCESS OF 3,000 ACRES NEXT TO US ON CAMP FLOWERS ROAD AND BEAR CREEK. HE HAD A DEER RANCH, SAWMILL AND GRISTMILL, AND WE'D TAKE OUR CORN TO HIM TO BE GROUND INTO CORNMEAL.

"THAT'S WHEN HE STARTED TO DEVELOP PANAMA CITY BEACH. HE WAS A MAN OF LONG TERM VISION BECAUSE HE ASKED MY FATHER TO COME OUT ONE DAY WITH THE INTENT OF WORKING FOR HIM AT THE BEACH.

"WHEREVER MY FATHER WENT, I WENT. WHEN WE GOT OUT THERE HE HAD BUILT A LOG CABIN AND WAS HAUL-ING OYSTER SHELLS FROM APALACHICOLA. HE BROUGHT IN THE SHELLS SO THAT PEOPLE WOULD NOT GET BOGGED DOWN IN THE DEEP SAND WHEN DRIVING OFF THE ROAD TO HIS BUSINESS.

"MY FATHER, WHOSE NAME WAS MANSEL MASHBURN, LOOKED AROUND AND PICKED UP A HANDFUL OF THAT WHITE SAND AND LET IT SLOWLY DRIP THROUGH HIS FIN-GERS. HE SAID 'MR. THOMAS, I CAN'T HELP YOU OUT HERE BECAUSE THIS SAND WON'T EVEN SPROUT A FIELD PEA. THERE'S NOTHING I CAN DO OUT HERE TO HELP YOU.'

"MR. THOMAS SAID, 'UNCLE MANSE, I'M NOT GROWING VEGETABLES OUT HERE. I'M GROWING PEOPLE. GIDEON THOMAS LOOKED BACK TOWARD THE JETTIES AND SAID, 'I SEE BUILDING AFTER BUILDING ALL THE WAY TO THE JET-TIES.' MY FATHER SAID, 'ALL I SEE ARE SAND DUNES, SEA OATS, SCRUB PALMETTOES, SCRUB MAGNOLIAS AND NOTH-ING ELSE.'

"MR. THOMAS SAID, 'YOU'RE RIGHT. THAT'S ALL THERE IS THERE NOW. BUT THERE WILL BE HOUSE AFTER HOUSE AND PEOPLE AFTER PEOPLE. IT WILL GROW.'

"AT THE CABIN THOMAS SOLD COLD DRINKS, SAND-WICHES AND SNACKS. IT WAS THE FIRST THING BUILT ON THE GULF IN THAT AREA. IT WAS SEASONAL. PEOPLE WOULD COME DOWN FROM DOTHAN AND OTHER PLACES LIKE THAT. BUT YOU COULDN'T GO DURING SEPTEMBER WHEN THE DOG FLIES CAME. THEY WOULD EAT THE MEAT OFF YOUR BONES. PANAMA CITY BEACH GREW FROM THAT EMBRYONIC START.

"CLAUDIA PLEDGER, THE FIRST MAYOR OF PANAMA CITY BEACH, IS STILL HERE DURING THE TIME OF THIS WRITING AT THE AGE OF 100. THOMAS RISKED IT ALL TO DEVELOP PANAMA CITY BEACH, AND IT WORKED OUT WELL."

J.M.

Amusement train rides and other type booths flank the walkway leading to the wooden pier at the "first" Panama City Beach, located where Sunbird Condominiums and Pineapple Willy's stand today. The waving flags most likely denote Memorial Day, the opening of the 100-day beach season after WWII.

LONG BEACH

To J.E. Churchwell, a banker in Panama City and a promoter of Long Beach, goes the credit for the catchy phrase, "The World's Most Beautiful Bathing Beaches," shortened today to "The World's Most Beautiful Beaches."

The story of Long Beach begins long before Churchwell became the owner, however.

In the l920s, turpentine operator Hubert Brown homesteaded the property that included Long Beach. W.W. Sharpless, who had been a deputy sheriff and Chief of Police in Panama City, soon joined him on the development of this land.

Sharpless and Brown purchased Sherman's Pavilion at Lands End (eastern end of Shell Island). They had it moved west over the deep sand by teams of mules and oxen to Long Beach where it was used for bathhouses and a skating rink.

Hathaway Bridge and sections of the Coastal Highway, now U.S. 98, opened in May 1929. That November, both Brown and Sharpless began

Long Beach, with its distinctive red-roofed buildings and cottages stretched over a large area just west of the Front Beach-Middle Beach road intersection. During the height of the season, when no rooms were available, visitors were permitted to set up tents or sleep in blankets on the beach. Circa 1965.

making several improvements that included drilling a deep well and erecting cottages. By the spring of 1930 they had wooden walkways running across the sand and many flowers planted throughout the resort.

But a reckless act by Sharpless ruined the lives of several people and resulted in the first murder involving someone from the beach.

Part of Sharpless and Brown's property stretched west along the highway and was undeveloped. Joseph Harrison,

a St. Andrews mail carrier, decided to take out-of-town relatives to the beach one day in the summer of 1930. They wanted a quieter place and were happily swimming and picnicking beyond Long Beach.

But Sharpless and one of his employees spotted them. Sharpless walked up and demanded 50 cents for the use of his property. Harrison refused, and the two brutally beat him so severely he remained hospitalized for several days. For many weeks Harrison could not walk or

Circus Day in Panama City was a big event. Here, circus wagons can be seen at the corner of Harrison Avenue and 5th Street. Circa 1920s. The circus held shows in Panama City, St. Andrews and Millville. In the 1970s, Long Beach's Deer Ranch added lions, tigers and leopards to their exhibit. These big cats were very popular with the crowds and gave their own circus shows.

The Long Beach Deer Ranch featured 73 of the "friendliest deer in the world." These animals came from different countries, including red deer from England. The deer were tame and enjoyed munching food from visitors' hands. The ranch also included a 1,700-pound buffalo, ponies, donkeys, sheep, goats, pigs and ducks. Circa 1965.

deliver mail.

When charges of attempted murder were dropped against the former law enforcement officer and his employee, Harrison swore vengeance.

On May 23, 1931, Sharpless was found shot to death on the desolate highway near what are now Beck Avenue and U.S. 98. Harrison and his son, Walter, 17, were indicted for Sharpless' murder. Their sensational trial captured the attention of Bay County and Northwest Florida.

The jury convicted both father and son for the crime.

A short tine later, Churchwell purchased 220 acres of Long Beach property on time from Sharpless' wife and the widow of Brown who had also passed away. He paid $10,000 for this huge piece of property. John McCall, another investor in Long Beach, also sold out to Churchwell.

But like many of the other developers of that era, Churchwell encountered slow

sales when he tried to sell beach lots. People were cautious and still not ready to invest in land for recreational purposes.

Sales improved in the late 1930s, and Churchwell installed a new well, telephone service and electricity. He built several more cottages, but everything

stood on hold when the government took control of all beach housing for shipyard workers and military personnel between 1942-1945.

The government packed 25 men into each cottage. They turned the pavilion into a mess hall that stayed open night and day to feed the hungry workers,

As early as 1950, the "Hang Out" had become one of the most popular spots on the beach. The building featured smooth concrete floors, perfect for young people to dance to juke box songs. The snack bar served soft drinks and other food items. Long Beach, the site of the Hang Out, offered merry-go-rounds, kiddie swings, bowling alleys, shooting galleries and a skating rink.

employed in round-the-clock, 8-hour shifts.

After the war people began taking vacations and enjoying more of their leisure time.

Sales improved. Long Beach became an incorporated municipality in 1953. Churchwell upgraded his resort by adding amusements such as a merry-go-round, swings, bowling alley and a new skating rink. But his most popular attraction became "the Hang-Out," which consisted of a smooth dance floor, jukebox and snack bar. During the 1950s hundreds of teenagers spent time rocking and rolling at the well—known spot.

In the 1960s, Churchwell, who became mayor, enlarged his attractions and advertised Long Beach as "the Coney Island of Northwest Florida." An air-conditioned waterfront motel room with a kitchenette rented for $12-$14 per night; a regular motel room, $6 per

During the 1960s and 1970s, train rides were popular on Panama City Beach. Both Tombstone Territory and Petticoat Junction (amusement centers named for TV shows) featured train rides.

night, in the height of the season.

Long Beach consisted of several restaurants, a railroad train pulled by an old steam engine locomotive, two supermarkets and scores of amusement attractions. By 1966 Long Beach stretched from the Gulf almost as far north as Back Beach Road.

As more and more buildings and motels were erected on the beach, Churchwell looked forward to the time businesses would remain open year round. After a few travelers stopped to

visit with him, while they were en route south for the winter, he equipped some of his cottages with heating units and hot water.

Long Beach evolved into "Petticoat Junction," a large amusement park with a Wild West theme, and the Long Beach Camp Inn. The Petticoat Junction name came from a popular comedy television show of the 1950s.

A gigantic one-eyed pirate figure drew tourists to the paddleboats in the small lagoon section near Front Beach Road at Petticoat Junction.

In the early 1970s after the state began eradicating the worrisome dog flies, the beach started attracting visitors year round from Canada and the Northern states.

But in the 1980s and 1990s, the land became too valuable for an amusement park and camping ground. Those who vacationed on the beach preferred new forms of entertainment. The park and campgrounds gave way to modern day condominiums and a diversified shopping center.

(Above) At Long Beach, those on the beach had a choice of umbrellas, sun cabanas, canopies and other type shields that offered partial or full protection from the sun. The famous Hang Out and other amusements can be seen in the background. Circa 1950s.

(Below) Swings, tetter totters, tilt-the-wheel and rental floats provide additional amusements for the crowd at Long Beach. Part of the life-guard's stand can be seenat the right. Circa 1960's.

Popular Laguna Beach, established in the late 1930s by J.B. and Carolee Lahan, drew people from Alabama and Panama City to the western end of the beaches. Here, beachgoers enjoy the sun and sand. A lifeguard's tower stands in the distance. Today, Lahan's son, Charlie and wife, Ann, operate the Carousel Supermarket and other businesses.

LAGUNA BEACH

depending on location.

Lahan urged investors to "profit while you play." For those who chose Laguna Beach, the development advertised "sailing, baseball, bathers under umbrellas, fishermen, horseback riders, shuffleboard and tennis courts."

Laguna Beach also claimed the "most beautiful tea room on the entire Gulf Coast." It featured a "fascinating roof garden overlooking the ever-changing Gulf."

*B*irmingham native J.B. Lahan made frequent visits to the beach in the 1930s. In August of 1936 he formed Gulf Properties, Inc. of Alabama. He and his wife, Carolee, developed Laguna Beach and offered beach lots for $100 to $600,

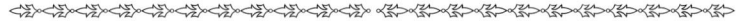

OTHER BEACHES

Several other beaches were developed before and after World War II. In 1938 Harry Edwards built Larkway Villas, 11 miles west of Panama City. He planned seasonal renting of his homes but found many of the people who came to see the homes wanted to purchase them and live in them year round.

In 1946, C.H. McGee began to develop his 180-acre Bahama Beach property that included 3,000 feet of waterfront. McGee purchased 35 surplus Army buildings from Macon, Georgia and had them moved to the beach where he

In the days before jet skis and parasails, beachgoers passed the time sunbathing and making castles in the sand. The beaches were wide open and people parked their cars anywhere along Front Beach Road. But drivers needed to pay attention. If they pulled into loose sand, it was no fun having to dig the car out to get it back on the blacktop road.

redesigned many of them for year-round use.

George Cowgill of Birmingham promoted Mara Vista Beach. Brown Howell and others made plans to subdivide Santa Monica Beach. J.P. and Fern Arnold completed Gulf

Beach Resort near the foot of Highway 79. Many other individuals or groups developed their own beaches.

In the 1950s, realtors such as Sam B. Hearn transported potential investors from Atlanta by plane to his El Centro Beach.

THE TARPON

The clear turquoise-hued water and the sugary-white sand of Panama City Beach make this area one of the premier destinations for diving in Florida. With numerous wrecks, sunken barges, an old bridge and other underwater sites, divers slip into their wet suits, tanks, masks and flippers to descend into the gorgeous undersea world of the bay, pass and Gulf.

For decades, the sunken S.S. Tarpon ranked as a top attraction 10 miles offshore from Panama City Beach in about 90 feet of water. Now, since 1997, when the State designated the famous steamship its sixth Underwater Archaeological Preserve, Bay County has moved higher on the list of world-class diving spots.

Captain Willis G. Barrow, of Pensacola, brought the 15-year old 130-foot freighter from Philadelphia in 1902 after need arose for steamer service between Pensacola, St. Andrews and Apalachicola.

The Tarpon sailed into St. Andrew Bay for her inaugural run of January 28, 1903 with Barrow at the helm. Thus began the first of 1,735 round trips she would take over the next 34 years. The pioneer vessel became a "lifeline along the Gulf Coast," bringing supplies to isolated communities with few roads and no rail service.

Barrow and his Tarpon soon expanded their route. The vessel operated round trip between

The popular steamship Tarpon under Capt. W.G. Barrow, made weekly trips between Mobile, Pensacola, Panama City, Apalachicola and Carrabelle from 1903 to 1937. The vessel racked up to a total of 1,735 trips before she sank in about 90 feet of water, 10 miles off Panama City Beach on September 1, 1937. Thirteen individuals survived, but 18 died in the disaster, including Barrow. In 1997 the Tarpon became Florida's 6th underwater archaeological preserve.

Mobile, Pensacola, Panama City, St. Andrews, Apalachicola and Carrabelle each week. Some years the steamer even docked at Millville and Lynn Haven.

The captain stuck to his schedule and guaranteed to make time in "rain or shine, storm or calm." He was often heard to say, "God makes the weather, and with His help, I make the trip."

The Tarpon brought many new families to the area. Travelers could book passage in the staterooms and dine on the sumptuous food with the captain at the head of the table.

Once the Bay Line was completed into Panama City in June 1908, Barrow faced stiff competition, but he always kept commerce flowing. The Tarpon often provided cheaper rates

than the rails. The fact that the captain carried his own stevedores to unload and load the vessel quickly while in port contributed to her speed. An annual overhaul kept the vessel in good repair.

Women and children loved to visit with the handsome skipper when he came ashore. Those who ate with Barrow at the Panama Hotel in Panama City always learned the latest news along the coast.

But deckhands knew the captain tolerated no foolishness. He never hesitated to give them a boot in the rear or strong tongue lashing if they did not perform their work with speed.

Over the years, Barrow and his Tarpon survived several hurricanes, which at times left the vessel high and dry. In March 1923, the ship caught fire at the dock in Panama City, but fire-fighters extinguished the blaze before much damage was done.

To families in this area and vessels plying the Gulf, the Tarpon was no mere ship. Barrow and his Tarpon became legendary through their remarkable schedule and dependable service.

The iron-hulled steamer carried all types of items from barrels of naval stores and building materials, to paper-mill products, new automobiles and the latest household supplies. Storeowners depended on the Tarpon to bring them groceries and green bottles of Pensacola's well-known Spearman beer.

But, as great as the 81-year-old captain was, he still clung to the ways of the past. Like other captains of that time, he over-loaded his vessel. When investigators tried to get him to paint a "load line" on the side of the ship, Barrow always had an excuse. He also never added a radio, which could have brought him aid from other vessels.

The evening of August 31, 1937, the Tarpon departed Pensacola en route east to Panama City. The weather turned bad and in the early morning hours, water began crashing over the sides of the steamer. The crew and captain battled heroically, but the vessel began sinking a little after 8 a.m. on September 1. They were able to launch only one of the three lifeboats. Thirteen men survived, but eighteen drowned. Barrow lost his life in the disaster.

Early divers retrieved hundreds of beer bottles and numerous other mementos from the wreck site. But in 1987, it became a third-degree felony to collect artifacts from shipwrecks.

By designating the steamer a preserve the State hopes the steamer will remain intact for future divers.

An underwater marker at the famous shipwreck gives some of its remarkable history.

RECOLLECTIONS *&* MEMORIES BY JACK MASHBURN

The Tarpon and Captain Barrow

"HERE'S A TRUE STORY ABOUT THE STEAMSHIP TARPON. CAPTAIN BARROW CARRIED HIS HANDS WITH HIM TO LOAD AND UNLOAD AT PORTS. ONE TIME A WOMAN WENT UP TO CAPTAIN BARROW WHEN THEY WERE HIRING. THEN, MEN WERE REQUIRED TO CARRY HEAVY SACKS OF SALT. CAPTAIN BARROW SAID 'CAN YOU CARRY 200 POUNDS OF SALT? SHE SAID, 'I CAN CARRY TWO AT A TIME.'

"SO THIS GUY STEPS UP AND SAYS 'I BET YOU CAN'T CARRY ONE SACK.' HE BET $1. SO SHE JUST REACHED DOWN AND GRABBED ONE AND WALKED OVER THE PLANK WITH IT. SHE SAID, 'GIVE ME THE $1.'

"THEN SHE SAID 'IF YOU WANT TO GET RECKLESS BET $5. I'LL CARRY TWO AT THE SAME TIME.' SO SHE DID AND GRABBED ONE UNDER EACH ARM TO GET THE $5.

"THEN SHE SAID, 'IF YOU WANT TO GET REALLY RECKLESS I'LL CARRY THREE AT A TIME FOR $10. WELL, THEY JUST KNEW SHE COULDN'T DO THAT. SHE SNATCHED UP ONE AND PUT IT UNDER HER ARM, THEN SHE GRABBED THE NEXT ONE AND GOT IT UNDER HER OTHER ARM. THEY THOUGHT THEY HAD HER BUT SHE GOT SOMEONE TO PUT A SACK ACROSS THE TWO SACKS, AND SHE WALKED THE PLANK WITH ALL THREE AND CLAIMED HER $10.

"THAT'S A TRUE STORY! CAPTAIN BARROW HIRED HER TO HELP UNLOAD. NOW IT WAS JUST FOR THAT ONE JOB. BUT MOST MEN WERE NOT REALLY HAPPY AT THE WAY SHE SHOWED THEM UP. I WOULDN'T WANT TO HAVE ARM-WRESTLED HER!"

J.M.

TYNDALL AIR FORCE BASE

Movie actor, Clark Gable smiled as he accepted his Silver Wings on January 6, 1943 at Tyndall Field. Gable underwent gunnery training at the base and created a sensation wherever he went into town. Favorite destinations then were Mattie's Tavern in St. Andrews and the Cove and Dixie Sherman hotels in Panama City. Col. W.A. Maxwell, the base commander, pinned on Gable's Wings and his Flying Bullet badge.

Col. W. A. Maxwell

When government officials came to Bay County in September 1940 seeking a site for an Army-Air Force flexible gunnery school, they first visited Panama City Beach. But they rejected that location in favor of the 18-mile long piece of property known as the East Peninsula. Water surrounded most of this land and it provided flyers an unobstructed view of the Gulf while training.

Hundreds of individuals and families lived on the peninsula in communities such as Cromanton, San Blas, Redfish Point, Beacon Beach, Auburn, Davis Beach, Belle Isle and Farmdale. They had until July 1, 1941 to vacate their homes and land.

The first small group of military personnel, transferred from Maxwell Field near Montgomery, Alabama, arrived

Long lines of motor vehicles traveled on and off Tyndall Field each day during WWII. Traffic became so heavy DuPont Bridge was closed in the early morning hours and then again in late afternoon and restricted to only cars and trucks bound for or departing Tyndall Field. All traffic came to a halt, however, when DuPont Bridge opened for vessels making their way over the Intracoastal Canal.

on August 26, 1941. Most were military police sent to guard construction and to patrol the beaches against invaders. These MPs were housed in 12 waterfront cottages at Beacon Beach on Crooked Island Sound until their barracks could be built. For the first few days, they lived the life of happy "beach bums."

While buildings were being erected on the field, the National Guard Armory on Sixth Street in Panama City served as the main headquarters. Col. W.A. Maxwell, the Base Commander, landed on the first aircraft, an AT-6, on the field on November 6, 1941.

Although small flexible gunnery schools existed at Las Vegas, New Mexico and Harlingen, Texas, plans called for Tyndall Field to become the largest and only permanent Air Corps Flexible Gunnery School in the United States.

On December 5, 1941, the first 600 troops arrived for training. Hundreds more followed the next day. They were temporarily housed at the Army recreational area on the west side of Watson Bayou, just east of what is now Bay Medical Center.

The new 26,000-acre base was named for Frank B. Tyndall, a Florida World War I flying ace. It officially opened on December 6, 1941, one day before Pearl Harbor.

After the war, Tyndall Field became Tyndall Air Force Base.

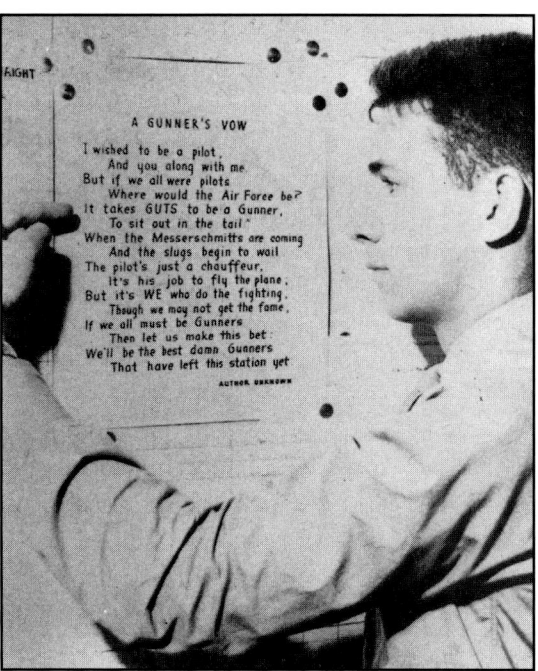

During WWII, Tyndall Field was the largest gunnery school in the Army-Air Force Training Command. By 1944, when wartime activities became routine, Tyndall trained 500 gunners per week. WASPs (Women's Air Service Pilots) often flew planes pulling tow targets for gunnery practice.

WAINWRIGHT SHIPYARD

Wainwright Shipyard employees launched Liberty Ship "Stephen Furdek" in May 1944. This vessel was the 40th built at the yard, located near Dyers Point. In June 1970 the Furdek was reported as heading for the scrap yard at Panama City. This ship was one of the few to meet her end at the same place she was constructed during World War II.

On April 12, 1942, the J.A. Jones Construction Company of Charlotte, North Carolina opened the Wainwright Shipyard, named for prisoner-of-war General Jonathan Wainwright. The yard covered 112 acres and was located on Dyers Point, near the east end of Hathaway Bridge. This piece of land had been the site of the huge West Bay Naval Stores & Lumber Company in the early 1900s.

Wainwright Yard became one of 18 in the country selected for the production of sturdy Liberty ships, which were capable of transporting 10,000 tons of cargo and reaching surface speeds of 11 knots.

With housing critical, spare rooms in St. Andrews were in big demand. Both men and women worked 8-hour, round-the-clock shifts to meet the tremendous need for vessels that first year.

On December 30, 1942, a few days after Christmas, the first Liberty, the E. Kirby Smith, slid down the ways. Workers at Wainwright built 102 Liberty ships and six T-1 tankers between 1942-1945.

At the end of the war, the shipyard closed. In September 1957, Port Authority Chairman, Mack Lewis announced that after 11 years of negotiations, the Department of the Navy agreed to sell the old shipyard to Panama City.

The Navy Base underwent several name changes before it became the Coastal Systems Station of today. The military base grew slowly with activity concentrated in the early days at the dock and shops' area (not shown in this photo.) The wooden buildings seen above the parking lot were removed years ago. The first Hathaway Bridge can be seen in the distance at the top right. Base housing and the marina were both constructed at a later date along the half-moon bay beach. Circa 1950.

THE NAVY BASE

For decades those knowledgeable about military affairs considered St. Andrew Bay a logical location for a naval installation. After World War I some even proposed that it become a submarine base.

But a definite need did not arise until 1942 when the government established the 373-acre Naval Section Base directly across the bay from Wainwright Shipyard where more than 100 Liberty ships were built during the war.

In 1945 this base became the U.S. Navy Mine Countermeasures Station. As workmen cut the winding entrance road from the U.S. 98 gate around thick swamps and pines that had been turpentined, bellowing alligators and snorting wild hogs voiced their complaints at the disturbance in their habitat.

Other employees doused themselves with liniment or "squita dote" to fend off millions of mosquitoes, yellow flies and gnats while constructing Buildings No. 1, 2, 3, 4 and 5, a renovated old homestead which the station converted to a work place. The base added 300 more acres in 1955.

The Administration and Operations Building, known as "110," was the first structure erected by a civilian contractor.

In the early days of the base, old Hathaway Bridge caused numerous problems for naval and civilian personnel. Tugboats and barges often rammed the long, low span, forcing it to remain closed several days for repairs. At other times the swing section stuck and would not close.

During these periods, employees of the Navy Base either parked at old Wainwright Shipyard and rode a boat back and forth across the bay, or they took the long drive around West Bay to reach the base.

Several "honky-tonks" stood near the intersection of U.S. 98 and Thomas Drive with the "Black Cat" one of the favorite watering holes.

Over the years the Navy Base underwent several name changes. The base is currently known as the Coastal Systems Station.

In the early days of the Navy Base, now Coastal Systems Station, a superintendent oversaw construction of all buildings on the military base. No outside laborers were employed until 1955. Building No. 110, the Administration and Operations Headquarters, was the first structure erected by a civilian contractor.

THE EMPIRE MICA

*A*t the beginning of World War II, German submarines prowled the East, West and Gulf coasts of the United States. These U—boats torpedoed hundreds of vessels with America unprepared for such attacks early in the fighting.

Several articles appeared in the newspapers about the enemy seawolves. They listed the sizes of the ships sunk, and the number of seamen saved or drowned. But exact locations for these losses never were identified due to the news blackout.

In this part of the country, all vessels sailing along the coast were warned to stay within the 10-fathom curve, where subs were at a disadvantage.

Late in June 1942, the freighter Empire Mica was sailing east on her maiden voyage from Baytown, Texas to her homeport in England. The large tanker carried 11,200 tons of petroleum distillate and planned to anchor the night of June 28 in either St. Andrew or St. Joseph Bay as she had been instructed to do for safety. But the Mica's heavy load prevented her from entering either harbor.

Hugh B. Bentley, the ship's 70-year-old captain, gave orders to speed through the waters that hot summer night. Bentley was unaware that German Capt. Gunter Muller-Stockheim pursued the Mica in his U-67 submarine.

About 1 a.m. on June 29,

one of the seamen who had just taken over watch, spotted a periscope in the moonlight. Before he could report his sighting, two torpedoes slammed into the Mica's portside, setting off powerful explosions heard for miles. Within minutes flames leaped high in the sky, and the ship turned into a burning inferno.

Fourteen seamen scrambled into one of the lifeboats and survived. But the 33 others either perished attempting to lower the other two lifeboats or burned to death, trapped in their bunks.

With the Coast Guard's only vessel undergoing repairs, rescuers from Apalachicola took their own private boats to the scene of the disaster off Indian Pass. They circled the wreck several times searching for men

but found none. They took those in the lifeboat to Apalachicola where the men spent a week recovering from their injuries before returning home.

About 40 years after the freighter sank, several divers attempted to retrieve its 32,000-pound propeller. After a number of blasts from explosives, a few salvagers succeeded in wresting the ship's propeller from the Gulf's floor.

Jimmy and Johnny Patronis, owners of Capt. Anderson's restaurant, purchased the propeller in November 1983. It stands at the entrance to their restaurant on Grand Lagoon.

The Empire Mica, a favorite dive site, rests in about 102 feet of water, 23 miles off Cape San Blas.

At its front entrance Capt. Anderson's restaurant displays the Empire Mica's propeller purchased in 1983 by owners Jimmy and Johnny Patronis.

THE SUNKEN U-BOAT

ENT GUNNER FIRING AT TOW TARGET
PANAMA CITY, FLORIDA
130-P

PHOTO BY SOUTHEAST
AIR FORCES TRAINING
CENTER, TYNDALL FIELD, FLA

Gunnery students at Tyndall practiced firing live ammunition at tow targets pulled by AT-6 trainers and other planes. The ink and paint used to tally scores were continually upgraded during the war. In 1945, gunners began firing "frangible bullets," which powdered like dust upon impact.

The Civil Air Patrol provided an invaluable service to the United States during World War II, patrolling the sea-lanes and uninhabited stretches of coastline.

The patrol was organized in 1942. The volunteers wore regular Army-Air Force uniforms that differed only with their badges.

Headquarters for this base, known as CAP No. 14, stood at the old municipal airfield near the northern end of Frankford Avenue in Panama City. Civilian Conservation Corps barracks from the 1930s were moved to the old airfield and served as housing for the pilots and mechanics.

The CAP pilots flew three missions each day, watching for enemy submarines and foreign agents coming ashore. They covered the long stretch of coast from Pensacola to Cedar Key.

CAP Base No. 14 consisted of 75 pilots and mechanics. They flew many different types of planes that included Fairchilds and Stinsons.

Longtime Panama City resident, Johnny Reaver came from Ohio to Panama City to join this CAP. As a flight officer and a mechanic, he earned $8 per day minus the cost of his uniforms. Reaver experienced several close calls, especially when switching from an empty tank to a full tank in flight.

One time, plane trouble forced him to land on a strip of sand next to a fisherman on Panama City Beach. The fisherman would not move so Reaver had to turn toward the water in order not to hit him.

Reaver witnessed one of the all but forgotten events of World War II. Although the government imposed a blackout on military activities and no information appeared in print, Reaver recalled the time some of the CAP pilots spotted a German submarine a mile off Panama City Beach at the foot of what is now Highway 79, in about 40-50 feet of water.

The pilots called Tyndall Field, but their gunnery school planes did not carry bombs. Tyndall, in turn, notified the Navy Base in Pensacola, which sent a PBY Amphibian Twin Engine equipped with several 100-pound bombs to sink the sub.

Before the bombing commenced, law enforcement officials ordered the Germans on board the sub to come ashore where they were arrested and taken to jail.

In the latter months of 1943, enemy submarine activity ceased along the Gulf. The CAP No. 14 group was transferred to California.

After the war ended, Reaver returned to Panama City to operate Skyland Airfield near the northeast corner of 11th Street and Balboa Avenue in Panama City.

During that time, the sunken sub became a hazard to navigation. The Corps of Engineers eventually dynamited the U-Boat, leaving parts of the vessel on the Gulf floor.

EDGEWATER GULF BEACH

*A*lfred I. DuPont and his brother-in-law, Edward Ball, began investing in Bay County in the 1920s. They owned hundreds of acres on the East Peninsula, now Tyndall Air Force Base, where they intended to build a huge resort west of what is now Mexico Beach.

When Dupont died in 1935, Ball carried on with his plans. But the federal government assumed control of most property on the East Peninsula in 1941 to build the military base, ending the DuPont estate's plans for a beach resort on the peninsula.

Edgewater Beach became one of the premier housing developments on Panama City Beach after the war. The DuPont estate purchased 300 housing units, known as the Gulf Shores Apartments. The organization improved these redbrick homes, built in 1945. The units offered one or two bedrooms, a living room, kitchen, dining room and a 'full tile bath.' They also featured air conditioning, room phones and reasonable rates.

The developers laid out the residential section with miles of wide, paved streets and walkways, adding shrubbery, flowers and grass lawns to give Edgewater a homey atmosphere. The complex maintained a huge beach-side-parking area for guests and visitors.

Edgewater Beach became a separate municipality in 1953. Included in the town were grocery stores, nightclubs, bars and other amusements within walking distance of renters and guests. The beach's popular "Jenkins Drive-In," a year-round dining and dancing center, attracted large crowds.

The Wakulla Edgewater Company, which owned the complex after the war, also operated the Wakulla Hotel at Wakulla Springs and Edgewater Gulf Hotel at Edgewater Park, Mississippi.

During the 1950s and 1960s, the complex thrived. Then in the 1970s the old brick buildings were slowly torn down. Edgewater Beach Resort replaced the former municipality, which became part of the City of Panama City Beach in 1970.

uring the Works Progress Administration and the Civilian Conservation Corps days of the 1930s, the state ordered an aerial survey of the coast to find a suitable location in Bay County for a modern recreation center and tourist camp.

In 1934, the engineers zeroed in on property surrounding the new pass, built that year and commonly referred to now as "the jetties." Once the pass was completed in November, the rock jetties at the entrance proved inadequate at controlling erosion. Over the next few years, the Corps of Engineers with the aid of the WPA widened, curved and lengthened the jetties by adding more rocks to them.

Little activity took place toward a park, however, as the channel and other projects took precedence while the country attempted to climb out of the Great Depression.

At the beginning of World War II, the federal government assumed control of the commanding location surrounding the pass to establish a coastal artillery unit. The military erected several buildings, a wooden water tower with a deep well, a wharf, observation tower and 10 small barracks, capable of housing about 12 men each, all on the west side of the pass.

Two six-inch guns were mounted on concrete turrets to fire on enemy ships or submarines attempting to enter the channel. Florida remained on high alert as German U-boats

prowled the Gulf sinking many ships, and enemy agents slipped ashore along the East Coast of the state.

Men on horses patrolled the beaches as far west as Phillips Inlet with different stations along the way. Entrance to the artillery unit came by way of boat or what is now Thomas Drive south to a rebuilt wooden bridge over Grand Lagoon. Then a narrow trail on the south shore of the lagoon led to the installation.

The Beginnings of the Park

After the war, the location attracted the attention of the Panama City Kiwanis Club and other civic organizations. Members from these clubs contacted U.S. Rep. Bob Sikes for his help in securing the land where the small military installation stood for the park, proposed before the war.

Acquisition of the 1,260-acre park came slowly, however, with the first 238 acres donated by a private citizen.

During the late 1940s, the park and bridge over Grand Lagoon remained closed to the public. Claude J. Willoughby became the park's first manager. He performed repairs and built "Gator Lake." He also obtained funding for the two piers, one on the lagoon and the other on the Gulf. In a few years, Steve Lee and a few others joined Willoughby to work at the park.

Eventually the bridge over Grand Lagoon was opened to traffic. Visitors slowly began

ST. ANDREWS STATE RECREATION AREA

The Turpentine Stills –
Turpentining was one of the main industries of this area during the early 1900s. In fact, the St. Andrew Bay area ranked as the number one producer of naval stores in this country in 1911.

Obtaining turpentine, a product of the distillation of pine gum, involved several steps. Workers had to dip the gum from slashed places, often called "cat faces," on pine trees.

The gum was transferred to 50-pound wooden barrels and taken to the still where cooking changed it to turpentine or rosin. Care had to be taken, however, because stills could explode if they became too hot.

"Scrape" was hardened rosin that collected on the face of a pine tree during the season. Here, a man is shown distilling the "scrape" in late autumn.

Turpentine was used for making paints, varnishes, medicines and many other products. Rosin saw similar use in the manufacture of soap, paper, inks, shoe polish, linoleum and several other items.

A restored old turpentine still can be seen at St. Andrews State Recreation Area.

entering the recreation area at no cost in 1951. Beginning in 1955, a fee of 25 cents was charged for admission to the park. The recreation area existed on both the east and a west sides of the pass, as it does today.

Campsites were established slowly, with the first 13 set aside in 1960. Through the years the wreck of the Percy Payne, a cargo schooner that sank in the early 1900s, lured swimmers and snorkelers at the edge of the Gulf between the west jetties and the Gulf pier. But little now remains of this wreck.

An old turpentine still was added to the recreation area and restored for exhibition. Signs explain naval stores and the way "gum" was tapped from the pine trees and distilled to make turpentine.

One of the six-inch gun mounts is still visible south of the concession stand near the beach, but little is left of the second mount, which stood closer to the jetties.

Camping sites at the park now number about 175. Along the recreation area's nature trail visitors can glimpse wading birds, alligators, deer and other wildlife. A convenient launching ramp provides boaters easy access to the bay, pass and Gulf.

Visitors flock to the park to enjoy the clear blue-green water, dazzling white sand and the superb camping facilities. Today, St. Andrews State Recreation Area is one of the most popular state parks in Florida.

RECOLLECTIONS & MEMORIES BY JACK MASHBURN

Brown's Beach

"IN THOSE DAYS THE STATE LEGISLATURE MET EVERY TWO YEARS. MY REAL INTEREST WAS POLITICS. I WENT TO TALLAHASSEE TO VISIT THE TWO BAY COUNTY REPRESENTATIVES AND FOUND OUT THAT GRADY COURTNEY WASN'T GOING TO RUN FOR REELECTION. AFTER THE 1951 SESSION WAS OVER, I ANNOUNCED TO THE WORLD THAT I WAS RUNNING FOR THE LEGISLATURE. I STARTED CAMPAIGNING WITH STUMP SPEECHES. THAT'S WHERE YOU GET UP ON A STUMP AND TALK TO ANYBODY WHO WILL LISTEN.

"I TURNED 24 ON APRIL 21, 1952 AND WAS ELECTED TO THE STATE LEGISLATURE THREE WEEKS LATER. I WAS STILL WORKING FOR ARIZONA CHEMICAL AT THE TIME BUT TOOK A LEAVE OF ABSENCE TO ATTEND THE LEGISLATIVE SESSION.

"THEN WHEN I FOUND OUT THE FEDERAL GOVERNMENT HAD RELEASED WHAT IS NOW ST. ANDREWS STATE RECREATION AREA I KNEW WE HAD TO DO SOMETHING.

"THE FEDERAL FOLKS HAD TOLD STATE OFFICIALS THAT IF THEY DIDN'T BUILD A PARK BY JANUARY 1, 1954, THEY WERE GOING TO SELL THE LAND. SO I PROMPTLY DREW UP A BILL TO CONSTRUCT THE PARK BUT INSISTED ON PUTTING IN THE STIPULATION THAT A PORTION OF THE PARK WOULD BE FOR BLACKS.

"THAT WAS NOT A POPULAR THING TO DO THEN AND A WHOLE GROUP OF PEOPLE CAME TO SEE ME IN TALLAHASSEE. THIS WAS DURING THE TIME WHEN NO BLACK MAN COULD EVEN PUT A FOOT IN THE WATER OR ON THE BEACH WITHOUT BEING ARRESTED, AND I THOUGHT I WAS GOING TO BE TARRED AND FEATHERED.

"I MET THE GROUP AT THE CAPITOL. NOW, I WAS TALKING WITH PEOPLE IN THEIR 40s, 50s, 60s AND UP. I REMINDED THEM THAT THERE WAS A KEY ISSUE BEFORE THE SUPREME COURT AT THE TIME. IT WAS A CASE CALLED BROWN VS. THE TOPEKA, KANSAS SCHOOL BOARD. I TOLD THEM THE SUPREME COURT MET EVERY FIRST MONDAY IN OCTOBER AND IN MY OPINION THEY WERE GOING TO RULE ON THE BROWN-TOPEKA, KANSAS CASE IN SPRING OR SUMMER THE FOLLOWING YEAR.

"I SAID, I THINK BROWN IS GOING TO WIN, AND IT'S GOING TO OPEN UP ALL OUR PARKS. I ASKED THEM IF THEY COULD SEE THE RAMIFICATIONS OF ALL OF THIS. I TOLD

*THEM IF WE HAD A PLACE FOR THE BLACK PEOPLE TO
COME THAT WE COULD WEATHER THE STORM. THE ONLY
PARK WE HAD THEN WAS WAYSIDE PARK WHERE THE DAN
RUSSELL PIER IS NOW.*

*"IN THOSE DAYS OF SEGREGATION AND POTENTIAL
INTEGRATION EFFORTS, I FEARED ALL OUR BUSINESS
WOULD BE GONE FOR YEARS. GOD BLESS THEM! OUR
TOURISTS WERE PEA PICKERS AND PEANUT SHAKERS.' AND
I DON 'T MEAN THAT IN A DEROGATORY WAY BECAUSE I
GREW UP AS ONE TOO.*

*"WE HAD A FEW FACTORY WORKERS COMING DOWN
FROM BIRMINGHAM AND ATLANTA BUT THEY WEREN'T
READY FOR INTEGRATION, AND I KNEW IF WE HAD A PARK
SET ASIDE WE WOULDN'T HAVE ANY PROBLEMS.*

*"AT THAT TIME BROWN'S BEACH ALREADY HAD ITS
NAME FROM THE PREVIOUS OWNER. IT HAD NOTHING TO
DO WITH THE BROWN VS. TOPEKA SCHOOL BOARD CASE.
BUT THAT MIGHT HAVE HELPED GET IT THROUGH.*

*"I SUGGESTED WE USE BROWN'S BEACH AS A SPECIAL
SECTION FOR THEM, AND CALL IT BLIND LUCK OR VISION,
IT TURNED OUT I WAS RIGHT. WHEN WE GOT THAT PARK
READY AND ACTUALLY OPENED IT FOR BLACKS, IF MY
MEMORY SERVES ME RIGHT, IT WAS IN JANUARY 1954.*

*"SO BLACKS THEN HAD THEIR OWN BEACH. IT WAS
JUST AS YOU GO THROUGH THE GATE TO THE RIGHT AND
IT WAS MARKED WITH A SIGN. IT WAS THE FIRST BLACK
BEACH ON THE GULF OF MEXICO FROM KEY WEST TO
BROWNSVILLE, TEXAS.*

*"IT AVOIDED A LOT OF TROUBLE. ONE TIME A FRIEND
CALLED FROM FSU-TV IN TALLAHASSEE TO INTERVIEW ME
ON BROWN'S BEACH. I TOLD HIM WHEN WHITE PEOPLE
FOUND OUT BLACK DIDN'T RUB OFF EVERYONE WAS OKAY.
I TOLD HIM NOW IF YOU WANT TO SEE WHERE THE
BLACKS ARE, GO TO THE JETTIES. THEY WERE ALL DOWN
THERE FISHING. IT WAS A GOOD PROGRAM, AND I'M GLAD
TO HAVE PLAYED A PART IN IT. I DON'T KNOW HOW SIGNIF-
ICANT IT WAS BUT IT FOCUSED THE ATTENTION ON THE
FACT THAT SOMETHING HAD TO BE DONE IN THOSE DAYS."*

J.M.

THE HERMIT OF ST. ANDREWS

The lure of the snow-white beaches, the mild climate and several excellent restaurants bring many to this area. But years ago at the turn of the century it was fishing that attracted people here when the Northern Gulf Coast had some of the greatest fishing grounds in the country.

Teddy Tollofsen's gravemaker in Greenwood Cemetery, Panama City.

During his life, Theodore Tollofsen of Norway took jobs as a seaman at various ports around the world. He was working in Pensacola after World War I when he heard about the fishing opportunities off St. Andrew Bay and sailed here in his 26-foot wooden boat.

Tollofsen began working for Bay Fisheries, one of the largest companies on the coast, and lived in a small house in St. Andrews. Being a foreigner, Tollofsen drew the curious who asked him many questions about his native country and the family he left when he came to America. Unmarried women considered him an eligible bachelor and brought him pies and other sweets.

Teddy never liked to talk much about his past. He grew tired of the many questions and began spending nights on his boat. He was asleep when the hurricane of Sept. 30, 1929 blew into the coast. The storm forced him ashore then whisked his vessel across the bay to Grand Lagoon where the battered hull wound up wrecked on the beach.

The heartbroken fisherman, whose main possession had been his boat, dismantled it and used the wood to build himself a 9 x 12 foot cabin on property that is now St. Andrews State Recreation Area. He lived in that location eking out an existence by selling fish and raising chickens.

Teddy passed the time salvaging relics from shipwrecks, which he used to decorate his hut. The Norwegian soon became known as the "hermit of St. Andrews." Even though Tollofsen sought solitude in this secluded location, people could not believe that he enjoyed being alone and continued to try and visit him.

When the park was established in 1946, Teddy received special permission to live out his life on government property. Tollofsen died in 1954. Inside his cabin, rangers found the wedding photo of a young couple and money he saved for his burial in Greenwood Cemetery in Panama City.

SIX SMALL MUNICIPALITIES ARE INCORPORATED ON PANAMA CITY BEACH

The year of 1953 dawned as a confusing and eventful time for many beach residents. Jack Mashburn and J. Ed Stokes served as State Representatives and George Tapper, State Senator. The changes that would take place on the beaches over the next few months would involve these three men and several business owners.

Ever since 1951, a number of people on the beaches had been pushing for "bridge to bridge" consolidation. When this movement failed the "Citizens' Committee," a group of 300, was formed two years later in 1953. The committee began working for incorporation of the entire 20 miles or so of beach area.

Tempers flared at many of the meetings held between those for and against consolidation. At issue was the availability of 20 new liquor licenses. The underlying concerns of the committee were stopping the sale of liquor on Sundays and controlling the hours when and if liquor could be sold on the beaches.

When the vote for consolidation failed again, the Citizens' Committee backed Panama City's plan to annex Panama City Beach, believing they could circumvent the incorporation issue this way and still achieve their goals.

But those in favor of such a move failed to consider the consequences. For some reason they believed they could obtain fire, police and water services from Panama City with little or no taxes paid by them.

Carl Gray, Mayor of Panama City, had been out of town when this issue was debated. When he heard about the proposal, he strongly objected and considered it "financially unwise." Gray also questioned the legality of such an annexation since the area was not contiguous to the city with St. Andrew Bay and Hathaway Bridge separating the two areas.

The wrangling between the two groups reached the point where the Panama City

The Panama City Beach Pier attracted fishermen year round. They caught flounder, pompano, ling, whiting, mackerel, sea bass and redfish in season. A light can be seen for night fishing. This first pier on the beach stood where Pineapple Willy's and Sunbird Condominiums are located today.

News-Herald called the ongoing battle, "The Great Incorporation Story."

Then the idea of consolidating small communities gained some popularity. But members of the Citizens' Committee accused those in favor of such a proposition in using it as a way to acquire the 20 new liquor licenses.

By May 11, 1953, the House had passed H.B. No. 954, creating J.E. Churchwell's Long Beach; H.B. No. 955 for M.C. Buckley's Edgewater Gulf Beach; H.B. No. 953 for A.W. Pledger's Panama City Beach; and H.R. No. 966 for C.F. Stiles' Dutchville. Then a day later, two more municipalities were introduced, involving the "microscopic municipalities" of Playville under H.B. No. 1098; and Julia, along Panama City Beach, under H.B. 1101.

At a meeting on May 13, Churchwell, Buckley and others admitted they favored incorporation of their small municipalities to protect them. They felt Panama City Beach, as a whole through incorporation, was too thinly populated for its residents to be able to afford the new tax burden for funding fire protection, police protection, garbage removal, an adequate water system, sewerage and the lighting of public areas.

One meeting finally reached the point where Churchwell told the opposition that they didn't know what they wanted and to "go home and wash your dirty linen and get to work," according to the Panama City News Herald of May 13, 1953.

As to problems over new liquor licenses, Churchwell, Pledger and Buckley all stated that they would have their charters amended to read that there would be no additional liquor licenses issued within their municipalities.

When some appealed to Tapper not to sign the bills, creating the six municipalities, he replied that he promised to support local legislation for counties when bills were approved by both representatives. Mashburn and Stokes each favored the creation of these small municipalities, and they became law.

RECOLLECTIONS *&* MEMORIES BY JACK MASHBURN

"BETWEEN 1948—1953 MOST PLACES HAD GAMBLING, EITHER ON A LOWER FLOOR OR CURTAINED OFF IN THE BACK. THAT INCLUDED ALL TYPES OF GAMBLING - SLOT MACHINES, ROULETTE WHEELS AND HIGH-STAKES POKER. GAMBLING WAS WIDE OPEN. THEY HAD IT ALL."

J.M.

The Dan Russell Pier extends into the Gulf, east of Hwy. 79. For many years, nearby Wayside Park attracted picnickers and swimmers to this location. The park contained several concrete tables and barbeque pits. In this picture, Wayside Shopping Center appears across Front Beach Road with one of the last huge sand dunes that once lined this beach. The location is now the site of the annual Seafood Festival, held each October.

WEST PANAMA CITY BEACH

In early 1959 the idea of creating West Panama City Beach, another new town, was debated by beach residents. A storm of criticism arose over the boundaries selected that included a large section of the beach all the way to Phillips Inlet.

An "island" of land between Long Beach and Edgewater Beach, along with a strip of property to make the island contiguous with the rest of West Panama City Beach, was included in the designated area.

Bill Harris and Dempsey Barron served as State Representatives that year. State Senator Bart Knight tackled the complaint problem about the size of the proposed town by appointing a committee to establish more satisfactory boundaries that excluded the island. This group reduced the proposed West Panama City Beach to half its original size.

West Panama City Beach was officially incorporated on June 30, 1959. The town extended about seven miles from just east of Laguna Beach to the western edge of Edgewater Beach. Knight added a clause that allowed the city commissioners of the new town to extend the sale of liquor beyond limits set by the state and to stop the sale of liquor on Sundays if the electorate of the new city voted to do so.

The new West Panama City Beach included the following beaches: Beacon Resort at the foot of Highway 79, Betty Lou Beach, Mara Vista Beach, Florida Beach, Larkway Villas, Bahama Beach, and the Old Dutch Beach area up to Edgewater Beach.

George Cowgill, Jr. was

elected mayor. When the tiny island in District 2 desired to become its own municipality, Knight backed the consolidation along with Harris and Barron. This new municipality, called West Long Beach, ran for three quarters of a mile along the Gulf and 500-600 yards inland.

In 1961, Clarence W. Sassard served as Police Chief of West Panama City and Lloyd Coram as Captain. By April the new City Hall was ready for occupancy. The city had installed two deep fresh water wells with overhead tanks for a sufficient water supply. During the summer an extra policeman was hired to provide 24-hour police service.

RECOLLECTIONS & MEMORIES BY JACK MASHBURN

The Old Dutch

"I WAS IN THE OLD DUTCH HUNDREDS OF TIMES. IT WAS OWNED BY CLIFF STILES FROM BIRMINGHAM. I HAD A COTTAGE AT EDGEWATER BEACH FOR A NUMBER OF YEARS. I KEPT IT YEAR ROUND FOR $75 A MONTH AND THAT INCLUDED UTILITIES.

THEY HAD SOME OF THE MOST UNUSUAL FLOOR SHOWS. A HYPNOTIST BY THE NAME OF DR. GRANT WHO APPEARED THERE WAS VERY GOOD.

WHEN YOU WENT IN THE FRONT FROM THE HIGHWAY, THE LOUNGE WAS ON THE LEFT WITH A HUGE FIREPLACE IN THE MIDDLE WITH DOORS ON THE RIGHT AND LEFT. IN BACK, THE PLACE HAD A RAISED STAGE.

ONE TIME A FRIEND AND I WERE SITTING THERE WHEN HE SAID HE THOUGHT HE SAW A WHITE ARABIAN HORSE GO BY IN THE BUILDING. I TOLD HIM HE WAS SEEING THINGS. BUT SURE ENOUGH THEY HAD A HORSE AS PART OF A FLOOR SHOW.

I AM TOLD THAT WHITE HORSES WERE USED DURING WORLD WAR II TO PATROL THE BEACHES BECAUSE THEY BLENDED IN WITH THE SAND."

J.M.

Old Dutch Tavern

America's Finest Beach — 10 Miles West of Panama City, Florida

In 1942, the "Old Dutch Tavern" was advertised as the only 2-story cypress log cabin in America, built entirely of cypress logs. Frank Burghduff listed himself as proprietor; his wife, Virginia, as mixologist. Guests were invited to enjoy the gorgeous moonlight nights from the dining room. Small planes landed on Panama City Beach as early as 1931. Pilots considered the sand a natural landing strip.

Legendary Sheriff, M. J. (Doc) Daffin, on the left, stands beside interim Sheriff Charlie Abbott and other deputies in this circa 1960s photo. Daffin was sworn in as Sheriff in 1953 and introduced markings on the department's cars. Doc died in office in January 1971.

CITY OF PANAMA CITY BEACH

In 1970 the idea of a "bridge to bridge" Panama City Beach again drew attention. J.R. Middlemas and Joe Chapman served as State Representatives that year and Dempsey Barron was State Senator.

They introduced a bill in late spring 1970 consolidating the municipalities of Long Beach Resort, Edgewater Gulf Beach, old Panama City Beach and West Panama City Beach into one municipality called Panama City Beach. This incorporation was the first step toward consolidation of the entire beach.

All three legislators realized that through one greater Panama City Beach residents would have a stronger voice and play more of an active role in government. They would receive better police and fire protection and obtain improved roads and public utilities. Through unification they also believed that the beach, as a whole, would become more attractive to promoters and grow at a faster rate.

But in the election held June 29 beach residents in four districts voted against consolidation. Only the little island between Edgewater and Long Beach favored it and voted to become part of Florida's newest city.

Another election was held July 28 to select officers. Dan Russell, who had been mayor of West Panama City Beach, was elected the first mayor of Panama City Beach.

Earlier that year West Panama City Beach claimed a population of 1,052; Long Beach Resort - 167; Edgewater Gulf Beach - 84; and Panama City Beach - 67.

Panama City Beach was established on Aug. 12, 1970. During the ceremony Russell removed the "west" from the West Panama City Beach sign on City Hall.

"I WOULD LIKE TO SAY THAT REGARDLESS OF WHAT'S PREVIOUSLY BEEN WRITTEN PRIOR TO THIS, THERE WERE NO INCORPORATED CITIES WEST OF HATHAWAY BRIDGE OR EAST OF PHILLIPS INLET UNTIL 1953. NONE; DURING THE FIRST PART OF 1953, AFTER I WAS ELECTED TO THE LEGISLATURE IN 1952, I SPOKE WITH A NUMBER OF PEOPLE AT THE BEACH. SOME OF THEM WANTED A CITY FROM BRIDGE TO BRIDGE AND SOME WANTED NONE AT ALL.

"I POINTED OUT THAT NONE OF THEM COULD AFFORD A BRIDGE TO BRIDGE CITY BECAUSE ANYONE LIVING IN AN INCORPORATED CITY COULD PETITION THE CIRCUIT COURT AND REQUIRE THAT CITY TO FURNISH ADEQUATE WATER, ADEQUATE SEWER AND ADEQUATE POLICE PROTECTION. THEY WOULD HAVE HAD TO LAY DOWN AN AD VALORIUM TAX SO HIGH, THEY'D RUN BUSINESS AWAY FOR YEARS AND YEARS.

"SO I TRIED TO COMPROMISE. I SAID, 'HOW ABOUT IF WE INCORPORATE A CITY FROM HATHAWAY BRIDGE TO THE "Y" (HIGHWAY 79), AND ONE FROM THE "Y" TO PHILLIPS INLET.' WELL, YOU NEVER SAW A MORE DIVIDED GROUP THAN AT THE BEACH IN 1953. THEY SAID 'WE WANT IT ALL OR NOTHING.'

"I SAID IT'S TIME THIS BEACH HAD SOME SELF AUTONOMY. DOC DAFFIN WAS ELECTED AS SHERIFF THE SAME TIME I WAS ELECTED TO THE FLORIDA LEGISLATURE. HE WAS SWORN IN, IN JANUARY 1953. HE CAME TO ME PERSONALLY AND SAID 'WE'RE GOING TO START MAKING CLUBS CLOSE DOWN AT 12 BECAUSE THAT IS WHAT THE LAW SAYS.' HE SAID 'WE ARE GOING TO SHUT DOWN THESE HOUSES OF PROSTITUTION AND WE'RE GOING TO START ABIDING BY THE LAW.' THEY WERE STAYING OPEN UNTIL 2 OR 3 A.M.

"THEY HAD 23 SUPPER CLUBS AT THAT TIME AND DREW A LOT OF PEOPLE. THEY BROUGHT IN A LOT OF GOOD VAUDEVILLE ACTS AND SOME THAT WERE NOT SO GOOD.

"ONCE HE STARTED CRACKING DOWN, TOURISTS STARTED LEAVING HERE FOR FORT WALTON, DESTIN, PENSACOLA AND GULF SHORES.

"SO I SAID 'IF I DO NOTHING ELSE, I'M GOING TO GIVE THE BEACHES A CHANCE TO MAKE THEIR OWN DECISIONS. WE'RE NOT GOING TO IMPOSE THEM.' AFTER WE SET UP THESE CITIES, THEY STILL HAD TO ELECT CITY COUNCILMEN TO DECIDE IF THEY WANTED BEVERAGES TO BE SOLD AND IF SO, HOW LONG.

"THE COUNTY COMMISSION WAS CONTROLLED BY AN UNUSUAL COLLUSION OF PREACHERS AND BOOTLEGGERS THEN. BOOTLEGGERS DIDN'T WANT ANY LIQUOR SOLD LEGALLY, AND THE PREACHERS DID NOT WANT ANY SOLD AT ALL.

"THE COUNTY COMMISSION HAD THE AUTHORITY TO OPEN THINGS UP, BUT THEY WERE TOO AFRAID OF THE TWO COMBINED GROUPS TO DO ANYTHING ABOUT IT.

"REPRESENTATIVE STOKES AND I ACTUALLY CREATED SIX CITIES ON THE BEACH- PANAMA CITY BEACH; LONG BEACH; EDGEWATER BEACH; JULIA, WHICH IS WHERE ANGELOS IS NOW; AND DUTCHVILLE, WHERE THE OLD DUTCH TAVERN WAS. THE DAYS INN AND RAMADA INN ARE THERE NOW. THE ONE IN BETWEEN WAS PLAYVILLE. THREE OF THESE-DUTCHVILLE, JULIA AND

PLAYVILLE NEVER ACTED AS CITIES. THEY WERE CREATED AS TOWNS JUST TO PROTECT THEIR RIGHTS.

"PANAMA CITY BEACH DIDN'T WANT ANY WHISKEY IN THEIR AREA, SO THEY PUT IN THEIR CHARTER THAT NO CITY LICENSE COULD BE ISSUED. THE DECISIONS WERE LEFT TO THE DIFFERENT CITIES.

"PANAMA CITY BEACH, LONG BEACH AND EDGEWATER ACTUALLY OPERATED AS CITIES FOR A LONG TIME. J.E. CHURCHWELL WAS VERY PROUD OF LONG BEACH. THE TOWNS COULD CONTROL THE HOURS CLUBS STAYED OPEN AND THE SALE OF ALCOHOLIC BEVERAGES.

"THE CITY OF WEST PANAMA CITY BEACH WAS ESTABLISHED IN 1959. GEORGE COWGILL WAS THE FIRST MAYOR. THE SECOND WAS MITCH YELVERTON AND THE THIRD DAN RUSSELL.

"WHEN THE CITY OF PANAMA CITY BEACH WAS FORMED IN 1970 BY MERGER OF OLD PANAMA CITY BEACH, EDGEWATER, LONG BEACH AND WEST PANAMA CITY BEACH, AN ELECTION WAS HELD TO SELECT A NEW ADMINISTRATION SO THAT EACH WARD WOULD HAVE REPRESENTATION. WITH THE INCORPORATION OF THE FOUR CITIES, THE ADMINISTRATION WAS NO LONGER A CITY COMMISSION, BUT A CITY COUNCIL."

J.M.

A SPANISH GALLEON "HIDDEN TREASURES BENEATH THE SAND"

Spanish galleons bring to mind thoughts of shipwrecks and lost gold. These galleons came into use in the 1600s when Spain needed larger vessels to transport the treasures from the New World. The wooden ships ranged in weight from about 300-1,200 tons and appeared sturdy and able to fight battles at sea. But these vessels, or "men of war" as they were sometimes called, were actually top-heavy. They were often overtaken by pirates or sunk in storms.

In 1961, while digging to construct the Escape Motel, now the Casa Blanca, workers uncovered old mahogany planks, pieces of metal and other types of debris. Additional shoveling revealed an ancient 700-pound cannon, made prior to 1756.

The motel owner, Dick Arnold, for whom the new Panama City Beach High School is named, oversaw the land preparation. He recalled finding timbers with square wooden pegs about 150 feet away from this location in 1954.

With the discovery of more relics, Arnold called for a full-scale excavation of what he believed to be an old Spanish galleon. Experts from the Navy Mine Defense Laboratory, now the Navy Base, assisted with a special metal detector, capable of searching as deep as 28 feet below the surface. Soundings were taken. They reported that the entire area where the cannon was found as "hot." But no other cannons or chests of gold were found.

Those studying the discovery determined that this vessel, which apparently burned at sea, must have blown ashore during a hurricane. They believed it was possible that the storm occurred in the early 1700s after four ships left a Spanish Armada in Havana and sailed on a course north, northwest, near the coastline.

At other locations along the beach, pieces of armor have also been found, leaving many to wonder what other artifacts may be buried beneath the sands of Panama City Beach.

THE NAVY TOWERS – STAGES I AND II

For more than 20 years the Navy Base's two towers, Stage I and Stage II, stood as familiar structures in Gulf waters.

The Navy ordered the construction of the two pre-fabricated platforms in 1957.

Since a Houston, Texas company built them, they were sometimes referred to as the "Texas Towers."

Stage I, which measured 105 x 105 feet, was located approximately 11 miles from the main pass in 105 feet of water. It housed a laboratory, storeroom, galley and copious amounts of test and evaluation equipment. The structure was designed to bunk 30 men.

Stage II, the one more people were familiar with, stood in approximately 62 feet of water about 1.75 miles offshore, just west of the main pass. This stage was smaller and measured 84 x 60 feet. It was equipped with less working room and contained sleeping quarters for four men.

The Navy began using these stages in January 1958 for dive support during at-sea operations and other tests. Both Stages I and II were built for helicopter landings with their lowest platforms 40 feet above the high water mark of the Gulf.

But salt water and Hurricane Eloise in 1975 took their toll on these towers even though they were designed to withstand winds of 125 miles per hour. By that time most of the sensor work had already been transferred to land operations.

On Aug. 27, 1984 the Navy demolished both structures.

RECOLLECTIONS & MEMORIES BY JACK MASHBURN

"I FISHED FOR MACKERAL UNDER BOTH STAGES. THE MACKERAL STAYED CLOSE TO FEED ON THE SMALLER FISH."

J.M.

The Navy's Stage II stood about 1.75 miles off shore from the jetties and was easily visible from Surf Drive and St. Andrews State Park on Panama City Beach. This photo shows cranes and men hard at work conducting tests for the government.

MIRACLE STRIP AMUSEMENT PARK

The Miracle Strip Amusement Park, the enlargement of a smaller amusement park, opened in the early 1960s. Located at the corner of Front Beach Road and Alf Coleman Road, the park boasted the fastest roller coaster in America at that time. The Miracle Strip also provided many teenagers their first summer jobs.

In 1963 Jimmy Lark enlarged his small amusement park, built after World War II, and changed the name to Miracle Strip Amusement Park. His towering roller coaster became one of the beach's biggest amusements. Additional rides and attractions were added to the Miracle Strip over the years, one being a spooky sensation, known as "the Haunted House." Popular Shipwreck Island Water Park followed in the 1980s.

RECOLLECTIONS & MEMORIES BY JACK MASHBURN

"JIMMY LARK OWNED A CONSTRUCTION BUSINESS, AND I KNEW HIM WELL, HE CAME UP WITH THE IDEA OF BUILDING THE MIRACLE STRIP AND IT'S TAKEN OFF FROM THERE."

J.M.

The Panama City Beach Observation Tower opened in 1965. An elevator lifted sightseers to the observation point, which offered a beautiful panoramic view of the Gulf and surrounding area. In 1995, Hurricane Opal damaged the structure. It was imploded and replaced with a condominium.

SEA CREATURES

St. Andrew Bay has been a seaport for almost 200 years, and stories about sea monsters became part of its lore.

Some of the tales described huge sea creatures 15 to 20 feet long that had curved wings, round eyes and two strange appendages on the sides of their mouths that looked like horns. These monsters supposedly had the ability to swim under boats, flip them over then swallow the passengers as they dropped through the depths of the sea. Once hooked, these great monsters could drag a boat for miles.

Through their appearances and the apparent damage they could inflict, these denizens of the deep became known as "devilfish." But in truth they were nothing more than giant manta rays.

Wallace Caswell, a local daredevil of the sea, spent most of his life working as a boat captain from the 1920s to the 1950s. In his off time he gave performances either riding or wrestling different forms of marine life. At that time people knew nothing about conservation. They thought marine life was so plentiful all types of it would last forever and never die out.

When Caswell had a party out and no fish were biting, he sometimes enlivened things by hooking a devilfish and giving his passengers unexpected fast rides into the Gulf. At first the fishing party would be frightened, but when it was all over

Popular dolphins, nicknamed porpoises, attract tourists at marine shows and boaters in Panama City Beach waters. These animals have a high intelligence and are easily trained to perform tricks for the crowds. Federal and State laws protect them and prohibit their feeding in the wild. Many years ago old-time sailors regarded porpoises as omens of bad weather when they bobbed and cavorted alongside ships while crews were at sea.

and the creature was shot and brought to the dock or released, they departed talking about their adventure for weeks. The local newspapers and those in Atlanta sometimes carried stories about these unusual fishing trips.

Mysterious Creature of Phillips Inlet

In the late 1950s one of the residents at Phillips Inlet found the remains of an unidentifiable creature on the beach of the lake. This "thing" reportedly attacked a boy near Avondale Mills' property the previous year.

Caswell was summoned to the inlet. He admitted the animal, which measured about 4-feet long and had a jaw with three rows of teeth, baffled him. Caswell sent the head to the Smithsonian Institute. They identified this strange creature as being nothing more than a black-tipped shark that somehow made its way into the inlet.

The Porpoise at Phillips Inlet

Porpoises abound in the Gulf and in St. Andrew Bay. They become playful, cavort in the air and captivate boaters who are not permitted to feed them under the law.

About 30 years ago, one named "Porpy" became a celebrity of sorts. During a high tide or hurricane this porpoise and his mate wound up in Lake Powell at Phillips Inlet. The female soon disappeared and made her way back into the Gulf, but the young bull porpoise remained at the lake.

He soon learned to love his new home where people living around the lake tossed him scraps and he performed for them. One of his enjoyments became following small fishing boats and bumping their motors out of the water as he played. Most laughed knowing it was only the friendly "Porpy."

But one fisherman became

so irritated with the playful porpoise that he cruelly plunged a harpoon into him.

C.H. Cain ran a fish camp at the inlet then and discovered the wounded animal near death. He felt so sorry for him that he built a pen where he nursed him for months until he regained his health. Then "Porpy" happily returned to the open waters of the lake.

But when he found the porpoise loose again, the same fisherman contacted the Department of Natural Resources and demanded they remove him from the lake. Men from the agency tried to catch the porpoise and take him to a seaquarium along the Gulf. Lake residents protested so much, however, that the state acquiesced and let "Porpy"

remain as long as he stayed in his pen.

But death came to the friendly porpoise in 1970. Cain and others mourned the loss of their little friend that made them laugh with his tricks. They knew Lake Powell would never be the same without their friendly porpoise.

CAMP HELEN STATE RECREATION AREA

With its jagged undeveloped shoreline, abundance of surrounding forests and miles of sandy beaches, tranquil Lake Powell is the perfect setting for Camp Helen, one of Florida's newest state parks.

Like most locations along the Northern Gulf Coast, the park's first inhabitants were various tribes of Indians. These Indians enjoyed the inlet and lake because it offered both fresh and salt water.

Through excavations of their shell mounds and middens, archaeologists determined the Indians visited here at least 4,000 years ago, connecting them with the Early Traditional, Deptford and Santa Rosa/Swift Creek groups.

During the Civil War, when this body of water was called Lake Ocala, saltmakers were drawn to its secluded beaches to make salt from seawater. One of the largest camps was known as Kent's Salt Works on the northeast shore of the lake. In recent years numerous artifacts from the saltmakers have been found.

After the war ended, saltmakers departed and the area reverted back to a primeval wilderness frequented by big cats, bears, deer and alligators.

At the turn of the century, families moved in to homestead around the lake. The McCaskill Co. of DeFuniak Springs attempted to promote the southwestern section of the lake as the retirement community of "Inlet Beach" in the 1920s.

The development met with some success, but the Depression wreaked havoc on the project. The Inlet Beach name remained, however. McCaskill sold out to R.E. Hicks, who planned to promote a similar community at this location. Hicks built a rustic home that many referred to as "the lodge," a stable, butler and maids' quarters, guest cottages and a water tower.

When he died in 1937, his wife, Margaret, acquired all the land. After eight years she sold to Avondale Textile Co. of Sylacauga, Alabama. That company erected several more cottages and duplexes, bathrooms,

a recreation hall, a fishing pier on the Gulf and a boathouse on the lake.

For almost 50 years employees of this company used the recreation area, known as Camp Helen, for summer vacations and weekend getaways.

In 1996, the state acquired 183.50-acre Camp Helen for $13.5 million. Fifty-five acres of the park lie north of U.S. 98. The remaining acres stretch to the Gulf at Camp Helen State Park.

During this time, Lake Powell received the prestigious designation as an "Outstanding Florida Water."

Plans are still being made concerning the park. Gulf Coast Community College's Office of Lifelong Learning has proposed a partnership between the Division of Recreation & Parks and the community college for the future development and operation of an Environmental Education Center on the property.

Helen Schroeder and Jack Mashburn (center of photo) appear at the ribbon cutting for Camp Helen April 19, 1997. Rick Hurst, a County Commissioner at that time stands on the right.

RECOLLECTIONS *&* MEMORIES BY JACK MASHBURN

Saving Camp Helen

"SAVING CAMP HELEN ACTUALLY BEGAN WITH A LETTER TO THE EDITOR BY HELEN SCHROEDER, TELLING THAT THE LAND WAS FOR SALE. SCHROEDER HAD NO PERSONAL MOTIVE; SHE JUST WANTED THE PROPERTY PROTECTED AGAINST DEVELOPMENT. SHE DISTRIBUTED FLIERS AND ORGANIZED A PETITION.

"IN MAY 1995 DANA BEACH RESORTS, INC. OF FORT WALTON BEACH HAD AN OPTION TO BUY CAMP HELEN FOR $12 MILLION WITH THE SALE SCHEDULED FOR COMPLETION IN APRIL 1996.

"LYNN GAGER, DIRECTOR OF THE LIFELONG LEARNING CENTER AT GULF COAST COLLEGE, HELPED ORGANIZE THE COLLEGE'S LOBBYING EFFORTS FOR CAMP HELEN. SHE ASKED IF I'D ASSIST THE COLLEGE TO PERSUADE THE STATE TO PURCHASE THE LAND, WHICH INCLUDED 180 ACRES. SHE EXPLAINED TO ME THAT THE COLLEGE HAD FOR SOME TIME BEEN DESIRING A PLACE FOR AN ENVIRONMENTAL EDUCATION TEACHING CENTER.

"THE NATURE CONSERVANCY, A NON-PROFIT ORGANIZATION INVOLVED WITH SENSITIVE LAND, FIRST HELPED LOBBY TO GET THE PROPERTY ON THE CONSERVATION AND RECREATIONAL LANDS LIST OR "CARL." THIS ORGANIZATION, WHICH SETS PRIORITIES FOR STATE LAND ACQUISITIONS, HAD IT RANKED NO. 25 ON ITS LIST. WE KNEW WE HAD TO GET THE NUMBER MOVED UP OR WE'D NEVER SAVE THE PROPERTY. THE GOVERNMENT AND ITS AGENCIES STICK TO THE RANKING NUMBERS AND CHANGE THEM ONLY AFTER CONVINCING PERSUASION.

"GEORGE WILSON, DIRECTOR OF THE CONSERVANCY, PERSUADED THE ORGANIZATION TO BUY THE PROPERTY FROM DOODLE HARRIS FOR $13.5 MILLION IN OCTOBER OF ONE YEAR AND TO HOLD IT UNTIL AFTER JULY 1 THE NEXT YEAR, SO THE STATE COULD THEN BUY IT FROM THE FLORIDA NATURE CONSERVANCY.

"IN TALLAHASSEE DOZENS OF PEOPLE PROVIDED TESTIMONY TO THE UNIQUENESS AND PRISTINE QUALITIES OF CAMP HELEN, LAKE POWELL AND THE SURROUNDING AREA. SHIRLEY BROWN, A NOTED UNDERWATER PHOTOGRAPHER, SHOWED AMAZING FILM OF THE LITTLE KNOWN BEAUTIFUL CORAL REEF ONE MILE OFF SHORE FROM THE INLET.

"I GOT A THOUSAND SIGNATURES FOR A PETITION THAT WHEN COMPLETED WENT TO THE STATE WITH ABOUT 10,000 NAMES. THE COUNCIL ALSO RECEIVED 1,200 DOCUMENTS IN SUPPORT OF THE PURCHASE OF CAMP HELEN, WHICH HELPED LIFT THE PROJECT NUMBER FROM NUMBER 25 TO NUMBER 6 ON THE "CARL" LIST.

"GAGER WORKED TIRELESSLY ON THE PROJECT TO HAVE THE LAND PRESERVED. IN THE SUMMER OF 1996, THE STATE CLOSED THE DEAL TO PURCHASE CAMP HELEN.

"WE ARE INDEED FORTUNATE TO ENJOY THE ONLY BEACH IN FLORIDA, TO MY KNOWLEDGE, THAT HAS A BEAUTIFUL STATE PARK ON EACH END - ONE FULLY DEVELOPED AND THE OTHER BEING DEVELOPED.

"I AM PROUD TO HAVE PLAYED A SIGNIFICANT PART IN SECURING TWO STATE PARKS FOR BAY COUNTY!"

J.M.

CAPTAIN TOM CORLEY

Captain Tom Corley holds several titles such as General Marine Surveyor, Marine Loss Specialist and Salvage Master. He has been a practicing Marine Surveyor for more than 50 years.

Captain Tom Corley, who was born in 1908 in Muskogee County, Georgia, had his interest piqued on sailing at the age of 11 when he took his first ride on the steamboat John W. Callahan on the Chattahoochee River.

Then during summer vacations from school he worked as a cabin boy on the steamboats.

In 1927, Corley acquired his license as Master 1st Class Pilot for Inland Waterways. After graduation Hemphill Engineering School in Memphis, Tennessee, his license was raised to include "Any Ocean."

During World War II, Corley served as a Commander in the Navy and later as a Ship's Master for the Merchant Marine, skippering tankers, cruise ships and freighters for different companies.

In 1954, Corley began construction of the Tom-Ric Motel and Marina. He also built Grand Lagoon Shipyard, now the Lighthouse Marina on Panama City Beach. According to Corley, these places were the first businesses of this type on Grand Lagoon.

During the summer of 1954, Corley formed Tom Corley & Son Marine Surveyors, Inc. For the next few years he worked part time as an independent marine surveyor. Assignments with the General Adjustment Bureau (GAB) took father and son to different departments around the United States.

Tom Corley advanced to receive the titles of General Marine Surveyor, Marine Loss Specialist and Salvage Master. He had charge of all marine claims caused by the catastrophic Hurricane Camille, which struck the Mississippi Coast in 1969.

Corley operated his business in and around Grand Lagoon until 1972.

In November 1998, Corley received recognition for 50 years of service from the Society of Accredited Marine Surveyors. As of this writing, Corley plans to retire from Marine Surveying on December 31, 2001, after serving 52 years and 7 months "as the longest practicing and oldest Marine Surveyor in the world."

CHRISTO

John Christo, Sr..

In 1912, John Christo, Sr. came to the United States from his native Greece with $19 in his pocket. The young man could speak no English, but had a burning desire for a business of his own. He earned 80 cents per day at his job. Through thrift and hard work he saved enough to open his first mercantile business in Quincy in 1914. Several months later, a second business followed in Marianna through a partnership with another family member.

In the early 1920s, real estate prices began to soar in Florida. Christo sold his business interests in the other counties and opened a "Five and Ten Cent Store" in the 200 block of Harrison Avenue in 1925. At that time, the first bridges across East and West Bay were being planned. The Cove and Dixie Sherman Hotels and Bay High were all under construction.

Christo's business prospered and during the next two decades, he averaged opening a new store every year, even through the Great Depression. By 1950, Christo owned 23 stores in Florida, Alabama and Georgia. One was located near Wayside Park on Panama City Beach.

Christo's sons played important roles in the development of the beaches. John II introduced armored car service to businesses "on the other side of the bridge." He also extended Small Business Loans to 15 years, giving many owners time to establish their shops, amusements, restaurants and other enterprises.

Jimmy, along with two partners, started the Spinnaker Night Club. He also helped establish Runaway Island. Both of these businesses were located on Thomas Drive.

Golfing – By 1923, golfing had become a national pastime in this country. In the autumn of that year, G.M. West, editor of the Panama City Pilot, urged community leaders to build golfing facilities if they wanted tourists to continue coming to Bay County.

H.L. Sudduth, the developer of the Cove, introduced his 9-hole course off Cherry Street in December 1925. One month later, in January 1926, sawmill owner W.C. Sherman opened his 18-hole St. Andrew Bay Golf Course. Depicted in this photo is the road to the golf course, along North Bay on the east side of Lynn Haven.

The Cove golf course, although popular, was gone by World War II. But the St. Andrew Bay Golf Course became the Panama Country Club. It is one of the more than 10 private and public golf courses located in Bay County today.

The Panama County Club is the site of the Sherman Invitational Tournament held each year.

The beautiful new West Bay Bridge was completed across the Intracoastal Waterway in the 1990s. Over the years a number of bridges crossed West Bay and West Bay Creek before the Intracoastal was cut through this section in 1938. These early bridges did not last long because they were built from wood. This new bridge replaced a concrete drawbridge erected after WWII.

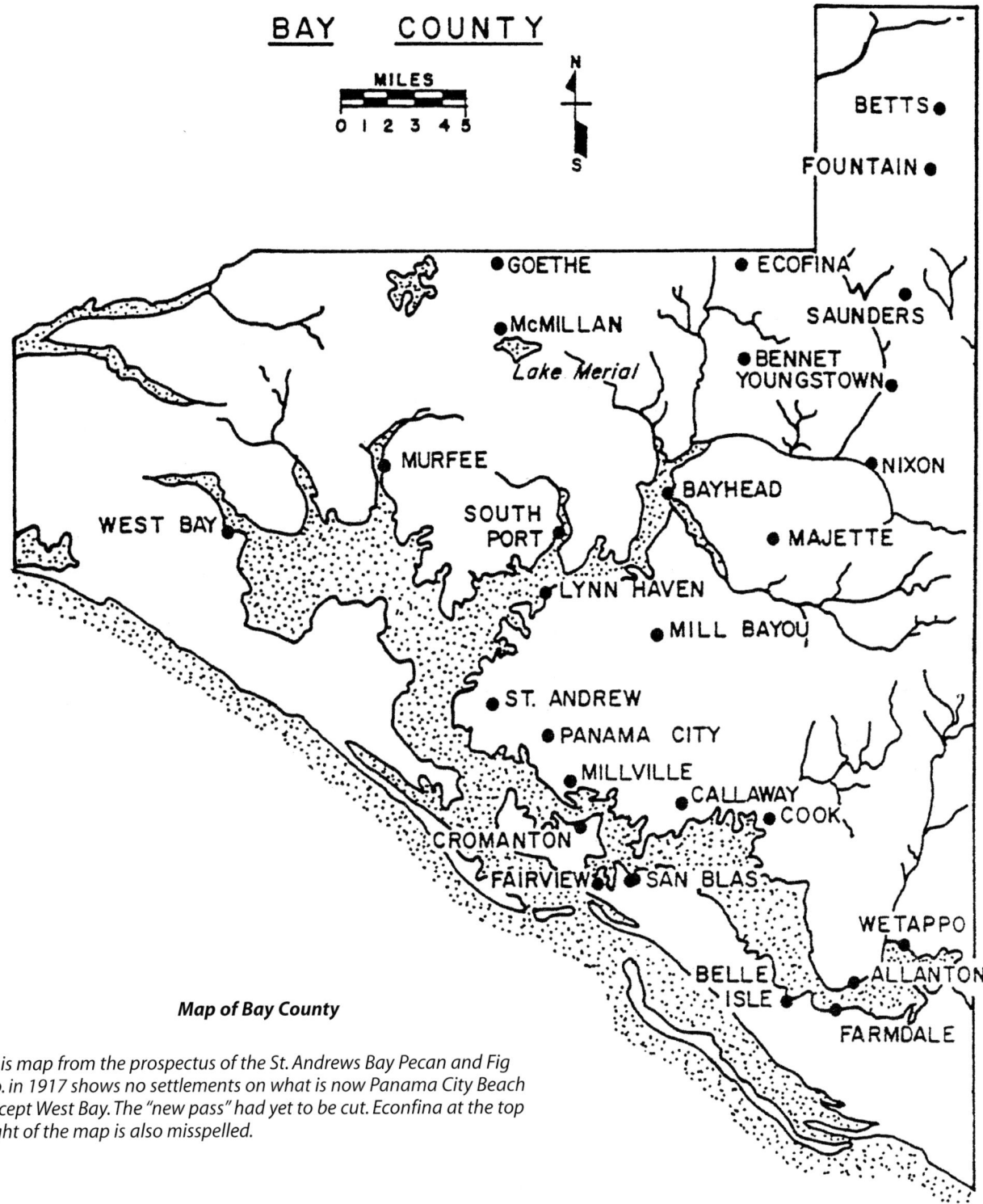

BAY COUNTY

MILES

0 1 2 3 4 5

N
S

BETTS •

FOUNTAIN •

• GOETHE

• ECOFINA

SAUNDERS

• McMILLAN

Lake Merial

• BENNET
YOUNGSTOWN •

• NIXON

• MURFEE

BAYHEAD

WEST BAY •

SOUTH
PORT

• MAJETTE

LYNN HAVEN

• MILL BAYOU

• ST. ANDREW

• PANAMA CITY

• MILLVILLE

• CALLAWAY
• COOK

CROMANTON

FAIRVIEW • SAN BLAS

WETAPPO

BELLE
ISLE

• ALLANTON

FARMDALE

Map of Bay County

*This map from the prospectus of the St. Andrews Bay Pecan and Fig
Co. in 1917 shows no settlements on what is now Panama City Beach
except West Bay. The "new pass" had yet to be cut. Econfina at the top
right of the map is also misspelled.*

PANAMA CITY BEACH HISTORICAL NOURISHMENT PROJECT

Jayna Montgomery Leach
Panama City Beach Convention and Visitors Bureau

For generations Panama City Beach has been recognized as a destination that provides its visitors with world-renowned white sand beaches. The emerald green waters and sugar white sands have beckoned millions annually seeking sun surf and sand. Little did those that frequented our destination for years know that one day our beaches would be faced with the effects of major beach erosion due to a combination of storms and natural causes.

More than twenty years ago, several community leaders had the knowledge and forethought to take an interest in the future of Panama City Beach. One such leader, Mr. Charles Hilton, Chief Executive Officer of Hilton, Inc., predicted erosion would wreak havoc on our beaches over time. Mr. Hilton, considered in some cir-

cles as the founding father of the city's history-making beach nourishment project, worked tirelessly over the years weeding through red tape and educating other townspeople. At first, it seemed national funding would not be available, but later, community leaders learned it would be available, but the city would have to form a Tourist Development Council (TDC) to qualify. In 1986, the Tourist Development Council was formed and levied a tourist development tax especially allowed under State of Florida law. The TDC requested that Continued Planning and Engineering be resumed and the Commission agreed to resume sponsorship, which they did by letter dated August 13, 1987. The TDC pledged to the commission that revenues from the designated taxes

would be used to provide necessary local funding for the project, and the Commission agreed to act as a non-Federal sponsor and provide legal authority.

Although a beach nourishment project had been in the works for years, it wasn't until Hurricane Opal hit in 1995 that those in opposition were convinced of a need for nourishment. Hurricane Opal, a category three storm caused significant beach erosion and seawall damage. Following Hurricane Opal, Panama City Beach incurred the wrath of Hurricanes Earl and Georges. With the surf now lapping at property seawalls, and sandy beach non-existent for tourists, the beach was about to undergo a complete metamorphosis.

The Panama City Beach Convention and Visitors Bureau in conjunction with the Bay

County Tourist Development Council embarked on the largest beach nourishment project in Florida's history. The project began in August 1998, and was completed in April 1999, just in time for the start of the city's tourism season.

The project included a massive reconstruction plan to restore the area's 16.8-mile stretch of sandy white beaches, which were almost non-existent in some areas due to Hurricanes Opal, Earl and Georges. The future of the tourist destination had clearly been in jeopardy. With the addition of 8.32 million cubic yards of sand, the beaches were extended to their new width of 100 feet and dune systems were created. The Panama City Beach CVB launched a major marketing campaign in feeder markets to let vacationers know that the $30 million beach enhancement project made the beaches wider and more beautiful than ever and that the effects of beach erosion due to some storms and natural causes were now non-existent.

The Beach Nourishment Campaign had a significant impact on the 1999 tourist season for Panama City Beach. Over one hundred articles were published in newspapers all over the United States on the positive effects of the beach nourishment for Panama City Beach. Titles such as "World's Most Beautiful Beaches Become Even More Beautiful" and "Beachfront Gets a Facelift That Benefits Tourism" hit in numerous markets during the spring of 1999. The Bay County Tourist Development Council reported a record year for bed tax collections in 1999, up 8.22% from 1998. The accommodations industry saw the return of repeat visitors who had, prior to the beach nourishment project, decided not to return to Panama City Beach. Due to the beach nourishment project and the beach nourishment marketing campaign, the future of Panama City Beach as a tourist destination was no longer in jeopardy.

Residents and visitors have always been aware that the beaches of Panama City Beach are some of the most beautiful in the world. However, it is nice to be acclaimed by others. In 2000, Panama City Beach became the recipient of two prestigious awards. The Travel Channel rated Panama City Beach the number four beach in America. The Surfrider Foundation, an international non-profit organization dedicated to the protection of the world's oceans, waves and beaches, rated Panama City Beach as the number three beach in America. The Surfrider Foundation recognized our beautiful beaches and identified our community as an environmental leader.

In addition to the most prestigious destination awards, Mr. Charles Hilton was selected to receive the Private Citizen Award from the Florida Shore and Beach Preservation Association for his more than twenty years of commitment and dedication to the Panama City Beach Nourishment Project. Mr. Hilton also received the leadership award from Coastal Living Magazine, who recognizes an individual that actively pursues and promotes the preservation of the land.

Because of the foresight and determination of individual community leaders, Panama City Beach will continue to attract visitors for many generations. Those who once played on our beaches as children can now return to see their children frolicking on the shores of "The World's Most Beautiful Beaches." As one of those children who vacationed on Panama City Beach every year, I am thankful for the nourishment project as I now watch my own children play on the sugar white sand beaches and emerald green waters of Panama City Beach, Florida.

PIER PARK

The St. Joe Company plans to develop "Pier Park" as a cooperative venture with the City of Panama City Beach. This park will be located on about 85 acres of land north of Front Beach Road and south of Panama City Beach Parkway (U.S. 98), just east of State Road 79. Part of this property is now the site of Aaron Z. Bessant / Wayside Park and headquarters for the popular Seafood Festival held each October.

This new, enlarged park will become the center of leisure activities in the community. It will appeal to individuals in all walks of life and stimulate economic development in the area.

Pier Park will offer high quality year—round shopping, dining and entertainment. As of now 50 acres will be dedicated to shops and restaurants. Thirty acres will be reserved for community events and other attractions throughout the year.

Pier Park's first phase, scheduled to open summer of 2002, will be anchored by a 200,000-square-foot retail center, composed of more than 80 stores. Included will be The Gap, Izod, Reebok, Vanity Fair, Disney and Converse.

Two of the Phase-one anchors are expected to be the Grand Old Opry Theater and Jimmy Buffet's Margaritaville as well.

Pier Park will feature ample lighted parking in its 500-space lot with an additional 10-acre overflow parking area available for events that draw big crowds.

From this complex, people will be able to stroll across Front Beach Road to 6-acre beach. In that location, they can sunbathe on the smooth white sand, take a dip in the turquoise-hued Gulf or fish from the popular Dan Russell Pier. A covered boardwalk is envisioned in the future along with volleyball courts and covered pavilion for weather-protected events.

St. Joe plans to utilize Pier Park as a gateway for growth in future decades.

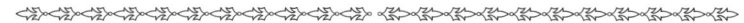

PHILIP GRIFFITTS AND FAMILY

Philip Griffitts served as mayor of Panama City Beach for 18 years from 1982 to 2000. During his time in office, Griffitts witnessed the tremendous growth of the beaches. He played a major role in this development, including the partnership between the St. Joe Company and Panama City Beach.

One of Griffitts' many achievements was the expansion of Frank Brown Park on Panama City Beach Parkway (U.S. 98). Through the improvement and addition of several, new first-class fields for baseball; softball, both slow and fast pitch; and soccer, Panama City Beach can now host national and international sports tournaments.

This family photo from left to right shows Griffitts, Sr.; his wife, Jerrilyn; son, Matthew; daughter-in-law, Laura; son, Philip Jr; and granddaughters, Katie and Anna Claire.

Left to Right
Philip, Sr.
Jerrilyn
Matthew, Laura (mother of girls),
Katie (big sister)
Philip, Jr. (father of girls)
Anna Claire (little baby)

LIMITED ACCESS CONNECTOR

*A*long with a Hathaway Bridge replacement and the expansion of State Roads 79 and 77, the Florida Dept. of Transportation is determining the feasibility and alignment for a new four-lane, divided, limited access road from Panama City Beach to the Alabama state line during the writing of this book.

The Alabama Dept. of Transportation is conducting a similar study from the Alabama state line to north of Dothan. With most of the land in the Panama City Beach area scheduled for commercial and residential development and a probable new airport north at West Bay, additional routes need to be planned for economic development and hurricane evacuation along the coastal areas.

Proposals under consideration bring this connector south from Dothan by one of three routes yet to be determined by the DOT. One road passes near Bonifay, the other by Chipley and the third runs west of Marianna. All merge into S.R.79 near West Bay.

EXPANSIONS OF ROADS

*I*n the near future, Panama City Beach expects the expansion of some of its main roads.

These changes will be based on traffic and traffic projections for growth along the beaches' coastal area. They will also be dependent upon a new airport planned for this section. This airport will increase the need for adequate roads and highways.

In approximately two years, the Florida Department of Transportation anticipates changing to a four lane for State Road 79 from U.S. 98 north to West Bay.

This highway will consist of two paved 12-foot travel lanes in both northerly and southerly directions. This expansion will include a grass median and 4-foot paved shoulders on each side of the highway.

The expected new airport will increase the need for expansion all of S.R. 79-north from West Bay to the Interstate. This route is currently being designed and prepared for right-of-way acquisition as funds become available.

State Highway 77 will also be widened to four lanes from Southport north in the same manner.

HATHAWAY BRIDGE REPLACEMENT

Artist rendering of Hathaway Bridge replacement.

Work is now underway on the construction of a Hathaway Bridge replacement. This project is being accomplished by the use of an alternative/innovative contract method, known as design building. Through this method, the contractor is responsible for the design and construction of the $80 million bridge project.

The two replacement spans will be segmental bridges with each segment weighing 200 tons. This type bridge permits construction without interruption of the boat traffic in the channel, which is part of the Intracoastal waterway.

The new bridge will have three 12-foot lanes plus a 12-foot auxiliary lane and a bicycle-pedestrian way running in each direction. In addition the new spans will be built with a vertical clearance of 65 feet, as required by the U.S. Coast Guard, and a horizontal clearance of approximately 287 feet. Permits must still be obtained from the Dept. of Environmental Protection, the Coast Guard and the U.S. Army Corps of Engineers. The current estimated completion date for the Hathaway Bridge replacement is July 2003.

Steel portions from the existing 1959 structure will be salvaged for scrap. The concrete sections will become artificial reefs in the Gulf.

PANAMA CITY BEACH
Color Portraits

Summer Leach, daughter of Jayna Leach, Director of Marketing for the Panama City Beach Convention and Visitors Bureau, enjoys feeding the birds while walking the beach near the surf on Panama City Beach.

A Great

Foundation...

Family

Panama City Beaches
brings generations of
families together.

Ties

Each day reveals a beautiful creation of Mother Nature.

Beauty and the Beach...

Natural surroundings

Recreation

Panama City Beaches provide the very best in recreational activities.

Spring Break

Spring Break activities for the entire community.

Miniature Golf plus more...

Golf

Beautiful waters
and white beaches
offer a variety of
activities...

Sports

Boat cruises at
Airboat
Adventure
Cruises

See the entire beach area from the sky—Fly with
Captain Skip Franck at Paradise Helicopter

More than
4,000,000
tourists visit
Panama City
Beaches each year

Some like
fast paced action...

...Others prefer a
slower pace

The Lady in Red
enjoys sunbathing on
the World's most
beautiful beach with
the sugar white sand
all around her.

Panama City Beach offers a great lifestyle...

...The best of seafood restaurants

...Luxury residences & condominiums

...Popular charter boats

Our greatest assets...

Our People

JACK MASHBURN

Thank You!

PART II

PANAMA CITY BEACH BUSINESS LEGACY

The Tradition - The Spirit - The Vision

Thank you to our
CORPORATE SPONSORS

Airboat Adventures
Allan G. Bense
Alvin's Stores
Angelos Steak Pit
Aquatic Realty
Bay Bank & Trust
Bay County Sheriff's Office
Bay Lincoln-Mercury-Dodge
Beach TV
Beachcomber By The Sea
Bennett, Campbell & Bennett
Bid-A-Wee Storage
Bikini Beach Resort
Billy's Oyster Bar
Black Angus Steak Restaurant
Breakers
Bronwen Dukate
Burke & Blue, P.A.
Captain Andersons
Carrillon Beach
Virgil Anderson
Carr Engineering
Cellular One
Century 21 Ryan Realty
Chateau Motel
City of Cedar Grove
Clear Channel Radio
Comcast CableVision
Condo World
Culligan Water
Dennis Pledger
Driftwood Lodge
Edgewater Beach Resort
Emerald Coast Bank
Florida State University
Gulf Coast Community College
Gulf Coast Medical Center
Gulf Power
Hamilton's Restaurant
Holiday Inn Sunspree Resort

Holloway House
Hombre Golf Club
J&J Enterprises
J.B. and Muriel Ellis
JRA Architects, Inc.
Kent-Forest Funeral Home & Cemeteries
Key West Bar & Grill
Kilgore Karpet & Ceramic Tile
L.D. Lewis, Jr.
Lee Sullivan
Marc Nolen
Marriott Bay Point Resort Village
Mikato Japanese Seafood Steakhouse & Lounge
Miracle Strip Park-Shipwreck Island
Montego Bay/C.E.T. Management
Panama City Beach
Panama City Beaches Chamber of Commerce
Panama City Beach Convention and Visitors Bureau, Inc.
Panama City Beach KOA
Paradise Helicopter
People's First Community Bank
Pineapple Willy's
Port Of Call Motel
Sandpiper Beacon
Schooners
Sea Witch Motel
Shuckums Oyster Pub & Seafood Grill
Signal Hill Golf Course
St. Joe Company
Stephen C. Myers, DMD
Sterling Beach/Cornerstone Development Group, Inc.
Sugar Sands Motel
Sunset Pass Condos
The Inside Story Interiors, Inc.
Treasure Island Marina
The Treasure Ship
Waitt Radio
Waste Management

CHAPTER I

SPOTLIGHT ON INDIVIDUAL SPONSORS

Marc Nolan

100

J.B. Ellis

101

L.D. Lewis

102

Virgil Anderson

103

The Pledgers

105

*Elbert & Gwyneth
DuKate*

106

Lee Sullivan

108

Allan G. Bense

109

MARC NOLEN
David Nolen Remembered as a Top-Notch Appraiser

While Marc Nolen also has left his mark on Bay County history, he prefers to talk about his late father, David T. Nolen.

Marc Nolen, Panama City Beach businessman, served the past four years on the Bay County Board of Commissioners and was chairman in 2000.

His father took a different route to success. David Nolen was a MAI (Member Appraisal Institute) and was among the early property appraisers in the state. In 1976, he was elected President of the South Alabama-Northwest Florida Chapter No. 49 of the American Institute of Real Estate Appraisers at that organizations' annual installation banquet on Panama City Beach.

The American Institute of Real Estate Appraisers is the oldest organization of professional appraisers in the United States and even in those early years was associated with the National Association of Realtors.

AT WORK — David T. Nolen, an MIA Property Appraiser, is shown at his desk at Nolen and Associates in Panama City.

When David Nolen died, on Wednesday, February 27, 1985—at the much too early age of 57—Bay County lost one of its most distinguished citizens. He had been a resident of the area since 1948, moving here from Nashville, Tennessee and was owner of Nolen and Associates.

In addition to his many other honors, Mr. Nolen was a member of the Bay County Board of Realtors, serving as Vice-President in 1980. He also was a veteran of World War II and a member of the First Baptist Church of Panama City.

David Nolen received a BA Degree in Major Economics from Maryville College in Tennessee in 1952. He was in real estate in Bay County from 1957 until 1963, and was a staff district appraiser for the Florida Department of Transportation, Northwest Florida District, and Central Florida District from 1964-1966. As the Chief Operating Officer of Nolen and Associates, Inc., he was an independent fee appraiser from 1967 until his death. He was qualified as an expert witness on property valuations in the Circuit Court of Bay County, Jefferson County, Escambia County, Orange County, Calhoun County and Leon County and also served U.S. Bankruptcy Courts in Atlanta, Tallahassee and Panama City.

In addition, Mr. Nolen was a former instructor in Real Estate Principles and Practices at what was then known at Gulf Coast Junior College. The Florida Real Estate Commission under the supervision of the University of Florida Division of Continuing Education sponsored the course.

The American Institute of Real Estate Appraisers conducted a voluntary program of continuing education for its designated members, and the MAIs and RMs who met the minimum standards of this program were awarded periodic educational certification.

COMMUNITY SERVICE—Marc Nolen of Panama City Beach, is shown with three members of the Under the Palms playground committee—left to right, Gayle Oberst, a member of the Panama City Beach City Council; Debbie Sasser and Gale Bradbury. Nolen, as Chairman of the County Commission in 2000, presented a check for $12,000 to Under the Palms, an ultramodern playground at Frank Brown Park in Panama City Beach.

Mr. Nolen would have been certified under this program through December 31, 1986.

Mr. Nolen was an expert on "people's property rights" and was noted for having written articles on that subject. When he was asked to write an article for Private Property Week in 1983, he said, "I have approached the task as I would an appraisal assignment –that is, first define the problem, research the market and then arrive at a conclusion."

When Mr. Nolen passed away in 1985, he left behind his wife, Winnie G. Nolen, who still lives in Panama City, Marc and a daughter, Kim.

While Marc Nolen, the owner of Mako's Restaurant at Captain Anderson's Marina on Panama City Beach, has taken a different route to success, he has, in many respects, followed in his father's footsteps as far as community service is involved. As a County Commissioner, he was helpful to many citizens in the area and represented the commissioners at many civic and community functions.

J.B. AND MURIEL ELLIS

The J.B. Ellis Story

hen J.B. Ellis' great grandfather came to this part of the country before the Civil War, what is now known as Bay County was still part of Washington County. His great grandfather, B.B. Brown, was buried in Millville, a small community that adjoins Panama City.

Although J.B. Ellis' father—once an engineer on the historic ship Tarpon—was born in Bay County, his mother lived in Newport, near Tallahassee and Joseph Brown Ellis was born in Tallahassee on August 6, 1930. The younger Ellis soon discovered the beaches, long before the area became recognized as Panama City Beach, and he hasn't been able to stay away for a long period of time since.

"When Muriel (the former Muriel Thomas) and I got married on January 8, 1971, we moved to Decatur, Alabama," J. B. revealed. "I hung my hat there after 25 years as a riverboat engineer on the Mississippi River. But we always kept coming back to the beach and spent half of our time here."

Actually, J.B. and Muriel are legally residents of Alabama and still own a house in Decatur and a fish camp on the Tennessee River. "We've got a lot of ties up there," he added. They now live in a house on Gulf Drive on the east end of the beaches.

However, J.B. and Muriel have stronger ties in Bay County. They came back to the beach in 1995 to live permanently when J.B. retired after 40 years on a riverboat. He made his first trip down the river as a galley boy when he was only 16 years old.

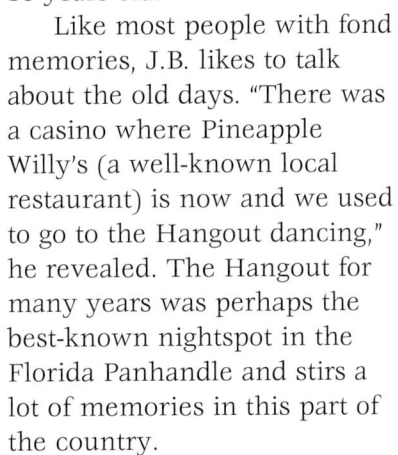

J.B. and Muriel Ellis

Like most people with fond memories, J.B. likes to talk about the old days. "There was a casino where Pineapple Willy's (a well-known local restaurant) is now and we used to go to the Hangout dancing," he revealed. The Hangout for many years was perhaps the best-known nightspot in the Florida Panhandle and stirs a lot of memories in this part of the country.

J.B. has lived in a lot of different places. In 1941, he moved to Tampa for three years while his father was working on a boat. He spent two years in Arlington, Georgia, when his dad was working on a tanker.

J.B. has a brother, John Ray Ellis, who lives in Decatur,

Alabama, but most of his relatives are in this area. "I have a lot of relatives around Southport," he said, "and I've got kinfolk all over the area."

J.B. is an Alabama football fan, although he says the last time he actually went to a game was when the Crimson Tide played LSU in Baton Rouge in 1973. He still has an Alabama tag on his car and waves the Crimson Tide banner. He also belongs to the Panama City Beaches Chamber of Commerce and knows just about everybody in town. Muriel is gaining a reputation as a pretty good photographer after purchasing a digital camera to pursue her career.

L. D. "SUNSHINE" LEWIS

ioneer businessman
L. D. "Sunshine"
Lewis didn't start his
career in Panama City
but, after he moved here in
1944, he certainly played an
important role in the business
life of the city.

He and his wife, Leona,
started with a small restaurant -
the Overpass Cafe - in Milton in
1934. He had previously, at
age 18, run a hot-dog stand in
Bagdad, and both ventures
proved his belief that "If you
take care of your business, it
will take care of you."

After retiring from his
restaurant, he formed a partnership with his brothers, E. W.
and James Elbert Lewis, which
resulted in the creation of the
Lewis Brothers Grocery
Company in Marianna.

Pioneer Built The Sunshine Chain

In one of many successful promotions, Mr. Lewis , right, awards keys of a new car to a lucky winner.

Mr. Lewis and his beloved wife, Leona, in the early days.

Two short years later, he
branched into the burgeoning
supermarket business by opening the first Jitney Jungle markets, establishing several in
Panama City in 1944, and then
others in Tallahassee,
Pensacola, Fort Walton (Beach),
Port St. Joe and Dothan, Al.

By 1953, Mr. Lewis realized
the growing need not only for
first-quality groceries and service, but for convenience. He
established a chain of Junior
Food Stores - with hours of 7
a.m. to ll p.m. - which gave
rise to their common name
"the 7-11".

Ten years later, in 1971, there
were 106 stores serving NW
Florida, Georgia and Alabama.

He left the Jitney Jungle
franchise in 1960 to concentrate
on Sunshine, and at the peak of
his business career, the

company was opening 30 new
stores a year!

Prior to his death in 1981,
when there were 364 stores
operating, he turned the operations over to his nephew, James
E. Lewis, Jr., and indulged himself in extensive overseas travel
with his son, L. D. Jr., and took
on wide community activities.

He served as President of
the Bay County Chamber of
Commerce, director of the Bay
Line Railway; director of the
Santa Rosa Bank in Milton and
was past president of the Retail
Grocers' Assn. In l962 he was
named Grocer Father of the
Year for the U.S. He served on
the Board of Baptist Hospital
(Pensacola), headed the ACS
cancer drive in Bay county
and was active in Boy Scouts
and Kiwanis.

CAPTAIN VIRGIL ANDERSON

Seafaring Family's Long Tradition

apt. Virgil Anderson, now 88 years old, is the only surviving son of the late Capt. Charles S. Anderson, who established a seafaring family in Panama City that is now a local tradition.

Virgil's brothers - all Captains - Walter, Max and Lambert, have all passed away, but the family tradition of owning and operating vessels continues. And the family shares its passion for the sea with tourists as well as locals, providing all kinds of recreational boating and opportunities to share the freedom and the mysteries of the sea.

Virgil's three sons - Carl S., Jerry C., and John D. all proudly bear the title of "Captain" and continue the family traditions.

Through their ideas and initiative, they continue to provide all kinds of recreational trips from deep-sea fishing to glass-bottom boats. They are also active in the commercial fishing industry, and even provide contract services to various government agencies - such as watercraft operations and maintenance at Tyndall AFB and beach cleaning for Bay County.

"This was all made possible by our father," Captain Carl recalls. "It was his guidance and leadership that opened up all these opportunities for us."

After discharge from the U.S. Marine Corps in 1938, Virgil married Mary Lowery and they had five children: Sarah Anderson Mason, Carl Stephen,

Virgil and Mary Anderson on their 60th Anniversary,

Jerry Collier, John David and Tillie Anderson Fowler.

Captains Virgil and Walter Anderson were among the first to tackle shark fishing, harvesting the huge sharks for their liver oil and other by-products, such as the fins, which were dried and shipped to the Far East.

The shark meat was never

eaten. The fins, highly prized as aphrodisiacs in the East, were dried for shipment.

"They hung them out on a spoil island in the bay,"

Captain Carl recalls, "and you could smell them for a long way!"

In fact, Captain Carl recollects that Panama City dwellers in those days were assailed by odors from several directions. "When the wind was from the east," he chuckled, "they got the paper mill.

"When it changed to the southwest, they got the sharks!"

Virgil descended from seafarers as well. His father, Capt. Charles Anderson, was actually born in what is now Southport, but which originally bore the name of Anderson. He married Sarah Gainer of the Gainer family, well known as pioneers of the Panama City area.

Originally, the family's fishing business was located at what

SHARK FISHING - Lower left, Carl, 7; with Capt.Walter, Judy Beth,5, Jerry, 5, and Sarah, 9.

Memories of Family Gatherings ....

FAMILY GROUP shows Lambert and Evelyn with son, Charles; Virgil and Mary with Sarah; Charlie and Sarah; Sue and Max, with Sanders and Betty Sue, and Captain Walter.

is now the site of the Federal Building in Panama City.

Virgil's brothers, Captains Walter and Max, were instrumental in pioneering the Grand Lagoon area of Panama City Beach in 1956 and in founding Capt. Anderson's Pier and the now-famous seafood restaurant, Captain Anderson's.

This is a family that has deep roots in the area and cares about its future.

At the same time, they all remain a vital part of the seafaring community - a family that has grown and prospered in Panama City, yet still sets out each day to seek out favorite fishing holes and bring home the fruits of the Gulf for everyone's enjoyment.

And while they continue the Anderson tradition of the sea, they are an important part of the tourist industry - sharing their excitement in the ever-changing Gulf and the freedom of going to sea with landlubbers

from all over the world.

Today, the family traditions continue, for instance, with Captain Ken Anderson, the youngest son of Captain C.M., who is also active in deep-sea fishing, dinner cruises and other sightseeing activities.

These days, Virgil enjoys

his retirement by gardening, golfing and remaining active in the First Baptist Church of Panama City.

"We hope that this article successfully reflects the love and gratitude that we feel for our parents," says their son, Carl. "Our father taught us about the sea; he taught us about business, and he continues to inspire us."

SHOWING OFF THE CATCH with friends (top), Mrs. C. S. Anderson, left and Capt. Walter Anderson, right, with his niece and nephews Carl, Jerry, Sarah and his daughter, Judy Beth.

THE PLEDGERS
And The Original Panama City Beach Resort

The Ferris Wheel was part of fun at old PCB Hotel.

hey advertised it as a place with "all the essentials for a perfect vacation" and indeed the original Panama City Beach resort, known in those days as the Panama City Beach Hotel, offered a little bit of everything. This was not the Panama City Beach, as we know it today, but rather a part of a four-town community that also included Long Beach, West Panama City Beach and Edgewater.

The hotel, developed by the Thomas and Pledger families on the property where the Sunbird Condominiums and Pineapple Willy's now stand, had only 12 rooms and a dining room, but there were 31 cottages on the premises and the entire project was built around a carnival atmosphere, which included a casino.

Perhaps the biggest attractions was a 1,000-foot fishing pier, which now is a much shorter pier behind Pineapple Willy's, a popular beach-dining place. The resort had a lifeguard and a bathhouse along with a dining room and a variety store, first-aid station and even a post office. The resort over a period of time featured theater-in-the-round with a carnival that included a Ferris wheel, merry-go-round and swings for the kids.

Actually, Angus Wilson Pledger, who passed away in 1963, was the first Postmaster of the Panama City Beach Post Office, and his wife, Claudia T., became the first mayor of Panama City Beach. Claudia, now 100 years old and still alert, eventually became the matriarch of the family.

The catalyst of it all was Gideon Thomas, Claudia's father, who looked at the blue-green waters of the Gulf of Mexico, dug his heels in the glittering white sand and dreamed a dream of the future. Mr. Thomas and the Pledgers donated a portion of land to the State of Florida and on March 31, 1953 Thomas Drive was named in honor of Mr. Gideon Thomas.

Angus and Claudia had two sons, Angus Dennis Pledger and Gerald Thomas Pledger.

The Thomas and Pledger families owned 104 acres of land in the area, and the Pledgers still own the property where the 18-hole Signal Hill Golf Course was constructed by the Shermans and the property where the KOA Campground on Thomas Drive is located, although the land has been leased for many years. Dennis Pledger, the son, and his wife Martha developed it in 1969, long before it became KOA.

Eventually all the waterfront property was sold.

Ceremony naming Thomas Drive for Gideon Thomas. Presented by Rep. J. Ed Stokes.

BRONWEN DUKATE
Dukate Name Part of History In Bay County, Other Areas

ong before the DuKate name became familiar to most people in Bay County, the family had built a strong foundation in other parts of the country. Bronwen DuKate recalls that her ancestors first made their arrival in this country when one came over with Lafayette. Being somewhat of a dandy, and having lost his leg in battle, he did not want to return to Paris. Her great grandfather subsequently moved to Biloxi, Mississippi, where the name is most recognizable.

Elbert "Duke" DuKate was a pilot in World War II and was shot down during the Ploesti air raid. He met Gwynneth's brother-in-law in prison camp in Sulmona, Italy, and subsequently met Gwynneth in England. After sweeping her off her feet, they were married and moved to New Orleans in 1946.

Elbert had worked as an announcer at a radio station in Austin, Texas prior to the war; he worked again as an announcer at WTPS in New Orleans while looking for a place to build his own station. He chose Panama City as he loved the pristine beaches and felt the area was ripe for growth. Having grown up on the water, he couldn't imagine living inland. They moved to Panama City and founded the Bay County Broadcasting Company in 1948.

"Duke" was a pioneer in broadcasting in this area. His first station--WPCF-1430AM— was the second radio station in Panama City. The first studio and office with the tower behind it was built on 15th Street and McKenzie Avenue. In the 1950s, the company purchased 20 acres on Magnolia Beach Road in order to increase the station's power. The transmitter went on the air in 1958, and WPCF became the most powerful station in northwest Florida. The in-town offices were moved to the City Marina until 1971 when all operations

SUCCESSFUL COUPLE—Elbert and Gwynneth DuKate came to Panama City to become pioneers in broadcasting in Bay County.

were relocated to the Magnolia Beach site.

In addition to WPCF, the company built the first FM station in the area—WMAI-108FM. It also owned a station in Valparaiso and acquired a Muzak franchise covering north Florida, south Alabama and two counties in Georgia. Muzak, an international corporation begun in the 1930s, morphed from huge tapes with one channel to 60 channels delivered via satellite during the time the DuKates owned the franchise.

The family sold its radio stations in the seventies, but maintained Muzak until Bronwen sold the corporation in 1996.

NEWS PATROL—Elbert "Duke" DuKate is shown at the microphone of his first radio station, WPCF, with live coverage of a news event.

Although Bronwen was never in the radio business, she returned to Bay County at the request of her father and brother in 1985 to work in the family business. Her brother, E. Laurence DuKate, lived in Tallahassee and was responsible for that office, while Bronwen was responsible for the Panama City and Dothan offices. Since his retirement in 1992, Laurence has returned to Bay County and now lives on Massalina Bayou.

Just as ancestors left their mark on Biloxi, the Elbert DuKate family played a distinctive role in business and community affairs in Bay County.

"Duke" was in the Rotary Club for many years, served on the Bay County Hospital Board, was an early supporter of Gulf Coast Community College and served on the Foundation Board. He also served on the Military Affairs Committee of the Chamber of Commerce and was widely known as a performer at Kaleidoscope Theater. In fact, the annual awards presented by Kaleidoscope are named the "Duke" awards in his honor.

In the early fifties, "Duke" left his mark on the Follies when he pantomimed C'est Si Bon. "He actually dressed like Eartha Kitt!" said Bronwen. Incidentally, Elbert DuKate named his boat in the fifties C'est Si Bon in memory of that special occasion and Bronwen currently has a boat with the same name.

Gwynneth DuKate was busy raising a family during the early years in Panama City. As the children grew, she began working in the company. In addition to being the "rock" that kept things stable while "Duke" dreamed, her beautiful English voice was often demanded by customers for their advertisements. She was a member of the Junior League, President of the Bay County Girl Scouts of America, active in the Heart Association, the Cancer Society, the Bay County Council on Aging and the National Association of Women in Broadcasting. A tireless worker, she was a valuable asset to any organization of which she was a part. The DuKates were both extremely active members of St. Andrews Episcopal Church from 1948 until their deaths.

Bronwen has continued her parents' community involvement. She was one of the first women asked to be in Rotary in Bay County and later served as President. She was a Florida delegate to the White House Conference on Small Business. She is a member of the Scenic Landscape Improvement Committee for the Beaches Chamber of Commerce; she currently serves as secretary of the Gulf Coast Community College Foundation and is a member of the Chemical Containment Committee of BEST (Bay Environmental Study Team for St. Andrew Bay). After her parents' death, she donated a scholarship in their name to GCCC and a garden in their memory to Kaleidoscope Theater.

DuKate Elementary School in Biloxi still pays tribute to her great grandfather. He also donated the DuKate Opera House to the city in the late 1800s. Bronwen has a gigantic mirror in her home that came from his home in Biloxi, which was described in a turn-of-the-century book, Along the Gulf, as a "veritable mansion and an architectural dream." Elbert DuKate grew up in a house on Beach Drive in Biloxi when that Mississippi city was known as the "Seafood Capital of the World." The house was destroyed by Hurricane Camille, but DuKate Street now runs alongside the property. When Elbert died in 1986, Tommy Thomas, a longtime friend, pulled some strings at the Pentagon and arranged for a "Fly-By" from Tyndall Air Force Base to St. Andrews Episcopal Church on Beach Drive. Tommy had always considered "Duke" a war hero, and the moving tribute was greatly appreciated by the family.

MAYOR LEE SULLIVAN

Seeks To Help His Community

t took some youthful irresponsibility and service in the Vietnam war to show Mayor Lee Sullivan where his future lay.

Born in Birmingham, Alabama, he lived for several years in Montana before moving to the Panama City Beach area in 1956.

"When we got here there were no schools on the beach," he recalls, "and we went to Drummond Park. I started the 4th grade in Hutchison Beach Elementary.

"I remember how hot it was in summer with no air-conditioning; but that didn't seem important."

After Jinks Junior High, Sullivan attended Bay High until the beginning of his junior year. He was injured when a horse fell on him. On his recovery, his parents sent him to Florida Military Academy,. He later entered the University of Alabama, then transferred to Florida State.

"I was intending to study law," he says, "but by that time the Vietnam war had started. I took courses during a summer quarter and decided to take the winter quarter off - that was when I realized the war was on and my deferment ended! I became a Marine."

The unthinking act of dropping out for a quarter changed everything for him.

"Realistically, that time period was the most significant of my life," he says. "The war taught me the things I hadn't considered of great importance before - and the things I considered important

Mayor Sullivan with his family

were not important at all."

In 1970 he spent several months in Pensacola Navy Hospital and credits "the Lord and some great doctors" with his return to health. But it was while he was hospitalized that the incident occurred at Kent State University.

"I had gone from a college campus to war and I just couldn't imagine anything that would cause soldiers to shoot students. I still can't.. If those guys wanted to fight, I could tell them a great place to go."

This made him decide that he wanted to do something to make things better. "I knew I couldn't do it on a global basis, so I chose law enforcement."

He started work with the Panama City Beach Police Department, working his way up from dispatcher to patrol officer to sergeant. In 1977, there was an opening for Police Chief and to his surprise, at 29 years of age, he received the appointment. He held the job for 20 years until retiring in 1997.

Although he created a successful security business, he still wanted to serve his community, and when the 2000 election for Mayor came up, he jumped into the race against an 18-year incumbent.

He took office in May, and regards his new job as an exciting challenge. "I am for truth, justice and the American way," he says, "and this is an opportunity for me to go home knowing that I have contributed something to my community."

Sullivan is married to the former Debra Thames, who was born in Washington County. He has a daughter, Shannon, who has 2 children; and a stepdaughter, Ginger, who has three. Their son, Philip, is 17, and twins Timothy and Matthew are rising 8th graders.

The family attends Woodlawn Methodist Church and the Bible on his desk testifies to the importance of God in the Mayor's life.

ALLAN G. BENSE

Allan G. Bense was elected to the Florida House of Representatives in 1998, becoming the first Republican chosen to serve District 6, which covers most of Bay County.

As a freshman, Rep. Bense has quickly established himself among the House leadership. Shortly after his election, House Speaker, John Thrasher named him to the position of Vice-Chairman of the powerful Judiciary Committee. Rep. Bense was the only first-year member to be appointed to serve on the equally powerful General Government Appropriations Committee.

A lifelong resident of Bay County, Rep. Bense and his wife Tonie own and operate several businesses.

Rep. Bense is a graduate of Florida State University, where he earned his Bachelors and Masters degrees in Business.

An active community leader, Rep. Bense recently gained national attention for his work in securing approval and funding for a Beach Re-Nourishment Program on Panama City Beach. He has been an active member of several civic organizations.

Allen G. Bense

St. Andrews State Recreation Area

 St. Andrews State Recreation Area is one of the most popular outdoor recreation spots in Florida. It's best known for its white sand beaches and crystal-clear water.

The park's uplands are characterized by rolling white sand dunes separated by low swales of either pine flatwoods or marshes. Dunes covered with sea oats abound. Dunes found farther inland are covered with sand pine, scrub oaks, rosemary and other hardy plants and play an important role in preventing erosion during intense storms and hurricanes.

The park opened in 1951 and now consists of more than 1,260 acres. During World War II, it was part of the St. Andrews Sound Military Reservation. Circular cannon platforms are still in place on the beach near the jetties.

An authentically reconstructed "Cracker" turpentine still is located in the park near Grand Lagoon. Charts and diagrams interpret the use and mechanisms of the still. Living history demonstrations are offered quarterly.

A nature trail starts at the turpentine still and winds through a number of different plant communities. Pine flatwoods, sandpine scrub, freshwater and salt marsh are encountered along the trail. Watch for alligators, wading birds and many small animals. A second interpretive trail is close to Gator Lake and the swimming areas.

Visitors may wish to sun or walk along the shores of Shell Island, a pristine barrier island situated just across the ship's channel from the mainland. This 700-acre parcel of St. Andrews State Recreation Area remains, for the most part, undeveloped. Shuttles run to the island in spring and summer. Tickets are available at the park concession.

Swimming is a favorite activity in the clear waters of the Gulf of Mexico where wave action adds to the excitement. Swimming in the shallow, protected pool behind the jetty is relaxing while snorkeling is an adventure in either swimming area. The extensive shoreline and rock jetties offer an excellent place to study marine life.

Fishing opportunities include deep sea, jetty and surf fishing. Two fishing piers and the jetties provide excellent vantage points year-round. Catches include Spanish mackerel, redfish, flounder, sea trout, bonito, dolphin and bluefish. A boat ramp is located on Grand Lagoon near the fishing pier.

A concession offers snacks, souvenirs and limited grocery items suited for campground guests. Two campground loops are situated in the pinewoods near Grand Lagoon. There are 176 sites with electricity, water, picnic tables and grills. Campfire programs are offered seasonally. A tent camping area for non-profit, organized youth groups is also available. Certain fees and restrictions apply.

Picnic facilities are found in several locations in the park with the main picnic area near the fishing pier on Grand Lagoon.

For more information, contact St. Andrews State Recreation Area, 4607 State Park Lane, Panama City Beach, FL 32408; (85() 233-5 140.

CHAPTER II
WORLD FAMOUS RESTAURANTS

Fine Dining and Culinary Delights

The Breakers

112

Pineapple Willy's

114

Hamilton's Restaurant

115

Key West Bar & Grill

117

Shuckums Oyster Pub & Seafood Grill

118

Billy's Oyster bar

119

Schooners

120

Mikato Japanese Seafood Steakhouse & Lounge

122

Angelo's Steak Pit

123

Captain Andersons

126

Montego Bay

128

The Treasure Ship

125

Black Angus Steak Restaurant

129

THE BREAKERS

Bishop Weathers Storms in Restaurant Business

HURRICANE OPAL—*The Breakers, one of the most popular eating-places on Panama City Beach received $1,600,000 in damages when Hurricane Opal hit in October 1995.*

 ack Bishop, who decided to settle in Bay County in 1976 after serving in the Air Force at Tyndall Air Force Base, has been the victim of three major natural disasters since opening The Breakers on April 14, 1971, but that hasn't slowed him down as his restaurant group has gotten bigger and better.

The Breakers, which offers casual waterfront dining on the Gulf of Mexico, once was considered one of the most popular clubs on Panama City Beach, relaxed, totally informal atmosphere. Harpoon Harrys is well known for its full-service double deck bar where you can enjoy sports events on television, not to mention the fantastic sunsets each day.

In March of this year, Jack where you can eat all you want from a seafood buffet that includes the ever-popular crab legs.

More recently, Jack has gone about the business of renovating the old Harbor House Restaurant, located at the Ramada Inn in St. Andrews. The St. Andrews Seafood House will employ approximately 125 people.

Altogether, Jack's four restaurants employ more that 275 people and many of them have been with him since he first opened The Breakers. The restaurant entrepreneur is moving his Corporate (or Chief) Executive Chef (CEC) Debra Warren Cook, who has been with him for 10 years, uptown to open the new restaurant in St. Andrews. "Some of the employees are kids I grew up with and went to college with," Jack pointed out.

Wife Sandy is heavily involved in the operation of The Breakers and Jack's daughter, Terri Whitehurst, now a nurse in Michigan, spent a lot of time helping make The Breakers the overwhelming success it is today.

BREAKERS TODAY—*Owner Jack Bishop made some structural and cosmetic changes to the Breakers after the storm.*

but in recent months has seen the pendulum swing more to unmatched seafood, prime rib and nightly chef specials. Harpoon Harrys, next door to The Breakers, opens daily at 11 a.m. and serves both lunch and dinner in an even more-

opened Captain Jack's on Thomas Drive, which is patterned after Bishop's, a popular seafood business he operated for many years across the street from The Breakers. Captain Jack's already has earned a reputation as a place

Despite his success with other ventures, The Breakers still remains Jack's operating point. One of the reasons might be that he has gone through so much with the highly acclaimed dining facility on Front Beach Road in Panama City Beach.

Hurricane Opal literally washed away the foundation of The Breakers in October 1995, inflicting damage in the neigh-borhood of $1,600,000. Jack was fortunate that he was in the good hands of an insurance man who wrote him a check without argument.

With Opal still fresh in the minds of Panama City Beach residents, Jack remembers well another hurricane that ravaged the Florida Panhandle 20 years earlier. Although the damage from Hurricane Eloise in 1975 came close to matching Opal, the dollar figure came out to a much lesser figure, $135,000—long before the days of insur-ance inflation.

Sandwiched in between Hurricane Eloise and Hurricane Opal was a fire in 1992 that virtually destroyed The Breakers and caused dam-age estimated at $1,200,000.

At times promoters used photos of Santa Claus dipping his feet in the warm Gulf waters to call attention to Panama City Beach during the winter months.

When cities were smaller and less populated, firemen drove their trucks around the neighborhoods, and Santa tossed candy to happy children waiting to see him.

PINEAPPLE WILLY'S *Ribs & Lots More!*

ith an unforgettable view of the Gulf, it's not surprising that the present location of Pineapple Willy's was the site of the original Panama City Beach Hotel - the "in" place for a vacation in the early days of the beach.

The Hotel burned down in due course, and the site became a bait and tackle shop with a pier, but again fate intervened in the form of a hurricane in 1975 which swept it away!

The present owner, Bill Buskell, came to the area in 1979, so Pineapple Willy's is marking its 20th anniversary.

The ribs for which the restaurant is famous were added to the extensive menu in 1984 - almost by accident.

Bill's brother owned a restaurant in Washington, D.C. and had a slow cooker "left over" which Bill acquired. A diabetic himself, Bill was sympathetic with the problems of people trying to stay on a low-fat diet.

"We kept experimenting to do away with the fat," he says today. "In our 8-hour slow-cooking process, all the fat drops to the bottom of the pan." To further decrease the fat, Pineapple Willy's only buys specially-trimmed ribs and when the Jack Daniels special sauce is added (16 ounces in every gallon!), there is a truly memorable product.

So memorable, in fact, that the restaurant sells over 1000 pounds of ribs a day to the customers who flock to the outdoor deck overlooking the water, or the tastefully-decorated inside area.

"People who eat our ribs just keep coming back," Bill says, so they are obviously happy with the result.

The lounge specializes in the "Pineapple Willy". This is described as a "world class, one-of-a-kind mixed drink known the world over." Inside the souvenir cup is a mind-bending blend of pineapple juice, cream of coconut and secret ingredients (including

Pineapple Willy's - Bill Buskell

Myers Rum!)

And the menu includes more than ribs - fresh gulf seafood, for instance, chicken and mouth-watering prime rib of only certified Angus beef. With a special menu for kids, Pineapple Willy's is truly a place the whole family loves!

HAMILTON'S RESTAURANT

Hamilton's Restaurant Carves Own Reputation

While other young boys were playing football or dreaming of becoming a fireman, Steve Stevens was well on his way to continuing the legacy of his illustrious father, Gus, a nationally acclaimed restaurateur. A culinary prodigy at the age of nine, Steve baked homemade delicacies for his family, the most discerning of food critics. Needless to say, he passed those early tests with flying colors and began his apprenticeship at the showplace of the Mississippi Gulf Coast, Gus Stevens Restaurant and Nightclub.

Hamilton's Restaurant, owned by Steve Stevens, on Panama City Beach.

Selected by Southern Living Magazine as the favorite restaurant of Panama City Beach!

Gus Stevens Restaurant & Nightclub on the Mississippi Gulf Coast, owned by Gus Stevens, Steve's father and place where Steve got his start in restaurant business.

"That was the strictest of training programs for any restaurateur," Steve recalled. "My father was very particular about his original creations and protected his recipes like the Crown Jewels of England!"

Steve remembers jokingly, "I am very fortunate to have studied under the best teacher. My father's words and teachings remain a daily part of my success at Hamilton's Restaurant here in Panama City Beach."

Despite the amazing education provided by his father, it wasn't a road paved with gold

for Steve. Equipped with little more than his epicurean tastes and a ramshackle Ford Fairlane, Steve arrived in Panama City Beach in 1984. "My greatest asset was my driving ambition and my undying passion for the restaurant business instilled by my dad," he pointed out.

That genetic passion has roots dating back to his father's childhood in his homeland of Patmos Island, Greece. The entrepreneurial fire that burned bright in Gus Stevens was ignited early in his only son, Steve. An extended visit to his father's island in the spring of 2000 gave Steve even more insight into the tenacity, determination and spirit that he inherited. "I have always been proud of my Greek heritage," he said. "But when I actually got the opportunity to live among the Greek people, I finally understood their thirst for life and the simple desire to please others by cooking a wonderful meal and serving it with joy. I experience that joy every day at Hamilton's. The smiling faces of my customers make my 12-hour days worth it!"

Amidst glowing critical acclaim, Hamilton's now boasts 250,000 smiling customers annually. Selected by Southern Living magazine as the favorite restaurant of Panama City Beach, Hamilton's caters to both tourists and locals. Seeing the potential for the landmark establishment when he first began managing it in 1986, Steve immediately began applying his father's recipe for restaurant success. "Delicious food prepared with the purest ingredients, great entertainment and treating each customer like a member of my own family has put Hamilton's Restaurant on the map here in Panama City Beach, the same way my father put Gus Stevens Restaurant on the map in Biloxi," Steve said.

Steve's mesquite grilled specialties, prime cut steaks, and the freshest seafood and a superb wine list are the headlines of his incredible menu.

After purchasing the restaurant from Bay Bank in the early 90s, Steve took his winning formula steps beyond anyone's

imagination. Located on North Lagoon Drive off Thomas Drive in the heart of the thriving beach community, Steve had visions of creating a complete family entertainment complex. In that true entrepreneurial spirit, Steve made his dreams a reality. Today, Hamilton's is a one-stop food feast and funfest for the entire family. A recreational haven comprised of everything from pony rides to pontoon boats, from wave runners to parasailing provides that great entertainment so essential to Steve's formula for success.

Hamilton's also provides full banquet accommodations for private parties of all sizes. On special holidays, such as Easter, Mother's Day, Thanksgiving and New Year's, Steve's culinary creations are in vast array in 100-item gastronomical buffets. Hamilton's annual Cajun Fest, where Steve and his talented staff feed and entertain more than 30,000 visitors in three days, is always a record breaking, history-making regional event!

Like his father before him, Steve has had his share of obstacles, overcoming the odds by seizing an opportunity, rather than experiencing defeat. "After Hurricane Opal left her $1 million mark on Hamilton's in 1995, I decided to remodel and really update every aspect of the restaurant," Steve revealed. "So we enclosed the large open deck and created a spacious dining area with a fireplace and a new deck where we feature live jazz on summer nights."

Active in many civic organizations, including the Panama

City Beaches Chamber of Commerce and the Tourist Development Council, Steve is a believer in the prosperous future of his community. That is why the restaurant visionary is already making plans to extend Hamilton's to include a downstairs music complex, gift shop and specialty food area, as well as marketing his original food items on the internet.

"Hamilton's has been a labor of love for me for the past 14 years," Steve concluded. "I am so thankful I have a well-trained and loyal staff and customers who keep coming back for the food I have prepared. I thank them all for their belief in me as a restaurateur. They are the ones who make Hamilton's."

"My greatest asset was my driving ambition and my undying passion for the restaurant business instilled by my dad."

—Steve Stevens

KEY WEST *Is Where 'LOCALS' Gather*

f, when you visit another city, you always ask someone to show you where the "locals" eat and drink, on Panama City Beach you'd be directed to the cozy Key West Bar and Grill.

Beverly Hill, who owns and manages Key West, says they get their share of tourists but "regulars" constitute the backbone of their faithful patrons.

"Of course," she adds with a smile, "someone who comes in for the first time one day is greeted as a 'regular' when he comes back for a second visit!"

The little hangout, built in the early '70's weathered Hurricane Opal and stood up to a tornado, and its sturdy oak pillars make it seem certain to outlast anything to come. It's the place to go for live music, friends and a comfortable atmosphere - filled, as it is, with souvenirs.

There are flags of many nations donated by past customers, signs, rock music memorabilia, and so on.

Beverly, who uses "we"

when she refers to future plans, includes her two sons, Joseph and David, who help run Key West, and all of her

Key West regulars find it relaxing and friendly.

employees. It's a team effort, she explains.

The California native came to Panama City Beach almost by accident, and acquired Key West in 1994.

She kept the name for the bar which had been given it by two German ladies, former owners, who wanted to create a casual, relaxed sort of place similar to those they had seen

in the Keys.

She enlarged the place, adding the enclosed front portion and a pleasant outdoor

patio. Her future plans include continuing regular live music and expanding the food service.

"We want to make it a place where people can come for good food (especially local seafood) at reasonable prices," she said.

Beverly herself adds to the welcoming informality. One day she may sport a baseball cap, another day a jester's cap for Mardi Gras or a Santa Claus cap. Tiny lights brighten the darkened interior, and tempting odors waft from the kitchen.

The Key West cat, a handsome grey stray who just walked in about three years ago, greets visitors with all the condescension of her breed. Whether she's lying in the sun in the doorway or inside waiting for leftovers, she is still a part of the team!

An outdoor patio adds to the informal comfort of Key West.

SHUCKUM'S OYSTER PUB & GRILL

Popular Place on the Beach

huckum's Oyster Pub and Seafood Grill is just one of those places people like to hang out on Panama City Beach. While the natives long have considered Shuckum's a place to go, the oyster pub at 15614 Front Beach Road, the main road that runs along the Gulf of Mexico, attracts thousands of visitors each year.

Florida Showcase magazine has cited Shuckum's as one of the premiere places to eat on the "World's Most Beautiful Beaches."

Shuckum's has been advertised as the oldest established oyster pub on Panama City Beach. According to Florida Showcase, the pub serves the freshest, shucked-to-order oysters of every description: raw, baked, sauteed or fried.

Shuckum's also serves grilled and fried seafood sandwiches and entrees, steaks and barbecued ribs, award-winning gumbos and seafood salads and appetizers. It has a full menu, a full bar, inside and outside dining and is open seven days a week the year round. Shuckum's also features a children's menu and accepts all major credit cards. Casual attire is just right for Shuckum's, a casual place to eat.

Shuckum's is family owned and operated and has been in the same location since 1967. For more than 30 years, the oyster pub has been providing

visitors and friends a great family atmosphere and a side range of fresh Gulf of Mexico seafood, along with the best fresh-shucked oysters in the area.

In 1985, Shuckum's expanded to a full-service restaurant and offers everything from fresh grouper to steaks and ribs, along with a full-service liquor bar.

Since 1996, Shuckum's has held the distinction of sole oyster provider for the annual Indian Summer Seafood Festival, which is held the second weekend of October. At the 1996 Seafood Festival, Shuckum's was awarded the "Peoples Choice Award" for its widely acclaimed gumbo. In addition, the oyster pub has participated in the Boggy Bayou Festival held in Niceville as well as the St. Andrews Bay Mardi Gras celebration in Panama City.

For many years, Shuckum's was the host and site for MTV's "Spring Break Panama City Beach" and has received national broadcast exposure. Shuckum's is also home to the famous "We shukum, you suckum" T-shirts. And, now, Shuckum's also has a gift shop

filled with T-shirt designs, caps, huggies and lots of cool quality stuff.

Shuckum's is owned by Brad-Cart Enterprises and is managed by owners Mack Carter and Johnny Bradley, with a lot of help from Chef Clarence Watson, who has been creating culinary delights for the restaurant for 12 years and came to Panama City Beach from Maryland. According to the owners, Clarence's expertise in the kitchen is largely responsible for the bar's regional fame. His range of culinary skills includes everything from Maryland crab cakes to steaks to homemade gumbo, all prepared with a snap of down-home taste.

BILLY'S OYSTER BAR *Is A Real Steamer*

f you want to have a "steaming" good time, the place to go on Panama City Beach is Billy's Oyster Bar and Crabhouse, a quaint little restaurant on Thomas Drive.

Billy's, owned by Billy and Eloise Poole, has been recommended by the *New York Times*, *Southern Living* and *Arthur Frommer's Florida and Our Customer*. It has also been featured in several news publications and on television in Bay County.

The words on the menu pretty well tell the story; "For the finest in steamed seafood," it reads. "It's A Steamer."

Billy's is an unassuming, friendly place located on one of Panama City Beach's busiest roads and customers readily agree that it truly does serve the finest in seafood, along with wine, beer and soft drinks. While Billy's serves what has been called the best steamed blue crabs and seafood gumbo in town, there is a multitude of choices on the menu.

"We have hamburgers and sandwiches for the kids and tantalizing steamed entrees for the adults," pointed out Eloise Poole, who runs the restaurant since husband Billy has semi-retired.

Little has changed since the restaurant opened seventeen years ago. You still get that old southern hospitality. The staff is congenial and greets customers with smiles all around.

The Pooles came here from Greenville, Alabama, 17 years ago after farming for many years. "The farmers were going broke," said Eloise, who has a Masters in psychotherapy from Auburn University Montgomery. "We had to find something to do. I had a little clothing store up there and I thought I would open one down here. That's why we bought this property. If someone had told me I was going into the restaurant business, I would have told them they were crazy."

"We had the first steamed seafood in northwest Florida," Eloise pointed out. "Everything we've got is steamed and everything we cook is fresh. We don't even own a stove."

Although a lot of restaurants have tried to duplicate Billy's Oyster Bar, none have succeeded. "I feel as long as you satisfy your customers, you have nothing to worry about," said Eloise, whose daughter Beth and granddaughter, Brandi also work in the restaurant. "We've got the greatest customers in the world."

SCHOONERS

hey've been blasting the cannon at Schooners every sunset for as many years as folks around Panama City Beach care to remember. The crowds roar in unison "10,9,8,7..." counting down to the precise moment the sun dips below the horizon; some lucky soul chosen from the crowd lights the fuse and the old cannon roars. It is the beach's official signal that one more beautiful day on the beach has ended and the real fun is just beginning!

They call Schooners the "Last Local Beach Club" and it really is the last of the old open-air hangouts left on the Gulf Coast. It started back in the late 60s, when it was known as "The Beach Party." In 1985, Jim Cannon purchased "The Beach Party" from Kenny Strickland and renamed it "Schooners." Most people think the name means a type of sailing ship, but actually Jim was sitting in Australia sipping an ice-cold "schooner" of beer when he learned that his favorite bar, "The Beach Party" was for sale! He cut his world

"The Beach Party" —Started back in the late 60s before it was purchased by Jim Cannon and renamed "Schooners."

Cannon Highlights Sunset at Schooners

tour vacation short and flew back to Panama City to buy the place.

Back then, Schooners was a rustic beach bar. You could get a plate of nachos or, if you were lucky, a cheeseburger. But, the locals loved it, and laid claim to the place. Atchafalaya and Telluride were the most-popular bands in those days, and, when they played, the crowds were so huge that the cops would have to direct traffic.

In 1995, Jim Cannon sold Schooners—just eight days

before Hurricane Opal blew into town. Schooners new owners, Sparky Sparkman and Toni Davis, were committed to rebuilding the historic original structure. Although it took six months longer to do so, the original bar along with every original floorboard, piling, wall and rafter was lovingly restored.

There were many days when it seemed General Manager Dan Plyler was going to rebuild the entire structure singlehandedly. The beach was in shambles after the devastating hurricane, and it was hard to find construction workers, so Dan did a lot of the work himself, and the longtime staff of Schooners pulled together and searched through the wreckage to find and restore old photos and historic memorabilia. Schooners reopened Memorial Day weekend of 1996, and locals were thrilled to see the "old Schooners" hadn't changed.

Schooners —After Hurricane Opal blew into town.

(Well, the owners pointed out, the bathrooms were also better.)

Over the years, not much has changed at "The Last Local Beach Club." The police still have to direct traffic when the crowds are in to see their favorite bands or attend the annual Lobster Festival. The beer is ice-cold, the pace is kicked back. There are wave-runners, sailboats and sandcastles..there is always a volleyball game on the beach. All day long, the locals wander up from their lounge chairs and umbrellas to grab a bite of lunch or cool off with a frozen margarita at the bar.

The band cranks up early every afternoon, so the dance floor is crowded before the sunsets, and it stays that way until early in the morning. Schooners is famous for its music and

local T-shirts—famous for the cannon at sunset and the good times at the bar, but lately the thing people are talking about is the food.

There is nothing "fancy" about Schooner's cuisine; it is simple, fresh and rated perfect. No sauces cover the unbeatable flavor of truly fresh grouper sizzled to perfection on Schooners grills. A platter of fresh fried oysters, hushpuppies and ice-cold beer blend perfectly with the salty breeze blowing in off the Gulf.

Every morning, the chefs buy fresh local seafood from local boat captains and, by lunchtime , they have created a menu of daily specials, which make the most of the fresh seafood and fresh local produce. There is a decidedly "Southern" flavor to the menu; gumbos and

blackened dishes from New Orleans, hushpuppies and slaw from the Mississippi Gulf Coast, succulent grilled shrimp and tomato Greek salads "stolen" from friends and restaurant legends at Captain Anderson's Restaurant. Homemade key lime pie and fresh baked bread from local pastry chefs are always featured. It is a magical mixture that keeps locals coming back for more.

Schooners, the Last Local Beach Club, is open seven days a week from 11 in the morning until the wee hours of the night. Lunch is awesome, dinner is awesome, the bands are awesome and the beach is awesome. And, of course, the sunsets are awesome. As a matter of fact, the owners contend this just might be the best place on earth.

MIKATO JAPANESE SEAFOOD-STEAKHOUSE & LOUNGE

The finest in Japanese Food

Rock Garden at Mikato—a favorite spot for sightseers.

hen Jong Lee came to America in 1976 after teaching for two years in East Africa, he was already a connoisseur of fine food and an outstanding cook. Today, he is the proud owner of the Mikato Japanese Seafood-Steakhouse & Lounge, generally considered one of the finest eating places on Panama City Beach, particularly for those who are looking for something a little different.

Jong, who came from a Buddhist family, was born in South Korea in 1946 but moved to Japan at an early age and studied Karate in high school.

He proudly boasts that he has been cooking most of his life. Although he has owned restaurants in other cities, primarily Anniston and Huntsville in Alabama and Nashville

Tennessee, Mikato has turned out far better than even the most optimistic entrepreneur could dare believe.

Jong estimates that Mikato serves between 45,000 and 50,000 guests annually, and he believes the number is about 50-50 between regular local customers and tourists. There is seldom a night during the busy summer season that Mikato is not packed, and the menu offers a bit of something for everybody. "We serve seafood and steak, lobster tails, scallops and shrimp, filet mignon and New York strip," Jong explains in his broken English. He said that he has found the biggest difference in dining in the United States and in some other countries is how people season their food. "It is more spicy in Korea and they use more sugar

in Japan," he pointed out. "In the United States, people use more salt and pepper."

While Mikato may be best known for its steak and seafood, there is a sushi and tempura special offered each day. The restaurant is open from 4 to 10:30 p.m. Sunday through Thursday and from 4 to midnight on Friday and Saturday.

Jong's wife and brother both work at the restaurant. He is the proud father of two boys, Walter, 19, an IB student at Rutherford who plans to attend Vanderbilt Medical School, and James, 9, a student at Patronis Elementary.

The family has just finished a renovation job at Mikato, including the construction of a rock garden that has attracted the attention of everyone who comes to the restaurant to dine.

Jong says he first fell in love with Panama City Beach while he was vacationing here in 1977. "They had the older bridge then," he revealed. "There was not much else and very few condos."

ANGELO'S STEAK PIT ®

You Won't Get a Bum Steer Here, and That's No Bull!

"Broiling over an open fire stands, in my opinion, as the remote starting point and the very genesis of our art. It has the primeval notion of our forefathers' drive for progress; and motivated by an instinctive desire to eat with greater pleasure. It was the first culinary method ever employed and, in my opinion, has never been improved upon." —Angelo.

hose were the enlightening words of Angelo Gus Butchikas, longtime Bay County restaurateur and the founder of Angelos's Steak Pit who died at a much-too-early age of 43 in a car accident in 1963.

Angelo Gus Butchikas

Today, George Butchikas carries on the tradition of fine foods his dad built after opening Angelo's Steak Pit in what was formerly the 98 Club in May of 1958. "You won't get a bum steer here and that's no bull" might sound like a cliche, but it typifies the high esteem Angelo's enjoys in Bay County and with tourists from all over the country.

Located two miles west of the Hathaway Bridge in Panama City Beach, Angelo's boasts clientele of literally millions, serving only the finest choice steaks, chicken, ribs and seafood cooked to renowned perfection over the restaurant's famous open hickory pits while you watch.

"We serve more than 200,000 people each season," George Butchikas said. That, despite the fact that Angelo's is open only from the middle of

March until the first week of October. The restaurant located on one of the main arteries leading to the beach, employs 150 people and it takes every one of them. We have tried staying open longer but with school starting earlier each year it has taken away from the Family Vacation and has not been busy enough to stay open.

To say that Angelo's steaks are different would be an understatement. "We cook our steaks on hickory and oak wood and one of our specialties is a 32-ounce T-Bone," George revealed. Little wonder that most people who come to the popular restaurant order steaks.

While Angelo's is one of the finest restaurants in the Florida Panhandle, it also is one of the most unique. Big Gus, a 20,000-pound steer in front of the building, has become quite popular over the years and has been chosen the leading land-mark in Bay County.

"We got Big Gus as an eye-catcher in 1970," George said. "They were four-laning Highway 98 and we felt people would be whizzing by so fast, they might miss us. They certainly have an identifying mark in Big Gus."

George acquired Gus in an unusual way. "We had to redesign that bull to make it a steer, but Big Gus has been part of our success ever since," Angelo's owner pointed out.

When you enter the lobby at Angelo's, you are greeted by the Prospector, a lonely raga-muffin in a chair who actually talks to you. "I was going to a lot of restaurant shows and I was at this show in Orlando in 1997 when I saw this man," George said. "I thought it would be good for advertising and peo-ple really like it. We even have a drink named for the Prospector and his picture is on our menu."

George has been the sole owner of Angelo's since 1989 when he bought brother Chris's share of the business. George said he figured it out and that

HAPPY DAYS!—Mr. and Mrs. Angelo Butchikas.

the average employee has been at the restaurant for 15 years. Wilma Fuller, pretty much a landmark herself, has been there since 1962.

George, carrying on the business philosophy of his father, seldom misses a day

being in the office at Angelo"s. "Sometimes I take off a night or two, but I am always here dur-ing the daytime," he said. Good food and fine restaurants have traditionally been a part of the family.

Angelo's Steak Pit—As it was in 1958.

TREASURE SHIP

he Treasure Ship, on Grand Lagoon in Panama City Beach, is a majestic 200-foot-long replica of a 17th century Spanish galleon similar to that of English adventurer, Sir Francis Drake's ship, The Golden Hind. Ships like this served both the Spanish, who looted the "New World" in the 17th and 18th centuries and the pirates who in turn looted the Spanish. They were known as treasure ships for they brought back cargo worth millions to their respective sovereigns.

The Treasure Ship was designed to give free reign to your imagination. Walk her decks, explore her hold, sample her wares, eat, drink and be merry! For here, everyone's childhood fantasy of pirates and adventures on the high seas is made real.

Swash a little, buckle if you must, be a pirate, the fair maiden, a cabin boy or a king. Finger your silver, toast her royal majesty, celebrate your latest victory, forget defeat. Climb her decks, sight her cannons, lash yourself to the mast in the driving wind. Enjoy the Treasure Ship, it was built for you!

The Dock Level of the Treasure Ship was operated as a popular nightspot called The Brig for many years, but has recently been transformed with Caribbean flair into Hook's Grille & Grog. Hook's features inside and outside dockside dining and is open for lunch and dinner. The well thought-out menu features

THE TREASURE SHIP located on Grand Lagoon, offers something special for tourists and sightseers on Panama City Beach.

outstanding offerings of local seafood and Certified Angus Beef™ dishes. A wide variety of appetizers, entrees and desserts keep a steady clientele of locals and visitors alike. Tropical drinks from the bar are made with fresh-squeezed citrus.

On Level II, in the main body of the ship, you'll find the Main Dining Room. Every seat offers an outstanding waterfront view of all the activity on Grand Lagoon. It's a favorite spot for families as the kids enjoy the pirates that freely roam throughout the restaurant, telling their tall tales, painting little faces and creating balloon art. The family atmosphere is colorful and creative, but does not overshadow the culinary talents of Chef Dee Brown when it comes to good food. Dee's award-winning cuisine has earned national attention. The success starts with the ultimate selection of fresh local seafood and masterful preparation methods that make The Treasure Ship a must for thousands of visitors each year.

On Level III, the Deck Bar has been recently renovated to

provide a spacious multi-level entertainment venue. This is the highest lookout point on Grand Lagoon. "Live" music is featured nightly during the high season. The family will enjoy the blasts of cannon fire as the pirates volley with the ships on the lagoon.

The Pirate's Playroom Arcade is a popular spot to test your skills on today's newest video games. The Treasure Ship Gift Shop is open year round with a great selection of souvenirs that will remind you of your wonderful visit to Panama City Beach.

In addition to The Treasure Ship's restaurants and entertainment offerings, the dock below hosts charter fishing boats, sightseeing boats and day-trips to provide you with lots of fun on the water.

You can keep up with all the excitement of The Treasure Ship by visiting its Web site at thetreasureship.com. You'll find all the menus, a "live" cam on the dock, pirate lore, recipes from Chef Dee Brown and complete information on everything you'd like to know about The Treasure Ship.

CAPTAIN ANDERSON'S RESTAURANT

 hen the Patronis brothers, Johnny and Jimmy, came to Bay County from Tallahassee in 1953 and opened the Seven Seas Restaurant at Fifth Street and Grace Avenue in Panama City, little did they know what treasures the future would hold.

They operated that restaurant for 14 years before the brothers got what turned out to be the opportunity of a lifetime.

"Jimmy and I had the opportunity to come out here (Panama City Beach) and buy Captain Anderson's Restaurant," Johnny revealed. "It turned out pretty good."

Johnny and Jimmy bought the restaurant, now ranked among the best in the country, from the famed Anderson brothers, Captains Walt and Max, who had built Captain Anderson's Marina and Restaurant in early 1958.

"Certainly, we've got to acknowledge what the Anderson family meant to this area," Johnny added. "They

Captain Anderson's Restaurant

One of the Very Best in the Country

made a unique contribution to local history."

The Patronis brothers haven't done too badly themselves. Captain Anderson's Restaurant has won numerous honors, including being ranked as one of the top 50 eating-places in America by Southern Living magazine. It has won a dozen Golden Spoon awards

from Florida Trend.

Since Southern Living started its poll of readers three years ago, Captain Anderson's has been chosen the top seafood restaurant twice and was second the other time.

Invariably, when newcomers come to Panama City Beach and ask about a good eating-place, Captain Anderson's is ranked right at the top. It wasn't always that easy.

"I remember when we bought the restaurant in 1967, we took out a $120,000 loan with Security Federal," Johnny laughed. "That was the biggest loan they had ever made at that time."

Since the Patronis brothers took over the restaurant, they have made three additions to the facility; in 1968, 1970 and the latest in 1996. The restaurant now has 35,000 square

The Patronis Family with Captain Anderson's Restaurant

feet, 640 seats and feeds approximately 250,000 people annually, despite the fact that it closes in November, December and January. That statistic is even more amazing when considering that Captain Anderson's serves dinner only.

Although the restaurant started with the two brothers, Jimmy's four boys, Theo, Yonnie, Nick and Jimmy, now are heavily involved in the business. There are 165 employees, including Chef Alonzo Keyes, who has been with the Patronis brothers since they went into business in Panama City in 1953. Lillian Lewis, the salad expert, has been with them almost that long.

"A lot of our employees have been with us for 15 and 20 years," Johnny said. "We've got our own bureaucracy."

Captain Anderson's has done so well because the restaurant specializes in fresh local seafood. "The fish from this part of the country (Gulf Coast) is the best in the United States," Johnny boasted. "They call us a seafood restaurant that specializes in real fish. We do it Greek style."

The Patronis brothers not only are highly successful businessmen, they are solid citizens as well. A few years ago, they donated land for the nearby Patronis School, which became the third elementary school in the beaches area.

Johnny has done a lot of work for the Chamber of Commerce and served as President of Bay County Chamber and also the Panama City Beaches Chamber of Commerce. Jimmy is heavily involved in Florida State University's scholarship program and is close personal friends with Florida Seminole Coach, Bobby Bowden.

Last year, Bowden wrote Jimmy Patronis, Jr. a letter in which he made the remark that "your Dad is Florida State."

In addition to Bowden, there are pictures of many famous people hanging on the walls at Captain Anderson's Restaurant. Included are former Alabama Coach, Gene Stallings, who won a National Championship with the Crimson Tide in 1992; former Tennessee Coach, Johnny Majors; NFL Hall of Fame Linebacker, Dick Butkus; Captain Max Anderson; and entertainers George Jones, the Oak Ridge Boys, Tanya Tucker and Pam Tillis.

Jimmy Patronis has a simple formula for success. "The thing I keep telling our people is good food and good service are really hard to come by," he philosophizes. "It doesn't just happen. You've got to make it happen. You've got to stay on top of it and you've got to baby-sit it."

While Johnny and Jimmy are not as active as they once were in the restaurant, it still is pretty much a hands-on operation for the brothers. "The four boys are pretty much running it, but we still come to work every day," Johnny said.

MONTEGO BAY

Montego Bay Became Instant Hit on Beach

n 1982, Roy Centanni wanted to open a lounge in Fort Walton Beach, but there were no liquor licenses available. So, the man who later affectionately would become known as "Rude Roy" moved to Panama City, bought the old Breakers from Jack Bishop and turned it into the Montego Bay Club, a night spot, on Beck Avenue. From that beginning, Centanni became one of the premier restaurateurs on the Florida Panhandle and Montego Bay became one of the fastest growing seafood houses in this part of the country.

Roy began his career in food services with Host International in a city famous for fine dining, New Orleans. From that restaurant, he moved to the position of food and beverage manager at the famous La Pavilion. While in New Orleans, he also managed Cafe Pontalbo in Jackson Square.

He later opened Brannigan's in Fort Walton and founded Jamaica Joe's, one of the most successful operations in north Florida. However, it wasn't until Roy opened Montego Bay Seafood House and Oyster Bar at "The Curve" on Thomas Drive, that his restaurant business began to boom.

He opened a second Montego Bay at 9949 Thomas Drive in 1985 and then three years later opened a third at what over the years has been one of his most-popular loca-

tions in the Shoppes of Edgewater.

In 1990, Roy formed a partnership with Jerry Senner of New Orleans and they opened Sweet Basil's, an Italian restaurant in the Shoppes of Edgewater. He then purchased Stoker's Restaurant on the west end of the beach and converted it into the fourth Montego Bay. The fifth Montego Bay became a reality on Cove Boulevard near the Panama City Mall when Roy bought the old Southeast Bank branch building and turned it into another seafood house. His restaurant business was going through a phenomenal rate of expansion.

In 1991, Roy opened Rude Roy's Marina Grill at the foot of the Hathaway Bridge. When he split with Senner, he opened Canopies, just across the bridge in Panama City.

"At one time I had seven restaurants," Roy pointed out. "But I downscaled and now own three original Montego Bays and Canopies. You might say I simplified life and got down to four."

At one time there was even a Montego Bay in Orlando and two in Alabama—one at Orange Beach and another in Montgomery.

Roy said he didn't realize what he had until opening the restaurant at Edgewater. "Two

nights after opening, we had huge crowds," he pointed out. "It was then I realized what a demand there was for good seafood. At that time, everything at other seafood places was either fried or broiled. I just put together a more diversified menu at a reasonable price. My food was grilled, or fried, and we added sandwiches and salads and offered lunch."

Today the three remaining Montego Bay restaurants offer both lunch and dinner seven days a week the year round.

The three Montego Bays in Panama City Beach have lured visitors from all over the world and Roy has pictures of numerous famous people hanging on the walls at the corporate offices on Clarence Street. An avid golfer for many years, he also has mementoes of some pretty good days of playing the great Scottish game.

"Cooking is a talent, just like everything else," Roy explained. Those who have tried the char-grilled amberjack and Oysters Montego at Montego Bay certainly have to agree.

128

BLACK ANGUS STEAK RESTAURANT

owe Smith has been a Bay County legend ever since he opened the Shrimp Boat in the St. Andrews area of Panama City in 1952, and he's still going strong. Lowe has owned and helped operate numerous restaurants in Panama City Beach since those days, and the Fireside Inn, in Panama City. In June 1990, Loren, who also is heavily involved in land development and construction, opened Pompano's on the eastern end of Panama City Beach and that restaurant now is considered one of the premier places to dine on the beaches. In addition, Loren is a partner

Lowe Smith a Bay County Legend

rant business that employs more than 175 people, including the popular nightclub, Boomer's, at the Black Angus. Lowe said that in the earlier years, there was always a big act in the club now known as Boomer's, including Barbara Eden, who sold out two consecutive nights.

However, the dignitaries who once visited the Shrimp Boat are probably even better

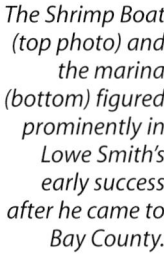

The Shrimp Boat (top photo) and the marina (bottom) figured prominently in Lowe Smith's early success after he came to Bay County.

perhaps even more significantly, he probably has been involved in more real estate transactions and developments than any other individual in this part of the country.

Lowe currently is partners with his son, Loren and son-in-law, Gary Paul, in operating the Black Angus Restaurant, which in the old days was known as with former County Commissioner Marc Nolen in the newer Mako's Dockside Restaurant at Captain Anderson's Marina.

Frances, Lowe's daughter, and husband, Gary are the primary operators in the Black Angus Restaurant, while Loren manages Pompano's and Marc operates Mako's. Altogether, the family is involved in a restau-known and included Susan Hayward, considered by many the greatest leading lady of all times in the movies, and Adlai Stevenson. "Miss Hayward was a beautiful lady and she was a frequent visitor to our restaurants," Lowe said.

While Lowe is the patriarch of the family, he is not as heavily involved in the restaurant

SWEET ANGELINE

Famed movie actress Susan Hayward is shown aboard a charter fishing boat during days Lowe Smith operated a marina in St. Andrews, Panama City.

operation as he once was, but has made an even bigger name in real estate development. Two of his most successful ventures have been Kingspoint, near the county airport, and the property around Lake Powell to professional golfer, Greg Norman, who plans to build two golf courses.

Other memorable real estate deals included the sale of the property where the Wal-Mart Super Center is located on the east end of Panama City Beach and where a relatively new Winn Dixie is located on the west end of the beach. He also sold property where one of the beach's most exclusive RV resorts was constructed, long before Winn Dixie made its arrival across the street. The

family once owned property in the area where the 33-story condominium, Sunset Pass, is scheduled to be constructed.

While at St. Andrews, Lowe also operated a marina and owned several boats. His early ventures in Panama City Beach, where he now lives, included the Driftwood Restaurant and two steak houses. Gary Paul started work for the Smiths as a bus boy at the old Shrimp Boat when he was only 13 years old and later became a member of the family when he married Frances. Loren started working around his father's restaurants when he was just a kid and made his first major independent move when he opened Pompano's.

Lowe came here and bought property in St. Andrews in 1949 after operating an automobile dealership in Montgomery for more than 30 years. He also was in the car business here and at one time owned the Toyota dealerships in Panama City and Marianna. Since that time, he has owned and operated numerous businesses, but the restaurants have always been something to fall back on. Loren, certainly one of the most successful young businessmen in the area, is a chip off the old block. "I will always be interested in the restaurant business, but I am getting more and more into real estate sales and development," he said.

CHAPTER III
WORLD CLASS LODGING

Hotels, Motels and Condominiums

Sea Witch Motel

132

The Driftwood
Lodge

134

Marriott Bay Point
Resort Village

135

Holloway House

137

Chateau Motel

138

Edgewater Beach
Resort

139

Port of Call Motel

141

Sandpiper Beacon

143

Bikini Beach
Resort

144

Panama City
Beach KOA

146

Sugar Sands Motel

147

Holiday Inn
Sunspree

148

Beachcomber By
The Sea

150

Sunset Pass
Condos

151

Sterling Beach/
Cornerstone
Development Group

153

THE SEA WITCH MOTEL *The Ship That Doesn't Float*

ince Roger W. Stephens developed The Sea Witch Motel thousands of guests have enjoyed this unique motel, finding great pleasure and relaxation in the friendly atmosphere that prevails at The Sea Witch.

In 1972, the west end of Panama City Beach was nurtured only by a handful of residents. But Roger Stephens had a vision. Many friends questioned the viability of the location. But Stephens had a long-term dream to provide visiting friends with reasonable cost lodging and vacation with unlimited access to the magnificent sand and surf. Roger knew the potential of this vacation dreamland. His parents, Mr. And Mrs. Ralph E. Stephens, had owned the beach house two doors down from the motel since 1946. Before being moved,

it was a latrine at Fort Benning, Georgia and was added to for a rest facility for the Stephens family and their employees and friends.

The younger Stephens grew up vacationing in this quiet paradise where gentle Gulf breezes stroke the towering dunes and miles of deserted white sand beach. The Auburn graduate acquired the Gulf-front

property in the 1960s. Construction began on the first phase of the Sea Witch in 1972 and it was opened for business in June 1973. He named his motel "The Sea Witch" for a well-known clipper ship that sailed from 1842 to 1856.

By the late 1980s, Stephens had more requests for rooms than he could fill. In 1988, he decided to enlarge his motel, adding a seven-story new section where his parents' family vacation cottage had stood. Today the seven-story tower of The Sea Witch Motel stands in place of two beach houses. This building was completed and opened for guests in 1988.

Located on the highest point of the beach, the motel

withstood both Hurricane Eloise in 1975 and Hurricane Opal, 20 years later in 1995. But as a result of these hurricanes, along with several other winter and summer storms, many locations along Panama City Beach lost considerable amounts of beachfront.

The beach renourishment project of 1999 added several yards to the motel's 500 feet of Gulf frontage.

Stephens died at the age of 49. His wife, Helen, took over as General Manager of the business in 1996. She acquired her knowledge of motel management in the 1970s and then married Roger in 1974. They had 2 children, Jennifer and Lee.

For many years, Helen pursued a career as a schoolteacher in Alabama. After retirement, she returned to the Sea Witch in 1996.

With a total of 143 rooms that include 64 two-bedroom units and 132 kitchenettes, it is easy to see that the Sea Witch continues to cater to families.

As a General Manager, Helen radiates enthusiasm and loves her job. She is quick to point out, however, that bringing the complex to this point was not easy. It took a lot of hard work.

She refers to the Sea Witch as "the ship that doesn't float." At any one time, several things are going on. Besides providing lodging, the Sea Witch also features a gift shop, guest laundry and a conference room that is popular for family reunions and convienience store with public laundry.

In the summer, the Sea Witch continues to cater to vacationing families who return year after year. The motel hires certified life guards in the summer to protect bathers and to enforce the flag system—blue means safe swimming, yellow—use caution and red—stay out of the water.

A beach service makes wave-runners, parasails and chairs with umbrellas available to guests.

During the fall, many families come from Tennessee, Alabama, Georgia and other sections of the country to enjoy a more quiet time on the beach.

Autumn and winter are when the water varies in changing hues of emerald green and guests enjoy watching the magnificent sunrises and sunsets on the Gulf that show gorgeous shades of apricot, rose, lavender and blue. At dusk, the sinking orange sun beneath the Gulf remains a magnificent, unforgettable scene.

In winter, it's the Snowbirds, who come from as far away as Arizona and the northern states like Minnesota, Michigan, and Illinois, as well as Canada. The motel hosts several events that keep guests busy such as potluck dinners, bridge, darts, golf tournaments, Christmas dinner, New Year's Eve party, Mardi Gras celebration and St. Patrick's Day.

Roger Stephens knew what he was doing when he constructed his motel. Waterfront and water view lots, of which few remain, sell at a premium. Like all places along the Gulf, this end of the beach is undergoing considerable growth. The Sea Witch has become one of the finest family motels on the Emerald Coast.

DRIFTWOOD LODGE

he Driftwood Lodge opened for business in 1955. The original building, constructed by Columbus, Georgia developer Ted Alford, was a two-story 12-room lodge. During the next ten years, the Driftwood Lodge expanded its main building, added beach level rooms and a fresh water swimming pool and snack bar. The current Big Horn Steakhouse was the Driftwood Restaurant and Lounge.

In 1968, Woody and Irene Miner were in central Florida visiting family, when they decided to take a side trip to the Panhandle. That was when they fell in love with Panama City Beach. In 1969, Woody and Irene sold their home and possessions, packed the car and moved to Panama City Beach from Connecticut. They arrived in Panama City Beach just as Hurricane Camille was bearing down on the Gulf Coast.

Yet, Woody and Irene loved Panama City Beach so much they encouraged their family to move here. In 1971, Doug and Lorraine Gilmore (Woody and Irene's daughter) and their young daughters moved to Panama City Beach. Doug and Lorraine took over management of the Driftwood Lodge, and purchased it from Woody and Irene in 1974.

In the 1970's Panama City Beach was a seasonal resort primarily for Southern families escaping to the beach for a week or two between Memorial Day and Labor Day. Today the Driftwood Lodge is a year-round resort destination for Spring/Summer family vacationers and our Fall/Winter "Snowbirds."

Doug and Lorraine ran the Driftwood Lodge as a family business. Lorraine would watch the front desk, while Doug took care of the building. In the evening the Gilmore family would cook out and eat dinner with their guests, a tradition that continues today.

Many of the Driftwood Lodge guests have been staying here for over 30 years. These guests consider the Driftwood Lodge their home away from home. As much as the Gilmore's love their "Old Drifters," as they affectionately call their old-time guests, they are thrilled to introduce new families to the city and motel that they love so much.

the Driftwood Lodge has seen Panama City Beach undergo tremendous growth in the past 46 years. What was once a sleepy summer resort has grown into a tourist Mecca. Mom, Dad and the kids, visiting for summer and spring vacation are our staple. Yet the market has extended to seniors, empty nesters and families with preschool children who can enjoy the great weather and water of the fall and late spring. Special events such as The Indian Summer Seafood Festival, the Gulf Coast Triathlon, the Isuzu Ironman Triathlon and the Gulf Coast Charity Celebration are bringing new people and national exposure to Panama City Beach.

Doug and Lorraine love Panama City Beach and have a vested interest in the community. Both Doug and Lorraine's mothers live here in town. Their daughters and their families also live here in Panama City Beach and are involved in Gilmore Resorts making this the third generation to own and operate the Driftwood Lodge. Doug and Lorraine are active in the Panama City Beach community. Both are involved in the Panama City Beach Chamber of Commerce. Lorraine is very active in Beach Care Services, Inc., Gulf Beach Presbyterian Church and the Chamber of Commerce. Doug is a councilman for the City of Panama City Beach and a Board member of the Tourist Development Council.

The Driftwood Lodge has been a part of Panama City Beach history for 45 years, and the Gilmore family wants it to be a part of Panama City Beach for years to come.

DRIFTWOOD LODGE in 1957 before the Gilmore family, Doug and Lorraine, purchased the motel and took over the operation.

MARRIOTT'S BAY POINT RESORT VILLAGE

Kids get special treatment when registering at Resort

arriott's Bay Point Resort, one of the truly plush places to stay in Panama City Beach, caters to groups and leisure-type customers. However, one of the things the Bay Point Resort does that attracts a lot of attention is the special treatment it gives kids.

"We have a special check-in for the kids," pointed out General Manager, David Bartek. "They really like that Jeep hood with stripes out there in the lobby."

When kids check themselves in they get special gifts. And, once they are settled in, there are a lot of special activities for them.

The Resort, which during the course of a year caters and services between 300,000 and 400,000 visitors, opened in 1986 with 199 guest rooms. Now, the facility has 355 deluxe guests rooms, including 78 garden suites and 10 handicapped-accessible rooms.

"All of the guest rooms in the main hotel have just been redone," pointed out Constance Harvout, Executive Secretary for the Resort. About a year earlier, all the suites in the Loch Legend Village across the street were completely redone. In that location, there are seven buildings, all named for famous golf courses. And, yes, the village has a St. Andrews and Augusta building.

The Resort offers countless opportunities for all visitors to enjoy themselves, including boating and dolphin encounters. Also popular are the bicycle rental and rides around the property and special activities like beach parties.

Guests have the opportunity to play two of the finest golf courses in this part of the country at Bay Point. You haven't really played the game until you take on the Lagoon Legend. Playing out to an awesome 7,080 yards, this 18-hole championship monster-of-a-course has been called "the second most challenging course in the United States" by the USGA and the "third best resort course in Florida" by Golf Digest. If the Legend is too tough for you, you'll find another outstanding course in Club Meadows.

Marriott's Bay Point Village probably is the most-popular meeting place in Bay County, primarily because of the 40,000-square-foot Convention Center and Ballroom. The Beaches Chamber of Commerce held its Business Expo-2000 at the Center and at the time this article was written, there were about 800 Rotarians on the property for a convention.

"I would say about 60 percent of our business comes from groups or conventions," Bartek pointed out. He said the Resort is working hard to reestablish its relationship with the community. The Resort also is involved in charities, working closely with the Bay Point Billfish Tournament, which donates proceed to the Anchorage Children's Home. Also, Marriott's "Charity of Choice" is the Children's Miracle Network.

It was about five years ago that Resort officials just about doubled the size of the Convention Center.

Bartek manages the property, which is owned by ALFA Insurance out of Alabama, for Crestline Hotels and Resorts. Altogether, the Resort has about 300 employees.

Bartek, who is originally from Pennsylvania, has been in the hotel business for 16 years and accepted the job with Bay Point in August of 1999. Before that he was general manager of the Tampa Airport Hilton. He lived in the Orlando area for 10 years and commuted to jobs in both Tampa and Nashville, Tennessee. He and wife, Amy have four children, from ages six to seventeen.

HOLLOWAY HOUSE

One of Area's Best-Known Motels

Left to Right—Richard, Patricia, Johnny, Jared, Myrtle, John, Aaron.

ohn Holloway, owner of the Holloway House, one of Panama City Beach's oldest and best-known motels, had no choice. He was born to be in the hospitality business.

"I was raised in it (the motel business)," he said. "My grandfather came down here in the thirties and built the Sea Breeze Motel."

Although John's dad was in the lumber business in Geneva, Alabama, John spent his summer vacations helping "Poppa," (Bill Holloway) at the motel.

"I joined the Navy after high school and spent five years in the service before getting into the motel business full-time," John revealed.

Shortly thereafter Poppa Holloway sold his motel to Billy Holloway, his other grandson and namesake. However, John Holloway later bought it back and wound up with two motels when he built the Holloway House.

John, in partnership with Bill, his cousin, built the Holloway House in 1969. By 1972 John had bought Bill out of his part of the business.

"We started the Holloway House before we sold the Sea Breeze," John pointed out. "We opened in July, 1970, and I will never forget that day. Myrtle (his wife) was pregnant and Patricia was born the same day we opened the motel."

Patricia is one of three children born to Myrtle and John Holloway. Patricia helps at the motel and is also a radiographer at Crest Clinic. Johnny Holloway, the oldest son, is a physicist at the Naval Coastal Systems Station here on the beach, and younger son, Richard, works full-time at the motel. "He's the head knocker," John said. "Without him, I wouldn't be here."

When the Holloway House first opened in 1970, there were 102 rooms and a gulf side restaurant. "We have since converted the restaurant into rooms and with a few other remodeling ventures, we now have 96 rooms of various accommodations," John pointed out. While most motels on

Panama City Beach are seasonal, John said his establishment is open year-round and employs between 20 to 25 people.

Also, like most motels on Panama City Beach, John said the Holloway House thrives on Spring Break. "It's different now than it was back in the forties and fifties," he said. "It used to be that kids on Spring Break came with their mothers and fathers. Now they have their own cars and a pocketful of money to spend when they arrive."

John probably gets a little homesick when he drives a little further west and looks at the Sea Breeze. "The place still has the old cedar shingles my grandpa put on the building," he pointed out. Obviously, some things have not changed.

137

CHATEAU MOTEL *Has a Warm Welcome*

he Chateau Motel, at 12525 Front Beach Road, has a long standing history on the beach - but it has changed considerably since its early days.

Originally opened in 1964, it was an extravagantly beautiful show place for its time— replete with wrought iron, red velvet curtains and a distinctly Gallic atmosphere. Started by a partnership of Kyser Wilson, Charles & Amy McCormick and others, the motel soon outgrew its modest beginnings, with a new wing built in 1968.

Now, new decor has changed the style to one more contemporary. Most of the 152 modern, spacious rooms boast private balconies. A glistening pool is centered in the motel and there is a private beach 500 feet long, with beachside chairs which can be drawn up right at the edge of the glistening Gulf waters.

Visitors vary from elderly winter snowbirds to the college crowd on Spring break; from starry-eyed honeymooners enjoying the moonlit waters to

The Chateau as seen from the ocean.

young families with children playing at the water's edge or hunting seashells up and down the beach.

With five different floor plans to choose from, the Chateau has the perfect room for anyone's vacation.

A warm greeting is extended to the visitor by the team operating the circular reservation area where Kevin Brackins presides as General Manager of the motel.

Kevin has been with the Chateau for the past eleven years. Originally from Kansas City, Missouri, he first managed a Holiday Inn in Ozark, Alabama, before moving south to Panama City Beach. Under his management, this thoroughly modern and comfortable beach-

side resort has become one of the favorite spots along the beach.

The warmth and friendliness of the staff, the luxurious accommodations just a step from the white sand make the visitor feel at home immediately on arrival. The addition of tropical birds preening themselves happily both inside and outside, gives the motel a special touch.

These birds are Kevin's special pride. Magnificent cockatoos and other colorful birds will even walk up your arm or sit on your shoulder. They are a sure magnet for every child in the area.

The Chateau has grown as the beach has grown, and has changed to meet the changing needs of its visitors. That's how the owners want it to continue in the years to come.

Pool view gives you different look.

EDGEWATER BEACH RESORT

he Edgewater Beach resort and Long Beach Resort are serious about becoming the premier destination resorts in the Panama City area. Last August, Andy Phillips, previously general manager of the 1,400-room

'New Team' Means Improvement For Edgewater, Long Beach Resorts

Westin Bonaventure in Los Angeles, was hired to tackle the challenge of turning this 110-acre beachfront condominium resort into the gem of the region.

Prior to heading the team at the Edgewater Beach resort, which was opened in 1985, Phillips' 14- year career with Marriott Hotels and Resorts and Interstate Hotels included such properties as the Marriott in Key West, Marriott at Sawgrass Resort in Pointe Vedra and Marriott's largest hotel, the 1,850-room New York Marquis in Times Square. According to Phillips, "the goal for Edgewater

Beach and Long Beach resorts is to continue to establish themselves as complete beach resorts with an emphasis on the wide variety of amenities and services available. This combination will allow guests to enjoy the previous diversions that made

Edgewater unique; the gorgeous beach and the famous Lagoon pool, championship golf and three restaurants and bars, along with the high level of service that our guests want and deserve."

Edgewater has just finished adding a 32,700-square-foot state-of-the-art conference center, which will more than double the size of the present indoor meeting space and continue to set the standard for resort meeting facilities and accommodations on Panama City Beach. The new conference center features a ballroom with

20-foot ceilings that seats 1,500 people theater-style, or 1,120 for formal dinner. In addition, the resort offers a full catering staff and unlimited outdoor venues, including a 45,000-square-foot lagoon pool deck and one half mile of private beach.

"We are pleased to offer bigger and better meeting facilities to all our guests at Edgewater," pointed out Phillips. "With this multimillion dollar improvement, we have solidified our position as the premier destination resort in Panama City Beach."

Flexible meeting space, state-of-the-art studio visual equipment and a professional staff ensure that all meeting events at the new Edgewater Beach resort Conference Center run smoothly. The catering staff and team of chefs satisfy even the most discerning palates as attendees enjoy fabulous luncheons and incredibly fresh seafood.

Edgewater Beach Resort offers a wide variety of accommodations: 500 fully equipped suites in all, spread over the

100-acre gated beach-front resort, situated along one of the "World's Most Beautiful Beaches", eleven pools including the resort's famous 11,000-square-foot lagoon pool, four spas, 11 tennis courts, access to executive and championship golf courses and on-property dining make Edgewater an attractive destination.

In addition to the new Conference Center, Edgewater is opening a brand-new fitness center and spa. "The fitness center and spa and our new conference center are critical elements to our resort," Phillips pointed out. "This is a very exciting time for us as we open these remarkable new facilities. The fitness center and spa will offer an aerobics room, aerobics classes, cardiovascular equipment, massage therapy and locker rooms. Guests can enjoy this new recreation option, in addition to Edgewater's many other facilities." Conveniently located above the golf and tennis pro-shop, the fitness center and spa is adjacent to the Conference Center and overlooks the tennis and shuffleboard courts.

Edgewater recently received one silver and two bronze awards in the 43rd Annual Adrian Advertising Award Competition of the Hospitality Sales and Marketing Association International (HSMAI) hosted in New York. The 1999 competition drew more than 1,800 entries from 51 countries and destinations worldwide. These awards reinforce the essential role that advertising and public relations play in the successful marketing of the travel industry around the world.

"We are proud that our efforts to provide quality advertising for Edgewater Beach Resort have been recognized," said Barry Hoehn, Director of Sales and Marketing for the resort. " Our advertisements reflect the class of our resort and we are thrilled to receive three HSMAI awards." Edgewater also has won Interiorscape Magazine's 15th Annual Best Project Completion for its hanging garden. The garden was chosen as one of the top 21 from more than 400 applicants and was featured in the January/February 2000 issue of Interiorscape Magazine. The solid and thoroughly constructed planter with a 5-foot radius and 18-inches of depth contains moss, nine 8-inch golden pathos, six 6-inch bromeliads (three yellow and three red) and one 10-inch Spathiphyllum.

Edgewater last year added the Golf Village at the nearby Hombre Golf Club, an 18-hole championship course developed by Wes Burnham, who also designed Edgewater. The Golf Village at Hombre offers fully-furnished 1,600-square-foot, two-bedroom/two bath villas located directly on the Hombre course, just minutes from the beach, and makes Edgewater Beach Resort truly a complete resort destination.

Burnham, who came to Panama City Beach from Birmingham in 1969, started construction on the $100 million resort complex at Edgewater in 1983. In order to build Edgewater, the Florida Department of Transportation, with approval of the City of Panama City Beach, moved a 3,000-foot-stretch of U.S. Highway 98 inland by 350 feet. At the time, Edgewater also built a nine-hole golf course around the lakes at Edgewater. Tennis courts also were part of this project.

In the late eighties, Burnham started construction on the Hombre, a golf course he designed and financed, along with three out-of-town partners. The course, generally considered one of the most competitive in the state, is located between Middle Beach Road and Back Beach Road close to the Edgewater Beach Resort.

It is generally agreed that Edgewater Beach Resort brings together the best of the land and the seas to create an oasis for guests of all ages. Here, Edgewater's 110-acre expanse incorporates an array of activities and amenities sure to make any vacation memorable.

PORT OF CALL MOTEL *The Schilleci Legends Live On*

Port of Call Motel viewed from the water.

t seems like a far cry from an ice-cream plant in Bessemer, Alabama, to a luxury motel on Panama City Beach, but the Schilleci family made the transition as easily as they made their original migration from Sicily to the United States.

They settled first in New Orleans, Louisiana but soon left for Bessemer, where they established their ice-cream business, supplying many grocery stores and restaurants.

Mark Schilleci, whose family owns both Port of Call Motel and the Fiesta Motel, recalls easily the changes that have occurred on the beach since his father, Frank, and his uncle, Dr. Vincent Schilleci, joined forces with Sam Rain, Jr., H. C. Springer and Otis Springer to buy the old Larkway Villa cottages in the early 60s.

The family retained the early partnership, built the Fiesta Motel and soon after-

wards developed the Trade Winds Motel . The partnership was eventually divided with the Springers taking the Trade Winds and the Schillecis taking complete control of the Fiesta.

Frank Schilleci and his brother, Don Schilleci, also developed the gulfside Port of Call Motel along with two restaurants across the highway. Mark now co-manages the Fiesta with Debbie McCormick who has been with the Schilleci family for over twenty years. Debbie also manages the Port of Call Motel and has been key in

reacquainting Mark with the beach area and motel business.

For Mark, it wasn't just a case of growing up and stepping into the family business far from it.

Like many other sons, he developed many different interests, and eventually chose to work with an Anheuser-Busch distributorship. Remaining in this business for 15 years he realized that he was ready for a change. The natural beauty of the beach, the sunsets and his love of scuba diving drew him back into the motel business like a magnet.

"As soon as I got here, I knew my blood pressure went down!" he says now.

The new philosophy the beach gave him was one of re-

Aerial Photo of Fiesta Motel.

laxing and letting the sea, sun and air do their magic. Since then, he enjoys the wide diversity of his visitors and his unending work to make them enjoy their stay.

And there's plenty to enjoy. Both motels have extensive frontage on the white sands and clear, clean waters of the Gulf. For those who prefer the calm waters of a pool, the motels also have crystal-clear swimming pools, one of those at the Port Of Call is seasonally heated for year-round use.

Rooms of every kind are to be found in these two motels, from fully-equipped efficiencies with kitchenettes to lavish suites—and many have private balconies from which vacationers can enjoy the spectacular view of the Gulf.

Panama City Beach's many attractions are within easy reach of both motels—from amusement parks to fine dining, from beachside shopping to all kinds of activities for the more adventurous.

And above all, the rooms at Fiesta and Port of Call are priced to appeal to all kinds of visitors.

Whether you're a spring-breaker on a tight budget, a "snowbird" escaping the winter storms, honeymooners looking for a once-in-a-lifetime memory, or a family intent upon relaxation, sunshine, the glorious Gulf and a safe place for young children, these two properties have something for everyone.

"My motels are places where individuals and families can get away from their everyday life,"says Mark Schilleci.

"They are places to slow down, enjoy and let go of your problems."

And at least once a day, he goes down to the edge of the Gulf and follows his own advice!

Port of Call Pool.

SANDPIPER BEACON RESORT

t is difficult to believe that two small beach motels of the 1950s, boasting a total of less than 20 units, could, by the millenium, become a bustling resort with 800 feet of pure white sand beach, four sparkling swimming pools, a hot tub and dozens of other amenities.

Yet that is just what happened at Sandpiper Beacon Resort—otherwise known as "The Fun Place"—and located at 17403 Front Beach Road.

The Beacon opened its doors in 1951 with 8 units, living quarters and an office.

The Sandpiper opened in 1955 with 9 units, living quarters and office. Neither motel had a swimming pool; each offered the same main attraction—the pristine beach and the blue Gulf waters.

The Beacon changed hands several times until finally

Two Motels Become One Resort

The original Beacon Motel was a single block building with no swimming pool but the Gulf.

being acquired by the owners of the Sandpiper, in 1960.

Thirteen years later, the improved motels merged, and later became known as the Sandpiper Beach Resort.

Nothing remains of the original motels except a tiny portion of the Sandpiper.

Everything else is completely modern, shining and 21st century. Beside the swimming facilities, there is a Lazy River

Ride, a bar right on the beach, waterslide and minigolf, playground and beachside diner.

There are rooms to suit everyone—families, honeymooners, groups and penthouses, many with private gulfside balconies.

A restaurant and gift shop round out the facilities at this truly luxurious resort!.

The original Sandpiper Motel, shown on an early postcard, bore little resemblance to today's busy resort.

BIKINI BEACH RESORT

hen John Gheesling got out of the Navy in 1950, he located in Pensacola (Fla.), married a New York City girl and landed a job as a one-man insurance investigator. In December of that year, two things happened that would lead him in an entirely different direction;

John Gheesling, III was born and the company he worked for transferred John to Panama City.

"We had three kids," disclosed John who quit using the name Jr. when his father passed away. "At that time there was a two-lane bridge between Panama City and Panama City Beach and when my wife wanted to go to the beach, traffic would be backed up for an hour and a half. She suggested we move to the beach."

John started out looking for a house, but wound up buying a tiny motel at the suggestion of his realtor. "He told me to buy this little motel which had four rooms in one building and two in another," John revealed. "I told him I didn't want a motel, I wanted a house. He said that if we took the motel, Rose, John's wife could rent rooms while watching the kids."

On March 3, 1957, the Gheesling family got into the motel business and soon built eight additional rooms. Two years later, they built another eight and had 22 rooms. A swimming pool was also added.

Eventually John sold the motel across the street and purchased property where the cur-

Bikini Beach Motel in 1960 when it was across street from present motel.

Bikini Beach Motel Had Humble Beginning

rent Bikini Beach Motel is located. "This used to be the Gulf Wind," he revealed, "and it was nothing but a bunch of little cottages."

So John tore down the cottages and built 44 motel rooms. For about three years the Gheeslings owned both the motel on the south (ocean) side of Front Beach Road and the one on the north side. John eventually gave in to selling the original property when a real estate dealer offered him double his price.

Once John put all of his efforts into the Bikini Beach, it continued to grow and now has 85 rooms.

Like many businesses on Panama City Beach, the Bikini Beach is a family affair. John, III who wanted to be a school-

teacher but was persuaded to become a motel operator, now manages Bikini Beach. Ann Gheesling Henry, his sister, and his wife Deborah are also

The Gheesling's Daughter Debra.

involved in the management of both Bikini Beach and the recently acquired Trade Winds Motel.

Momma Rose also worked there until she "fired herself" in 1993.

The elder Gheesling remembers when tourism on Panama City beach was a 100-day season. "It ran from Memorial Day to Labor Day and that was it," he pointed out. "We closed our doors after Labor Day."

Then something happened that affected the entire motel industry on Panama City Beach. A man from Canada asked John if he would stay open the year around if he were guaranteed occupancy. "When the Canadians first started coming,

we charged them $90 per month for one month, $80 for two and $70 for three," John revealed.

When other motels saw what the Gheeslings were doing, they began to call, wanting to know if the Canadian, whose name was Anderson, would help them fill up their rooms in the off-season.

This was the beginning of the "Snowbird" season on Panama City Beach, and John Gheesling actually invented that word because the Canadians were coming here to get out of the snow.

Things have changed drastically since John Gheesling got into the motel business and a lot of it centered around the

humble beginning of the Bikini Beach. The motel has been renovated and added on to since 1988 and currently employs between 25 and 30 people, depending on the season, and has 12 maids at peak time.

John Gheesling has held every office in the motel and restaurant association and was on the founding Board of the Tourist Development Council, whose main responsibility is promoting tourism.

John, III has followed in his father's footsteps in the matter of community service and is serving as President of the Chamber of Commerce. He was also on the Civil Service Board until resigning to run for the Panama City Beach City Council.

BEACH KOA *Has Links to the Past*

anama City Beach KOA at 8800 Thomas Drive is a charming second home for hundreds of beach lovers who are lured by the crystal-clear waters of the Gulf, abundant sunshine and pure white sandy beaches.

Although it is one of the oldest resorts on the beach—having been started in the late 70's—its owners have an even longer history in the area.

The present owners, Ruth Glenn and her brother, John Starling, were born to an old Panama City family. Their father, Willard Starling, graduated in 1919 in Panama City High School's second class—consisting of just two students! Their teachers came in from Chipley and DeFuniak Springs.

Ruth and John's mother, Estelle Cawthon, was an English teacher who retired in favor of her family. But Ruth

carried on the family tradition in education by becoming a teacher herself in Okaloosa and Washington Counties.

Ruth remembers the 70's as a time when the beach was almost deserted in the winter. "I remember when a plane landed on Thomas Dr.," she recalled, "and took off again with no trouble!"

She also remembers the days when Labor Day marked the absolute end of activities on the beach. "It was like a mass exodus!"

Ruth and John's brother, Winston Starling, ran the campground until his death in 1988 and "we reaped the benefit of all his hard work," Ruth comments.

The campground went with the KOA franchise in 1987 and offers 114 sites as well as mobile home sites, tent areas, camping cabins and storage facilities.

Winston Starling, who died in 1988, built up the KOA.

There is gasoline and L.P. on the property along with a handy store attached with a small deli where campers frequently gather. Winston Hall is a popular spot with visitors for various social activities.

Like other beach properties, the campground has weathered many storms, but Opal was probably the worst, leaving heavy damage in its wake.

Today, it is hard to imagine a more attractive welcome than Ruth has created—with flowers in abundance in crisply painted containers which mark the entrance.

Helping to run the business are Ruth's two sons, Scott and Greg Atkins, and John's son, John Starling, Jr.

No matter who is on duty when a camper checks in, he can be assured a warm welcome and a wonderful stay at KOA!

Willard and Estelle Starling donned old-time costumes to pose outside one of the KOA's rustic cabins.

SUGAR SANDS *Grew With The Beach!*

It all started here ...

ugar Sands Motel is just the latest in a series of properties that have graced the site at 20723 Front Beach Rd.

Its owner, Philip Griffitts, grew up on the beach and acquired the old Bell-Mar Court Motel in 1974. A year later, its 15 units—one of which was occupied by the Griffitts family—were swept away in Hurricane Eloise.

Undeterred, Griffitts built it back, and three years later acquired the adjoining Gulf-front lot and added a 2-story building with 12 additional units. As protection against future storms, this building was constructed on pilings

The property was further enhanced when Griffitts bought land across the street and added more units.

Then, in 1984, he decided to tear down the old two-story building and two of the original Bell-Mar cottages, replacing them with a new two-story building which sufficed for ten years.

In 1994, Griffitts made the decision to build again. This time, the old 2-story building was expanded to 5 floors—and it was completed just in time for Hurricane Opal's arrival!

After Opal the building was somewhat damaged, but the seawall next door was breached, and 34 units were lost.

Patiently, Griffitts rebuilt again, and today's Sugar Sands Motel has 82 units, each with a large kitchenette.

"They're more like condo units than a motel," Griffitts comments, "with balconies overlooking the Gulf and every possible convenience."

The business is mainly family vacationers—and much of it is repeat business, the owner says. "People who came here as children are bringing their children here now," he commented.

Sugar Sands is also a favorite place for groups. Bay High recently chose the motel for its 50th class reunion, and several families make it their choice for their annual reunion.

Griffitts has been an important part of the community as the beach grew. He was a member of (before it merged with the Chamber of Commerce) the former Bay County Motel and Restaurant Assoc., and was on the Resort Council. Most importantly, he served as Panama City Beach's Mayor for eighteen years!

He is married to the former Jerrilyn Phillips and they have two sons, Philip, who runs the motel, and Matthew, a student at FSU who works at the motel in the summer.

The Griffitts family just purchased another Gulf-front Hotel and is doing extensive renovations. The new property will be known as the Islander Motel.

Now there are 82 units around the pool ...

HOLIDAY INN SUNSPREE

Paradise Found Means Award Winning Hotels

n the sugary white sands of Panama City Beach is a legendary service team committed to creating a paradise of fun-filled memories especially for you.

More than 30 years ago, Charles and Lela Hilton, and their children, Julie and Chip—along with Lela's mother, Katherine Boatwright, built their first hotel on Panama City Beach. Today, with their six award-winning properties, convention center and 18-hole championship and par-3 lighted executive golf course, the Holiday Golf Club, the Hilton's Paradise Found Resorts & Hotels feature premier accommodations, lush tropical gardens, positively outrageous service and an array of planned, supervised activities, island characters, and musical entertainment to enliven your stay on the playful side of Paradise Found!

The Hiltons' hotels have won an array of awards, including over 20 for the Holiday Inn Sunspree Resort, which has repeatedly been selected as a Torchbearer, one of Bass Hotels

& Resorts' top 20 hotels. Other honors claimed by the Holiday Inn Sunspree include the prestigious Quality Excellence Award and the coveted Members Choice-Best Family Vacation Hotel Award.

The Ramada Beach Limited once again received the Gold Key Award for exceptional service and quality accommodations.

Volcano waterfall at Days Inn & Ramada Pool.

The Days Inn Beach was again the recipient of the Five Sunbursts Award of Quality. The Best Western-Del Coronado and the Casa Loma both have received Directors Awards for quality assurance.

Team members always welcome guests to their premier resorts with hospitality Southern style. The Holiday Inn Sunspree Resort, highlighted by deluxe oceanfront accommodations and a guest activities program for the entire family, is the Hiltons' dream vacation paradise. The resort, located at 11127 Front Beach Road, has 340 luxurious rooms with private balconies and long ago became one of the primary destinations for people vacationing on Panama City Beach.

The Ramada Limited and Days Inn Beach also feature guest's activities along with tropically casual guest rooms, a magnificent Convention center and a spectacular cascading mountain waterfall pool.

As with all of the Hiltons' Paradise Found Resorts, the Best Western Casa Loma and Best Western Del Coronado have award-winning views of the sparkling clear turquoise Gulf of Mexico waters and pristine sugar white sands, complemented with an intimate inn atmosphere and a spectacular sunset.

"We are really proud of our team's awards, but our most important reward is having our resorts filled with happy guests who take beautiful memories of fabulous vacations home and return to our properties again and again," President Lela Hilton pointed out.

"Cleanliness, friendliness, good price value and 100 percent guest satisfaction are our top priorities and not extras."

The Hilton family is one of the best-known and most involved families in Bay County and has numerous other business interests, including Gulf Asphalt Corp., GAC General Contractors and the La Valencia Beach Resorts, which features vacation homes. In addition, Charles Hilton and daughter, Julie are members of the law firm Hilton, Hilton, Kolk and Roesch. Chip Hilton teaches golf and also is a well-known artist in this area. Charles Hilton, one of the strongest supporters of tourism in Bay County, served as chairman of the old Resort Council, forerunners to the Beaches Chamber of Commerce.

Julie served as President of the Beaches Chamber in 1994-95. Mother Lela served as a member of the Bay County Tourist Development Council and chaired the first TDC Beautification Committee and was instrumental in starting landscaping of public beach areas.

Charles Hilton was charter president of the local Optimist Club and later served as Lieutenant Governor of the state Optimist Club. He also has been a leader in the Methodist Church and has served with the Governor's Tourist Advisory Council as Chairman of Florida Tax Watch, the Florida Transportation and the Builder's Association. In addition to his numerous other local and state services, Charles, a former Eagle Scout himself, has been a leader with the Boy Scouts of America.

Both Charles and Julie have served on the Florida Hotel and Motel Association Board.

Julie, who is well known for her community, civic and state accomplishments, is a member of the Federal Reserve Bank of Jacksonville and has served as President of Bay County Motel and Restaurant Association, the Miracle Strip Council, and the Scenic 98 Association.

BEACHCOMBER HOTEL

hen three Enterprise, Alabama businessmen decided to venture into the hospitality field, they chose what some thought was a most unlikely site. Thanks to Hurricane Opal, the Beachcomber Hotel, built many years before by Ted Alford and later owned by Thea Fredrickson, lay in total devastation, with sand and sea taking over in the two years following the storm.

The first thing the partners did was to raze what remained.

The Beachcomber, at 17101 Front Beach Rd.—the newest hotel on the beach—is owned by T. E. Lee, William and Jerry Carr with Larry Williams as Vice-President and managing partner.

Less than a year in construction, the hotel opened on July 3, 1998—with some of its rooms still unfinished. Since then, of course, everything has been completed, even down to the final touches of luxury—like hair dryers, massaging showerheads, irons and ironing boards, TV sets in every room and art work by local artist Paul Brent. An effective security system gives guests peace of mind.

The fully-equipped kitchens have everything but that doesn't really matter because a free, full continental breakfast is served every day, there is coffee in the room, and restaurants nearby.

Each of the 96 suites has about 500 square feet of living space, with a private, ocean-front balcony. A free newspaper is delivered each day.

Larry Williams brought expertise from several nationwide chains, most especially the Marriott, and added special touches unique to the Beachcomber.

Two of these are special attention to the needs of the disabled, and to making the stay a specially happy one for children.

The children's pool is not a wading pool tucked away in some obscure corner. It is a specially-constructed shallow pool just like the adult pool but ideally designed for children and the handicapped. There is ample sunbathing space around so that parents may get their tanning time in while the children play.

A member of the Snowbird Committee of the TDC, Williams has many snowbirds who return each year to the Beachcomber. He finds that snowbirds and families mix well together and the spring breakers that choose the Beachcomber seem to be those who prefer a more relaxing, less frenetic lifestyle!

Williams believes much of the hotel's success lies in the friendly hospitality extended by every member of the staff—25 of them in the busiest times.

Beautiful Beachcomber is a #1 Hotel

SUNSET PASS PREMIER

*Sunset Pass
You've Earned Your
Place in the Sun*

f you have ever con-
sidered owning your
own Florida beach
resort vacation home,
or if you're ready to retire to
the good life, it's time to take a
look at Sunset Pass, a condominium resort with all the features and amenities you want
and deserve. Sunset Pass is nestled in 43 acres and hundred
year-old oaks, pines and magnolia trees. It features walking
trails, more than 1,000 feet of
shoreline alongside pristine
Lake Powell, and two-acres
adjoining the sugar-white
beaches of the Emerald Coast.
More than fifty percent of the
property is devoted to open
space and preservation areas.

The huge development
received words of praise from a
Department of Environmental
Protection official who called
Sunset Pass a textbook project.
According to Bay County officials,
the developers did everything by
the book and the environment
has been a prime consideration
in planning the project.

Sunset Pass features 10
unique designs in luxurious
one, two and three bedroom
layouts. Resident amenities
include 9 ½-foot ceilings in the
living, dining and bedroom
areas, spacious walk-in closets

with storage shelving, oversized
sliding glass doors opening to
private balconies with views of
both the Gulf of Mexico and
Lake Powell, and many additional unique features that
make condo living a real pleasure. An elegantly detailed two-
story lobby overlooks a garden
terrace, adding beauty and convenience to the resort.

Resort amenities include a
grand meandering river-style

super pool, whirlpool spas, convenient beach access with a
planned beach pavilion with
heated pool*, tennis courts,
nature trails, a health club with
aerobics room, a game room
and gift shop in the lobby, and
a private parking garage, all
confined in this spacious gated
community.

The leTriomphe develop-
ment on Panama City Beach
Parkway is adjacent to the

Walton County line and Camp Helen Park, offering convenient access from several major metropolitan areas. It is 300 miles southwest of Atlanta, 265 miles south of Birmingham, 395 miles southeast of Memphis, 290 miles east of New Orleans and 140 miles west of Tallahassee. Atlanta and Memphis have direct commercial flights into area airports.

leTriomphe Property Group, L.L.C. are quality developers and property managers specializing in residential developments, including condominiums, retirement communities, luxury hotels and resort properties. leTriomphe has rapidly grown to become one of the leading companies of its type in the country with over one billion dollars in its portfolio in various stages of operation, development and construction. leTriomphe has projects in New Orleans and Baton Rouge, Louisiana, Houston,

Texas, and Destin and Panama City Beach, Florida.

leTriomphe's commitment to excellence, diligently protecting its relationships and assuring quality products, has been the genesis for the growth and prosperity of the company. The team of 145 individuals who helped create the company and the unique partnerships that have been formed as a result of that commitment enable leTriomphe to recognize, capitalize and focus on only the most outstanding development opportunities available.

"Welcome to Paradise...a place where the sun meets the sea in an explosion of brilliance and color, where pure white sand beaches run for miles alongside the crystal azure waters of the Famous Florida Emerald Coast." Those who have seen it agree that Sunset Pass is the place to visit, the place to live, and the place to call home.

PENDING PERMITS.

SUNSET PASS
This resort community on Lake Powell will be one of the largest condominium complex's in Bay County.

TWO PREMIER COMMUNITIES
Sunset Pass, located on the Panama City Beach Parkway, and Majestic Sun in Destin are two of the largest developments for leTriomphe Property Group.

CORNERSTONE DEVELOPMENT GROUP

The Family Ties That Bind

he owners and operators of Cornerstone Development Group believe in keeping it all in the family. Almost everyone in the McNeil and Runnels families is involved in some capacity in the premier development group. The cohesion of older and younger family members has increased the success of this Destin-based consortium.

Cornerstone originally started developing in the Destin/South Walton area, but has recently branched out to include developments as near as Panama City (Sterling Beach) and as far away as North Carolina (Kelsey Preserve).

John McNeil's family is deeply rooted in the development business. His son, Garrett, is Project Director for the latest Cornerstone development, Sterling Beach. Beverly, his wife, is the Director of Community Affairs at Kelly Plantation.

Davage "Buddy" Runnels, Jr., has also incorporated his family into the operation. His eldest son, Trey, is an attorney and manages legal concerns of Cornerstone. His son, Scott, is an orthodontist with aspirations to assist with the business including post-construction aspects of the future Kelly Plantation Office Park. The professional building will be located at Kelly on Commons Drive. Buddy's nephew, Chet Walker,

is the Sales and Marketing Director for Cornerstone.

"We are bringing family in so we can pass on twenty years of experience to the next generation of youth and continue the tradition in our families," Runnels said.

John and Buddy encourage the younger generation's

affiliation with Cornerstone because of their astute knowledge of new technologies and their awareness of changing trends in the marketplace. The partners believe the guidance and wisdom they have garnered over the past decades will serve to complement the contributions of the younger

Left to Right—John McNeil, Jr., Davage "Buddy" Runnels, Garrett McNeil.

153

Architect's Rendering: Sterling Beach Condominiums, Panama City Beach , FL.

family members. Interwoven and interchanged, the family's diversified elements create a lasting tie that binds.

"Family is important to us, and not just our immediate family. Our employees have become a part of our extended family," John McNeil said.

Cornerstone previously built Sterling Sands Condominiums, located at 1080 Highway 98 East, Destin on the Gulf. Also located in Destin is Sterling Shores Condominiums, currently under construction directly across from the Gulf at 1751 Highway 98. In the future, Cornerstone hopes to expand the idea of community through the use of technology by starting a Cornerstone television station, a bulletin linking the projects together via the Internet and by integrating the technology into the master plan of the houses and various communities. The Sterling Beach project was begun to expand opportunities and create diversity for the development group.

John McNeil said: "We are very proud of the new development because it is a qualified development in a lovely place. It is a beautifully designed building."

The McNeil and Runnels families will continue to focus on guiding future generations into the business, thus perpetuating the partnership. "This is the heart and soul of our families," stated John McNeil. The promise of the future is clasped firmly in the hands of these local families, who meld friendship with faith to create a lasting legacy.

—*Written by Cynthia Burton*

CHAPTER IV
THE MARKETPLACE

Retail Marketing and Service Industry

J&J Enterprises

Alvin's Stores

Bid-A-Wee Storage

The Inside Story

*Kilgore Karpets &
Ceramic Tile*

Culligan Water

*Waste
Management*

J & J ENTERPRISES, INC.

J&J Enterprises Started in the Basement of Motel

&J Enterprises, known for its quality screen printed T-shirts, caps and jackets, had a humble beginning. As a matter of fact, J&J, owned and operated by Jim Patterson, first came to light in the basement of his Panama City Beach motel.

Of course, it was not surprising that Jim, who holds an Industrial Engineering degree from Auburn University, would eventually market something that best suited his education after serving as an elementary school teacher and a motel owner.

Although Jim, still an avid Auburn sports fan who attends many of the Tigers' football games, is a native of Dothan, Alabama, he claims practically growing up on Panama City Beach, spending as much time here as he could.

In 1961, there was a teacher shortage on the beach and Jim decided to try something new. "They would take anybody," he laughed, "so I went to Gulf Coast Community College (in Panama City) and took some educational courses." While Jim was teaching during the day, his wife Wanda was operating their motel on the beach. He taught for about six years, but when Wanda became pregnant with their third child he decided to resign his teaching position.

QUALITY SCREEN PRINTING — J&J Enterprises on Panama City Beach is widely known for quality screen printed T-shirts, caps and jackets.

However, the teachers went on strike and the principal had a heart attack, so Jim served as Principal of Beach Elementary School for "two or three months." He eventually sold the motel in 1978, not before something dramatic happened.

"We started dabbling in T-shirts in the basement of the motel," Jim revealed. "My daughter, Karen, who was in junior high, was putting transfers on shirts and the business just began to grow." He rented space in a building underneath a shopping center and went to work. "We were there about three or four years."

Eventually, the family had to find something larger and a 12,000 square feet building was constructed on Moylan Road. Construction began in 1980 and the new facility opened in 1981. J&J employs approximately fifteen people and Karen is one of the three graphic designers. Jim's wife Wanda is office manager.

"At one time, about 90% of our printing was done for gift shops," Jim said. "However, times changed and now our printing is mostly at the corporate level, although we also print for a lot of events." All of the work is done at the Moylan Road Facility.

Because of the company's early connections with the Naval Coastal Systems Station on Panama City Beach, J&J now ships items to Navy divers all over the world. Jim said his printing business continues to grow. "We have a lot of loyal customers who just keep coming back year after year," he explained.

In addition to Karen (Mrs. Ted Davison), Jim and Wanda have another daughter, Kellie Haselden, in Tampa, and a son, Robb, who is an actor in New York City. Jim is well known on Panama City Beach and once served as the local Optimist Club President.

ALVIN'S STORES, INC.

The Alvin's Island Story Sounds Like A Movie

he Alvin's Island story is a fascinating one that probably could be turned into a successful novel, or maybe even a movie.

Perhaps the most popular "all-purpose" beach shop in Bay County, Alvin's started as a five-and-dime store back in the fifties.

The late Alvin Walsingham was working for a 5 & 10 chain and got a bonus for selling the most merchandise. He took the bonus and started his own business, opening a 5 & 10 store on Beck Avenue in the St. Andrews section of Panama City.

"My mother (Marion) was a big part of the business," pointed out Gary Walsingham, now President and Chief Operating Officer for the company. "She really worked to make it go."

So did Gary, who had moved to Panama City with his family when he was in the second grade. "I think we had moved about five times before we settled here," he revealed. "We were constantly moving."

However, the Walsingham family found a permanent home in Bay County.

The new Alvin's 5 & 10 store on Beck Avenue did well until the boat captains moved out of the St. Andrews Marina in Panama City to Captain Anderson's Marina in Panama City Beach. "That just about killed the type of business we had in St. Andrews," Gary said.

By that time, Gary, who had

grown up assembling toys (particularly at Christmas time), learned to do a lot more around the store. "I also learned to hate Christmas," he laughed.

When Alvin's 5 & 10 opened its first store in Panama City Beach in the mid-fifties, there wasn't a whole lot on the beaches and the 5 & 10 was a new concept of doing business.

Alvin's was strictly in the small-item business until the family bought Tom Prater's clothing store and combined it with the 5 & 10. However, it was not until Alvin Walsingham opened the store on Thomas Drive, across from the popular club, Spinnaker, that the name Alvin's Island came to fruition.

"The building was on what looked like an island and we just started calling it Alvin's Island," Gary revealed.

It was the son, Gary, who suggested that the family put everything together and use a bamboo and tropical theme in

its stores. Whirlwind growth was just around the corner. Today, Alvin's Island sells just about anything and everything to do with the beach, including a wide variety of gifts; clothing (particularly T-shirts), toys, souvenirs and you name it.

In addition to nine stores on Panama City Beach, including the one that fronts the Company Corporate Headquarters at 14520 Front Beach Road, Alvin's has expanded to Destin, Fort Walton Beach, Pensacola Beach, Orange Beach and Gulf Shores (the latter two in Alabama). In the old days, the family even had a 5 & 10 in Quincy, (Fla.), which was a popular gathering place for farmers when they came to town on Saturday. "Today, our stores cover a 155-mile radius," Gary pointed out.

Although Alvin's has been highly successful with all its merchandise, Gary said Beanie Babies represent the all-time hot seller. "This is the only thing we've ever had to limit for our customers," he explained. "Usually, we try to get customers to buy more than one item. Beanie Babies often were limited to one and there were times when we couldn't provide them."

The Walsingham family is well known in Bay County and most recently has been recognized throughout the country. Earlier this year, Gary was elected president of the Florida State University National Seminole Boosters with 8,000 members. No one else from this part of the country has ever ascended to that lofty position.

While Gary, an avid golfer and fisherman, stays plenty

busy just serving as CEO of Alvin's, somehow or another he has worked in time to fulfill his new responsibilities at his alma mater.

The Alvin's CEO plays golf regularly at the Panama Country Club and carries a 12 handicap. One of his favorite playing partners is legendary FSU Coach Bobby Bowden, who also owns a condo on Panama City Beach. Gary's son Mike, who is in charge of buying clothing for Alvin's Island, is an even better golfer and plays to a four handicap.

While Gary Walsingham still plays golf, his big thing right now is fishing—big-time fishing. "We bought a sports

fishing boat and we compete in billfish tournaments," he revealed. "It's something all of us can do together."

Something else the family can do together is work. As a matter of fact, the family—Gary and wife, Cumi, Mike and Gary's daughter, Sherri—does virtually all of the buying for Alvin's Island. Bill, Gary's brother and Vice President of the company, and wife, Sylvia also are key personnel in the corporation.

BID-A-WEE *Works With Its Community*

hen Jean and Don Shafer came to the beach from the Greater Chicago area in 1990, their main desire was to fit in with their new community. "We wanted people to welcome our business," says Don today.

That's why the 384 units of Bid-A-Wee Storage are painted in pastel colors, with Victorian wood railings and metal roofs—because that is the decor of the surrounding subdivision.

While Don and Jean were both active in the community, Jean, as President of the corporation, worked more closely with the Chamber of Commerce and was a Chamber Ambassador.

In fact, Don has recently learned that the Ambassador of the Year Award will be named to honor his late wife.

Although the business has grown from 10 to 384 units and now includes all kinds of shipping services, Don still runs it himself, 7 days a week, with the

assistance of his new wife, Jenny, who was one of the first people to greet the Shafers in 1990. She, too, is active in Chamber work.

Bid-A-Wee Storage is located at 13911 Panama City Beach Highway.

THE INSIDE STORY
First In Home Decorating Since 1983

Verna Burke/Amy Armstrong

n 1983, anyone with a home to furnish had to visit several different stores all over town but Amy Armstrong and Verna Burke changed all that.

In furniture emporiums—mostly run by men—sofas stood in military formations; tables were marshalled into a separate area, and one might find a mirror among the bedroom suites. Amy and Verna envisioned a place where a homeowner could go and find wallpaper, furniture, accessories and, most of all, help with their interior design. The Inside Story, at 7829 Front Beach Road, was the result—one-stop shopping for every decorating need!

Each of the owners brought vast experience in interior design to the partnership. Amy had lived in Panama City prior to opening a decorating venture in Houston, TX—When she returned to this area, Verna was already involved in decorating condos. "I felt there was a need for a single place where people could find everything," Amy

recalls, "and naturally, I asked my best friend to go into business with me."

From 3600 square feet across the street from its present location, The Inside Story soon outgrew its accommodations and was moved to 11,000 square feet at its present site.

Here the partners introduced their new displays—furnishings arranged in cosy, home-like arrangements, complete with magnificent floral arrangements, mirrors, accent pieces, and accessories.

Panama City was impressed with the new store—and so were national trade publications. The Inside Story has been written up on several occasions. The well-known furniture maker, The Lane Company, asked the two partners to advise on furniture design, colors and fabrics. They hosted a seminar in Panama City for all U. S. Lane Store galleries.

Not surprisingly, more than

half of the store's business is with customers outside Northwest Florida. On several occasions, they have been asked to design the interiors of condos or houses sight unseen—working only from the blueprints.

The new owner of a penthouse in Destin did not even see his furnished condo until he and his wife arrived to move in—and Amy and Verna had lighted candles, laid out trays of hors d'oeuvres and had soft music playing! The owners were thrilled with the finished product.

A "turnkey" project of 7 new condos in Virginia is the latest in many projects statewide and nationwide which have earned this unique store an enviable reputation.

Amy and her husband Larry Armstrong have three children—Parker, Courtney and Nicholas. Verna and Les Burke (a Panama City attorney) have two sons, Michael and Todd, and are thrilled with a new grandchild, Catherine Grace.

KILGORE'S KARPETS & CERAMIC TILE

ilgore Karpet and Ceramic Tile doesn't really describe the rambling business at 11509 Back Beach Road.

A stroll through the beautiful showroom provides glimpses not only of carpet and tile, but of laminated flooring, hardwoods and marble to please the most discriminating shopper.

The new hardwoods have gained so much popularity that from doing one a month a few years ago, Kilgore's is now doing 10 a week! Once, there were just two crews working on ceramic tile and marble—now there are 12. Tile, in fact, accounts for 56% of their business.

Things weren't always going so well for Jim Kilgore, who came to Panama City Beach in 1964 from Mississippi. For the first year, he operated a carpet cleaning franchise which, he says, "starved him to death". He had always been independent—he boasts that he has not received a paycheck signed by anyone else since he was 17— so, of course, he opened his own business.

It was a small building on 6th Street and not very successful but he hung on until 1970 when he was forced to call it quits.

"Everybody told me I would never make it again in Bay County and I might as well go back to Mississippi," he recalls, but I moved to the Beach and opened in a 'hole in the wall' beside the old Ocean Opry. After about a year, the business burned—the victim of arson. Not dismayed by the repeated reversals, Jim moved into a trailer, then found the property he currently occupies. "I started with nothing and no help from anybody—and precious little from banks," he recalls, but today his business is grossing $3.5 million a year and he employs 30-35 people, including sub-contractors.

The first carpet installer on the beach, Kilgore's is now first stop for owners of condos, motels, private homes and even prisons! "I figure I did the floors for two-thirds of the

Jim Kilgore

places on Thomas Drive," he says.

Jim's son, Mike, is operational manager of the business, and Mike's wife, Brenda is a key employee.

"I have great employees," Jim reports. He admits he expects a lot of them, but says he doesn't interfere with them if they do their job.

Although he admits to having "seen the top of the mountain and the bottom of the sea" in business, Jim Kilgore is optimistic about everything. He keeps up with the latest trends in flooring and is obviously knowledgeable about all the changes.

***Kilgore's Showroom
Has Variety!***

Kilgore Karpet and Ceramic Tile has grown enormously since it opened in 1975.

CULLIGAN WATER *Simply Call and Say- "Hey Culligan Man"*

 Culligan Water has a strong and distinguished place in the history books of Bay County, but few people know the whole story.

Our local Culligan franchise is owned and operated by the Trumbull family. In the Panama City area Culligan first got its start in 1950 when Denslow (Den to everyone) Trumbull joined forces with his father and his brother-in-law, Jack Stout, to purchase a franchise from Culligan and locate in our beautiful area. A very interesting link from the Trumbull family and the national Culligan Corporation is that over 50 years ago Den's uncle actually went into business with Emmett Culligan, who was the founder of the now famous water-conditioning, water-supplying company. It was this relationship that forged the path for Den and Jack to move their families to Panama City.

When Den's father retired, Den was named the president of the company and he was recently presented with his 50 year award for his work with water conditioning. The proud legacy of the family continues through the work of Den's youngest son, Jay Trumbull, who heads their newest venture, the bottling of the Econfina Spring water which began in 1995.

Econfina Springs is located in a North Florida setting. The spring is surrounded by miles of rolling hills and live oaks in Bay County. It is just north of Panama City (25 miles). Econfina is only one of the 75 First Magnitude Springs in the entire United States and one of only 27 in the state of Florida. A First Magnitude Spring flows a minimum of 64 million gallons of water a day! The water at Econfina far exceeds all FDA and EPA water quality requirements. The spring is considered so pure because it only contains a total of dissolved solids (TDS) of 49 parts per million, when the national average is 190 TDS!

For hundreds of years, Creek, Cherokee and Seminole Indians drew water from this icy clear spring...they called it "Econfina," which means "Natural Bridge," after a natural limestone arch which crossed the sparkling creek at the mouth of the spring. Hundreds of years later, General Andrew Jackson's army crossed the Apalachicola River and Econfina Creek. In 1821, when the Florida Territory opened for settlement, one of Jackson's men returned to the beautiful spring he remembered from the long sojourn through the South. William Gainer, Jackson's surveyor and mathematician, settled his family along the west side of the swift flowing Econfina.

Econfina Springs is also owned by another local family, the Patronis'. Together with Den and Jay, they bottle this remarkable pure water for sale throughout the (Southeast)

United States. The purity of the water is "...unheard of," states Jay Trumbull. The Patronis family is committed to protecting the integrity and natural beauty of the spring. Culligan picks up the water daily on 6,000 gallon trucks that take it to the processing plant where it is bottled in its truest form.

While bottled water is the rage all over the world, Culligan does a lot of other things that make your drinking water better. You can have an accurate, visual evaluation of your water supply. What is its degree of hardness? Does it contain Iron? Sediment? Excessive Chlorine? The great people and tradition at Culligan will be happy to serve your water needs. The Culligan offices are located at:

315 East 15th Street
Panama City, Florida 32504
(850) 763-1721

Culligan has additional franchises in Fort Walton Beach, Florida and Dothan, Alabama. They are in the business of serving Bay, Jackson, Calhoun, Gulf, Walton, Holmes, Washington, Santa Rosa, Okaloosa and Escambia Counties in the state of Florida and Houston County in Alabama.

Ever since the founding of Culligan in 1936 by Emmett Culligan, the company has continually developed new technologies to treat hard water and rid water contaminates. All the products offered have been perfected through research and development, and

are used by homes and businesses the world over. Always advancing with new technological developments, their products continue to set the standards for the water treatment industry.

Den Trumbull states, "After being in the business for over 50 years, we know water. Our mission is to deliver high quality water treatment products that will benefit every part of consumers' lives. We have seen about every water problem imaginable and we have solved all those problems. You can trust us for well designed prod-

ucts that are built to last. And everything we do is backed by courteous, dependable, Culligan man service."

If success is measured in numbers, then there is no comparison to the success the company has enjoyed...Culligan employs more than 50 people and has a fleet of over 30 trucks.

So, think about your water and the quality and purity you require for yourself, your loved ones and your customers, then pick up the telephone and say "Hey, Culligan Man." Start with the best and your satisfaction is assured!

WASTE MANAGEMENT

aste Management of Bay County, located at 6319 East Highway 22 in Panama City, has been providing solid waste management in the area since 1984. Since that time, both Bay County and Waste Management have experienced changes due to an expanding community.

Waste Management of Bay County is an active member of the local Chambers of Commerce and Home Builders Association. The goal is to be a good corporate citizen and to actively participate in numerous civic organizations and functions. Through the years, this company has held fast to fundamental values that have guided its growth from the beginning. Waste management has worked diligently to build relationships based on trust, service and commitment to the community. The company has attempted to keep these rela-

tionships strong through trust, hard work, dedication, integrity and pride in what it does.

Waste Management of Bay County is part of Waste Management, the largest solid waste environmental services company of its kind. It currently operates in 49 states,

WASTE MANAGEMENT OF BAY COUNTY

the District of Columbia, Mexico, Puerto Rico and 14 other foreign countries. It is with great pride that the company aligns itself with the largest provider of waste management services in the world, officials contend. "But, more importantly than our size is our focus to continually

maintain what has made Waste Management the number one solid waste company in this area," they said. This represents a commitment to every customer and every community served by the company.

The growth in Bay County is a direct result of dedicated hard-working people and their commitment to their jobs and community.

Waste Management of Bay County officials said they are proud to be a part of a dynamic and changing team and that they look forward to a continued partnership with Bay County into the New Millennium.

"If we can be of service in any capacity, please feel free to contact our office at 874-1019. Our customers and this community are very important to us."

CHAPTER V

BANKING & LEGAL PROFESSIONAL SERVICES

EMERALD COAST BANK

Division of The Bank

Home Office on Panama City Beach.

hen Emerald Coast Bank opened on September 1, 1996, it was the only bank with home offices in Panama City Beach, but that wasn't the only thing noteworthy about the new financial institution on the east end of Front Beach Road. Emerald Coast is a bank that has built its reputation on doing things differently.

Although the bank adheres to all the established principles of sound banking and investment, convention is broken when it comes to customer service-and the customers love it.

"Frankly, the people make all the difference in the world," said Hunter Daffin, President of Daffin Mercantile and a member of the Board for Emerald Coast Bank. "This bank is designed and operated by people who are committed to making a better bank. They are not just talking the talk; they're walking the walk. You can feel it when you walk through the front door, and, most importantly, you can feel it on the bottom line every month."

From the very beginning, it was obvious that Emerald Coast, affectionately known as "the Beach's Bank" by locals was designed for customers, not bankers. Even more importantly, it is a local bank run by local people, with all decisions made locally.

At one time, local banks were the standard for America, but they are rare commodities these days. Therefore, Emerald Coast Bank was a welcome change for the residents, especially the local business community. As Wes Burnham, developer of Edgewater Beach Resort, the Hombre Golf Club and Long Beach Resort and a member of the bank's Board puts it: "For me, it's simple. I want a local bank that can make local decisions and I want a bank that understands local business. This is the bank."

When Emerald Coast Bank opened, it was the fastest-growing state-chartered bank in Florida, and it was the only bank in state history to open in three different locations on the same day. In addition to Panama City Beach, Emerald Coast has offices in the nearby town of Seagrove, in Sandestin and in the Bay Point community. Expansion is expected to continue through 2001 with offices opening in Destin, Santa Rosa Beach and Panama City.

From its humble beginning, Emerald Coast Bank grew quickly and, by the turn of the century, the bank held $120 million in assets and employed 48 people.

Perhaps the most significant contribution to the long-term success of the bank is the unprecedented strength of the Board of Directors.

With the following people, a winning team of investors and supporters were assembled:

Earl Durden, Rail Management and Consulting Company; D. Terry Dubose, banker; Elke McCoy, real estate management; Dr. Curtis Williams, a retired cardiologist; Gary Walsingham, CEO of Alvin's Island Tropical Department Stores; Gus Andrews, real estate broker and developer; Harry Sipple, residential contractor for SIBCO South; Hunter Daffin, CEO of Daffin Mercantile; Jerry Dunkle, Dunkle Properties, Inc.; Mike Bennett, Bennett Enterprises; Dr. Mike Reed, orthopedic surgeon; Reggie Lancaster, owner of the Flamingo Motel & Tower; Steve Counts, real estate developer; Tommy Milligan, JTM Corporation; Wes Burnham, developer of Edgewater, Long Beach Resort and Hombre Golf Club; Yonnie Patronis, general manager of Captain Anderson's Restaurant and Waterfront Market; and Mark Barrett, Design/Build Systems, Inc.

"One of the first things Emerald Coast Bank did to begin changing the way banking was done in Northwest

Florida was to introduce the All in One checking account," pointed out Board member Curtis Williams. "When I first heard the idea, I couldn't believe it hadn't been done before! I mean, why worry about which checking account you should pick? Just put all the best features in one account and make it available to everybody. That's beautiful. All in One Checking pays interest and there's no service charge. If you're a little older, you make a little more on your money. What else could you ask for?"

All in One Checking, local directors and management, customer-based services—the differences Emerald Coast Bank have brought to banking in Northwest Florida are remarkable; and the bank remains highly competitive with rates on savings and certificates of deposit products designed to help maximize the customer's hard-earned dollars while providing the safety and security that customers expect for their investment. "The response from the community during the past four years has been phenomenal and we appreciate the patronage favored from the citizens of our community. Our customers realize that their experience with us will be unique and we place great emphasis on providing distinguished customer service to all who bank with us," stated Brian K. James, President and CEO of Emerald Coast Bank.

Emerald Coast Bank's primary mission is to provide the best service and return the power of banking to the customers. Emerald Coast Bank is

committed to being fair to all people, regardless of race, religion or financial status and to making this a better community in all areas of life.

THE PEOPLE WHO RUN EMERALD COAST BANK:

Brian K. James,
President & CEO

Charles Harper,
*Bay County President/
Senior Vice President*

Mike Leonard,
Vice President

Barbara L. Haag,
*Executive Vice-President/
Chief Financial Officer*

Bradford F. Beauchamp,
*Senior Vice-President/
City Executive*

Jeffrey K. DiBenedictis,
*Senior Vice-President/
City Executive*

Jeremy M. Shields,
*Senior Vice-President/
Chief Operating Officer*

John Sumrall,
*Senior Vice-President/
Senior Lending Officer*

Mark Dutram,
*President EC Financial
Management*

Melinda M. Brown,
*Vice-President/
Human Resources Director*

Stacey Palmer,
*Vice-President/
Mortgage Loan Officer*

Jessica Thompson,
Credit Administrator

Cindy Hooks,
Cashier

BAY BANK & TRUST CO.

hen Bay National Bank was chartered in May 1935, capital stock of the association was $50,000. Today, the county's oldest locally owned, independent financial institution, now known as Bay Bank & Trust Co., has assets of more than $160,000,000.

Located on Florida's northwest gulf coast, Bay Bank & Trust, Co. has been an integral part of the economic fabric of Panama City, Panama City Beach and the surrounding area for 65 years. The bank helped the local community following the dark days of the Depression and World War II and has played a significant role in the development of the area into one of Florida's most popular vacation destinations and newest growth markets.

There are six branch banks and employees number more than 100. The bank also has nine Bay Banker ATMs located in the county.

Over the years, the people at Bay Bank & Trust Co have witnessed a lot of change in the community as well as in the banking industry as a whole. Although the bank has grown as the community has grown and has changed business procedures to meet new banking challenges, the locally owned financial institution is still the same community-minded bank it was in 1935. It is still dedicated to delivering quality financial services the way they should be, through personal attention and commitment. The bank is known by many residents as a good neighbor that strives to know the customers and to provide the financial products and services those customers want.

According to bank officials, employees are the backbone of the bank. Bay Bank & Trust Co. employees donate many hours of personal time to community projects through their civic and charitable organizations. Employees believe in the old adage that by helping to build the community, they also build the bank.

There have been many milestones since nine stockholders started the bank on May 24, 1935. Bay National Bank of Panama City opened in the small building across from City Hall, but moved to new offices at the old Marie Hotel in 1939. During World War II, officials opened a bank facility at Tyndall Air Force Base. In 1950, the bank moved to a new building at the corner of Fifth Street and Mercer Avenue. In 1982, the bank moved to its present location at Fifth Street and Harrison Avenue.

It was a red-letter day in 1951, when Bay Bank & Trust Co. introduced drive-in banking to Bay County. Trust powers were authorized in 1956 and Small Business Administration Loans were authorized in 1961.

In 1966, Bay Bank & Trust Co. started an Armored Car Fleet and in 1969, the bank introduced MasterCard to Bay County. In 1980, Bay National Bank & Trust Company became Bay Bank & Trust Co.

BENNETT, CAMPBELL & BENNETT

JULIAN BENNETT

Boys of the Depression Recall the Early Days.

llis Fowhand, 86, was born in Bay County and has been in the furniture business here just about as long as he can remember.

"There weren't many people in Panama City in those days," pointed out Ellis. "No pavement on 11th Street and Harrison Avenue. I remember an old flagpole downtown that had water on either side where the animals could drink. One of our real delights was to go down there and put our feet in the water."

In his many other recollections of the early days in Panama City, Ellis remembers an outdoor bowling alley and a big oak tree near a cafe that produced a controversy because the owner didn't want to cut it down. "They came in and bored holes in the tree and poured salt in the holes and they killed it," Ellis said.

Ellis is a member of some elder statesmen in Panama City who often refer to themselves as the "Depression Boys."

Bubba Nelson, who also is 86, is another. Bubba once owned Nelson Chevrolet and Buick and one of his favorite employees was Ralph Julian Bennett. "He was the sales manager of the car dealership there where the TV station (Channel 13 on Harrison Avenue in Panama City) is located," Bubba pointed out. "Ralph Bennett was one of the greatest sales people I've ever met. And he also was a great sportsman."

Ralph Bennett's son, Ralph Julian Bennett, Jr., today is a prominent attorney in Panama City and also has various business interests, including motels, on Panama City Beach.

Bubba was one of the original organizers of the Panama City Downtown Rotary Club and he and Travis Childs are the only two surviving charter members. Bubba, who has been in the automobile business most of his life, also was prominent in the organization of the Bay County Chamber of Commerce and the Committee of 100.

"In those days, we were scratching for a living," Bubba said. "I bought the dealership from my father in 1937."

Bubba also served as president of what was then the Commercial Bank and eventually wound up owning the bank.

He sold out to SunTrust Bank.

Bubba remembers Panama City as a little old country town that made its living off of timber and turpentine. "In those days, most of the tourists were fishermen," he said, "but it just kept growing." Like Fowhand, Bubba remembers if you wanted to go to Hurricane Island, where everybody went swimming, you had to leave the city dock on a boat and pay a fee to get there. Like the other two members of the "Depression Boys," Bubba lives on West Beach Drive. He did own a house on the east end of Panama City Beach before Hurricane Opal wiped it out in 1995.

Jimmy Hentz, who is a little older than Nelson and Fowhand, also was one of the old-timers who went through the Great Depression. Jimmy, like Bubba, remembers catching the launch at the city dock and

going to where the Old Pass (that leads to the Gulf of Mexico) is today. "There was a pavilion there and you could rent a bathing suit for 10 cents and swim all day," he said.

Jimmy recalled hearing and reading about the Federal gunboat that shelled houses on what now is West Beach Drive during the Civil War. He also remembered that mill workers toiled for 10 cents an hour.

Jimmy studied to be a teacher, but transferred and studied business administration. He completed his studies at Southern Business College in Atlanta in 1928. When Wall Street crashed in October of 1929 (Black Tuesday), Jimmy had a hard time finding a job. "Everywhere I went there were no help wanted signs," he said.

However, Jimmy had worked for A & P Tea and was hired by his old company during the Depression. He eventu-

ally started Hentz's Cut-Rate Grocery and moved his bride, the former Harriett Robertson of Americus, Georgia, to Panama City in 1937. Those were the days when coffee sold for 29 cents a pound and they threw in a five-pound bag of sugar free.

In 1955, Jimmy got the Piggly Wiggly franchise and formed the Hentz Company. He later served as President of the National Piggly Wiggly Association. Ten years later, he owned and operated the Holiday Shopping Plaza near Hathaway Bridge.

Like many of the older citizens in Panama City, Jimmy is a member of the Downtown Rotary Club and has a perfect attendance record of 35 years. He does a lot of volunteer work, particularly with the Red Cross and also is a Mason and Shriner and a lifetime member of the Elk's Club.

BURKE & BLUE *Law Firm is in Traditional Style*

The law firm of Burke and Blue is an integral part of Panama City's business and professional life.

A stone's throw from the beautiful *circa* 1914 Bay County Courthouse, the firm's offices are located at 221 McKenzie Avenue, overlooking the Massalina Bayou. The view from the building in the late afternoon is like a picture postcard with a vermillion sunset streaming across the outline of sailing vessels.

The firm consists of eleven attorneys, Les W. Burke, Rob Blue, Jr., Nevin J. Zimmerman, Edward A. Hutchison, Jr., Timothy M. Warner, Elizabeth J. Walters, Sherri Denton Mallory, Douglas L. Smith, Sharon Dinwiddie, Michael S. Burke and M. Todd Burke, Jeffrey Bassett; of counsel, and Jessica Kisin, and a supporting staff of twenty-five legal assistants and paraprofessionals.

The attorneys represent clients in areas of the law including Administrative, Governmental, Condominium, Banking and Financial, Insurance and Real Estate, Corporation, Probate, Estate Planning and Personal Injury. They represent clients in all Florida and Federal Courts in both civil and appellate matters.

Burke & Blue also maintains a law office in the rapidly-growing area of Destin and South Walton County and concentrates in the practice of Real Property, Commercial and Transactional, Land Use and Environmental, and Condominium law.

Established in 1973, the founding partners learned that by being involved in the affairs of the community, they could become more sensitive to the needs and desires of their clients.

Shaped by purpose, the partners lead by example and others model themselves after what they do. Teamwork and going the "extra mile" has set them apart as a tradition. The attorneys and staff consider it a privilege to be known through a heritage of service to their community, schools, churches, and many diverse charities.

They volunteer for dozens of organizations and take part in a mentoring program at an elementary school.

In other words, family and community are important; it's the soccer or basketball team you coach or the youth choir you direct that matters—or just being there to fill a need.

Burke & Blue accomplishes this purpose with the highest standards of integrity, quality and professionalism.

Burke and Blue, P.A. is very much a local tradition.

Traditional ethics and the beauty of Panama City combine at the offices of Burke and Blue on Massalina Bayou.

KENT-FOREST LAWN FUNERAL HOME

Youngest and Largest in Area

ent-Forest Lawn is the youngest funeral home in the Panama City area. In 2001, they will be celebrating their 20th Anniversary in the month of November. It also is the largest-by far. As a matter of fact, Randy Hudgins, Manager of the funeral home at 2403 Harrison Avenue in Panama City, pointed out that Kent-Forest Lawn does as much business as the other two local funeral homes combined.

The funeral home was founded in 1980 by Greg Brudnicki, accountant and comptroller, and Charles Kent, a Licensed Funeral Director, and is operated in conjunction with three area cemeteries. The funeral home is located on the grounds of Forest-Lawn Cemetery, which has been in business since 1960. Evergreen Memorial Gardens, located at 3733 Highway 231 North, the oldest and largest of the cemeteries, has been in operation since 1955. And Garden of Memories Cemetery, located at 5435 East 15th Street, has been part of the business since 1982.

"Our business was not handed down like most funeral homes," pointed out Kent.

Kent was born and raised in Panama City and attended Rutherford High School and Gupton-Jones College of Mortuary Science in Atlanta. He started in the funeral business at the age of 16.

Brudnicki, a former Florida State University baseball player and avid Seminole supporter, has been in the area since he was nine years old and attended public schools here before

Kent-Forest Lawn Staff.

graduating from FSU in 1977.

Brudnicki has been involved in many business ventures in the Panama City area and is on the Board of Directors for Peoples First Community Bank. He also is chairman of the Bay Medical Center Clinic Board and is a member of the State of Florida Board of Funeral & Cemetery Services.

Hudgins, who joined the funeral home two years ago, handles the day-to-day operation. He is a graduate of Gupton-Jones College of Funeral Service in Atlanta, and Asbury College in Wilmore, Kentucky. He grew up in the funeral business and has been a Licensed Funeral Director for 11 years.

Other key members of the staff include: Joe Gainer,

Assistant Manager; Laina Hicks, Cemetery General Manager, five other Licensed Funeral Directors and/or embalmers:

Jim Teuton, Hugh Duke, Jimmy Boyd, Bill Jones and Sam Kuhns; secretary, Linda Cooper, and Family Services Counselors: Deborah Kanes, Mimie Mikolay and Debbie Shaffman. The latest addition to the staff, J. Ray Southerland, Founder of Southerland Funeral Home, brings a wealth of experience to the staff.

Kent-Forest Lawn may be the youngest of the area's funeral homes, but its staff can boast a combined 266 years in serving the funeral and cemetery needs of the Bay County area. That's experience you can trust.

Kent-Forest Lawn also operates Emerald Coast Funeral Home in Fort Walton Beach, and Kent-Thornton Funeral Home in Dothan, Alabama.

PEOPLES FIRST BANK

Apples and Lemonade—A Tradition

 ts beautiful new building and the banking technology which is being used, make Peoples First an institution heading with confidence into the 21st century.

Yet inside its doors, the traditions upon which the bank has been built still prevail, as customers sip the cool lemonade which is always available, and crunch a juicy red apple out of the basket.

The bank operates on the belief that "Times change; Values endure", and its success has been built on the abiding policy of "One Customer at a Time."

"Peoples First has seen significant growth and earnings in a very short time, but that's not the amazing part," says President and CEO Raymond Powell. "What makes Peoples First so unique is that we've achieved our success one customer at a time, unaided by merger or acquisition."

Peoples First has built a solid foundation on customer service and satisfaction.

The bank's motto: "We put People First" has paid off as it has become one of only 27 in the state to achieve the billion dollar mark.

Peoples First, in fact, which began as Peoples First Financial Savings and Loan Association in 1983 has become the fifth largest thrift institution in Florida. Under the leadership of Joseph F. Chapman, III, Peoples First has grown to include banking

Joseph F. Chapman, III

centers and loan production offices throughout North and Central Florida. Headquartered in Panama City, there are also operations in Pensacola, Fort Walton Beach, Destin, Marianna, Tallahassee, Jacksonville Beach, Palm Coast, Orlando and Niceville with many more scheduled to open in the near future.

In January, 1995, the bank's name was changed to Peoples First Community Bank, which more completely represents what the bank is—a full service bank with a full range of banking products, focused on having the most satisfied customers.

Mr. Chapman enlisted the help of close friends, who invested in his idea of a community bank with old-fash-

ioned customer service. He also persuaded the most experienced and well-respected bankers in the business to offer their help.

They discussed ways of making Peoples First the best it could be, and one of those ways was the development of the Prime 55 account.

Mr. Chapman felt strongly that the banking needs of senior citizens should be handled with the utmost care and respect. In order to reach this goal, he created a board of Advisors, made up of successful and influential senior citizens from the community. This group of distinguished individuals was given the task of advising the bank on the best ways to fill the needs of mature customers. They did.

From the beginning of the Prime 55 Account and the Prime 55 Advisory Board, there are now 118 Prime 55 Advisors and eight Boards, statewide. The mission of the Prime 55 Advisory Boards boils down to this: to represent the interests of senior citizens everywhere Peoples First does business. It's a simple concept that the bank takes very seriously.

The stability of the Board of Directors and the senior management team has greatly contributed to the growth and profitability of the bank. The Board of Directors is a solid group of professional and business people who are involved

Corporate Center Opens ...

Corporate Center Dedication
May 1, 2000   Panama City, FL

in making contributions to the development and improvement of the community. Peoples First is committed to a strategy of controlled, but continued growth.

This growth has helped the bank meet its goal of $1 billion by 2000 and the bank has surpassed several other milestones since its inception. Peoples First was recognized by Florida Trend magazine as one of Florida's fastest-growing financial institutions and ranked fifth in total assets among Florida thrifts. By offering flexible terms and unbeatable rates, Peoples First has also become one of Northwest Florida's residential lending leaders.

And it has maintained its belief in the importance of being a good corporate citizen by providing volunteer support and financial assistance to over 200 organizations annually.

The hiring practices, training programs, coaching, motivation/reward system and truly believing that people are the company's greatest asset, assure the bank of the best employees.

From lemonade and apples in the lobby to the latest in computer technology serving the customers, Peoples First will continue to be a strong, solid and expanding company that really does... *put people first!*

August 4, 1984 Panama City, FL

CHAPTER VI

SPORTS, RECREATION & TOURISM

On Land, Air and Water

Paradise Helicopter

176

Treasure Island Marina

177

Hombre Golf

179

Airboat Adventures

181

Signal Hill Golf Course

182

Miracle Strip Park-Shipwreck Island

183

PARADISE HELICOPTER

Paradise Offering Certified Helipad

aradise Helicopters, Inc. has operated from the only certified helipad on Panama City Beach for the past five years. The helicopter service is owned by Skip Franck, an experienced and multi-rated pilot with more than 10,000 hours logged flight time. He has flown nearly every part of North America, from the Alaska Pipeline to the southern areas of Florida, mountains, shorelines, rivers, plains and all in between.

Paradise Helicopters brings you tours in movie filming, television coverage, aerial photography, and power line patrol to construction site reviews. Florida residents and guests have enjoyed, requested and

required the services of Paradise while seeing the region from the "best seats in town."

Paradise is the only Federal Aviation Association Part 135 helicopter operator in the Florida Panhandle. That is a coveted and highly regarded rating in the aircraft industry and a federal flight rating unsurpassed throughout north Florida. Most importantly, it is extraordinarily noteworthy and a community and customer guarantee of first-rate service and safe flight at all times.

A visit to Florida should be complimented with a birdseye view of the countryside, shoreline and the spectacular Panhandle. The historical area to Shell Island, St. Andrews Bay to Seaside and on to New Orleans, leaves an impression on visitors and encourages them to seek more and find

their way around when they return from their flight.

Business trips, fine dining, special occasions, tailgate parties, golf matches, the races...all can be reached from the helipad of Paradise Helicopters. Aerial photography has never been easier, or as well done as it is with Paradise. Skip Franck has flown with many of the top photographers, from the west coast to the east coast, and is often requested as pilot in command for major photo trips.

Franck, owner and operator of Paradise, has flown his entire life, beginning from his earliest years as a co-pilot with his father. He has owned and operated helicopters and many diverse aircraft. Trained as a pilot, he also has an extensive background and education in every phase of aircraft ownership and management.

TREASURE ISLAND MARINA
A Landmark on the Beach

EARLY BOATS AT TREASURE ISLAND MARINA-These wooden boats, with Gale engines, are docked at the Treasure Island Marina many years ago. Today, more-modern boats are still docked at the spacious marina on the Grand Lagoon.

reasure Island Marina, considered by many to be the fishing head-quarters for deep-sea fishing in Bay County, has been a landmark on Panama City Beach for a lot of years. Ted Davison, General Manager of the marina, proudly points to the fact that Treasure Island stores about 700 boats at the facility, including a multitude of fishing vessels.

Rich in history and heritage the 13-acre Treasure Island Marina property, once owned by Gulf Oil and Venture Out

Resort, was sold to Mr. And Mrs. William Nomberg in 1976. The sleepy little lagoon had a few fishing boats and locals were frequently seen water skiing from the Pass all the way to the bridge on Thomas Drive.

The Treasure Ship Restaurant, with General Manager, Dave Schaler at the helm, completed construction and opened in 1978. The main dining room, famous for seafood and steaks, has been a family favorite since its open-ing. The outside decks, gift shops, lounges and ever-famous

Pirates have been entertaining children and families for more than 20 years.

Charter and excursion fleet is famous for all types of fishing and family adventures, including big game grouper, mackerel, snapper and all types of bay fish.

The marina, with its 24-hour fuel dock and seafood market, also has grown from one building and 25 boats to one of the largest complexes in the state of Florida. It is the exclusive Sea Ray Yacht dealer for the Florida Gulf Coast, as well as a dealer for Boston Whaler and Scout boats.

In addition to servicing and storing hundreds of boats from all over the country, Treasure Island Marina has grown up to be a true entertainment complex, according to Davison. "The marina now is a true landmark on Panama City Beach," Davison pointed out. "We have a lot of good people here and all of them are part of the success we have enjoyed."

Present day, Treasure Island Marina.

TREASURE ISLAND SKIING TEAM-In 1959, Treasure Island Marina had its own skiing team and members are shown above Left to Right—Steven Dehart, Donnie Long, John Murphy, Ronnie Fouse, Rick & Karen Mainous, Karen Solomon, Barbara Thames, Renee Roberts. This was before the old Thomas Bridge, near the marina, was replaced. The skiing team is a thing of the past, but the history of Treasure Island Marina lives on.

HOMBRE GOLF CLUB

"Bad Hombre is one of the Toughest Golf Courses in Northwest Florida"

he Hombre Golf Club opened for play on December 1989 with the foursome of Hubert Green, Hal Sutton, Donnie Hammond and Buddy Gardner teeing it up on the par-5 first hole. The course, often referred to as "Bad Hombre" when played from the longer tees, features water on 15 of the 18 holes but is meticulously manicured to PGA Tour standards the year round.

Considered one of the toughest courses in Northwest Florida-indeed in the entire state-Hombre, designed and developed by Wes Burnham, is both scenic and challenging. The course is nestled amidst wetlands, marshes, lakes and preserves and beautifully framed with a stunning

assortment of palms, pines and azaleas. The Burnham design challenges every aspect of a player's golf game, making sure that almost every club in the bag is used.

Wes Burnham, a native of Birmingham, moved to the "World's Most Beautiful Beaches" to live in 1969 and to build Gulf World. Years Later he returned to Birmingham and then in 1981 the Birmingham investor joined with a Canadian business associate to purchase what had been the Town of Edgewater Beach. Three years later, the Edgewater Beach Resort

became one of the Gulf Coast's premier resort developments. Burnham's voracious appetite for golf led him to build the Hombre and The Glades, a 238-acre residential community surrounding the course.

The Hombre's four sets of tees, ranging from 5,275 yards to almost 7,000, allows golfers to choose the level of difficulty that best fits their game and handicap. From the "Bad Hombre" tees, the course plays to 6,820 yards with a 73.4 rating and a slope of 136.

For several years, the Hombre was home to the Panama City Beach Golf

currently is one of the top players and leading money winners on the Senior Tour.

Few golf courses in the country get the opportunity to host one to the PGA Tour Qualifying Tournaments, but the Hombre has been host for several second-stage events, starting in 1992. For the first time, the local course will be the site of a first-stage Qualifying Tournament in October of 2000. There will be 23 spots open for about 80 players.

Dan McGrath, longtime General Manager of the Hombre, is especially proud of the Hombre's Golf Village, which opened in 1998. The Golf Village features 1,600-square-foot, two-bedroom villas with a magnificent view of one of Florida's finest championship golf courses. The Hombre is also home of the Martin Green Golf Academy.

Kenny Eastham was club pro at the Hombre when the

course opened in 1989, but left to pursue a career in real estate and Steve Childree became the pro in July 1992. Darrell Smock, a Class A PGA professional, came aboard as pro in August 1996.

Construction has started on another nine holes at the Hombre, which will make it the first 27-hole golf course in Panama City Beach and only the second in Bay County. The three nines will be known as "The Good, The Bad and The Ugly."

Classic, first a part of the Ben Hogan Tour and then the Nike Tour. The event drew many aspiring pros, and a number who were already well established on the Pro Tour, to the Hombre. Buddy Gardner, a former Auburn University golfer, who at the time was the touring pro for the Hombre Golf Club, appropriately won the inaugural Ben Hogan Tour event. That, incidentally, was the only tour victory for Gardner, who grew up in Montgomery and later moved to Birmingham, despite the fact that he had some degree of success on the PGA Tour.

Hubert Green, a former Florida State University golfer from Birmingham, currently lives on Panama City Beach and now is the Hombre's touring pro. Green, who ranks among the 33 all-time PGA tour winners with 19 victories during his 26 years of competition on the regular tour,

AIRBOAT ADVENTURES

Enjoying a Journey through the Everglades

n May 1999, Rod Rosser and family, natives of Birmingham, brought a new adventure to the Panama City Beach area. His business is called Airboat Adventure and his feature attraction, the powerful Swampvette, USCG approved, carries 18 passengers and a crew of two.

The Swampvette is an airboat similar to those used in touring Florida Everglades and it can go just about anywhere known to man...as long as it is on water.

"This business is one of the finest experiences on Panama City Beach," Rosser said. "When we think of airboats, the Everglades come to mind. We're just like the Everglades and our goal is to give people the thrill of being there while letting them experience wildlife in a natural setting; alligators, osprey, pelicans and the open air represent the beauty of West Bay."

Rosser's boat operates out of an old house located at the beach side of West Bay Bridge just off Highway 79, five miles from the Panama City Beach city limits. Next-door is the popular Boondocks Restaurant, operated by Hillary Head, daughter of the man who owns the property along the bay.

"Local support for the Swampvette has been great and tourists from all over the country and abroad have seen our website and called or come by to ride the airboat," Rosser pointed out. Check out our website at:

www.swampvette.com.

The Airboat Adventure location even resembles the picturesque Everglades with Spanish moss hanging from the trees and plenty of sawgrass and water around it. And customers who sign up for the 30-minute nature tour through the marshland, swamp areas and creeks of West Bay get a little extra education from Rosser, the experienced narrator.

Rosser said he first got the idea of starting the business when he was in Kissimmee (Fla.). "I took an airboat tour while I was there and liked it so much I felt it would go over big here," he added. "We didn't have anything like this on the beach." The Telephone number for Airboat Adventures is (850) 230-3822.

SIGNAL HILL GOLF COURSE

Signal Hill Golf Course is home for Snowbirds

ust like Spring Break is the lifeblood of many motels and restaurants on Panama City Beach the Signal Hill Golf Course has its season when the Snowbirds are in town.

"We have tons of players when the Snowbird-winter guests are here, but Spring Break really hurts us," pointed out Beth Langford, one of the owners of Signal Hill.

Beth and her brother, John Henry Sherman, estimate that between 40,000 and 50,000 golfers play Signal Hill "during a good year."

There is good reason why. Signal Hill, challenging, but not brutal like some courses in the area, is an experience golfers can afford. Signal Hill is 5,259 yards long, from the white tees and the toughest hole is the 479-yard par-5 14th, again playing from the popular white tees, which most casual golfers use. Par is 37-34-71. The 327-yard par-four sixth hole carries a handicap of two.

Signal Hill, which was built by John Henry Sherman, Sr. almost 40 years ago, is family owned and operated. In addition to Beth and Bubba (that's what the family calls him), sister Kathie Carter of Birmingham is a partner. And Beth's two sons also work at the course, which is located on County Road 392, but also fronts Front Beach Road and North Lagoon Drive at various points.

When the elder Sherman leased the property from Claudia Pledger in 1962, he started off with nine holes on the backside. In 1970, he added what is now the front nine-holes and a driving range. He also had a four-unit motel, a

Original Clubhouse—Now Office Space.

swimming pool and a snack bar on the property, but later tore the motel down.

Unlike many business people who have come here to make their fortunes, the Sherman family was born and raised in Bay County.

The elder Sherman also developed the exterior part of his property, which covered 125 acres.

On October 5, 1994, the year before Hurricane Opal struck the Panama City Beach area, the family built the new clubhouse that now ranks as one of the course's truly outstanding features. However,

the little building that once served as the first clubhouse now offers office facilities on the north side of the property.

"While we didn't have the kind of damage some people did, the year Hurricane Opal hit (1995) was the worst year we ever had," Beth pointed out. "That row of sand berms daddy put in acted as a natural barrier and protected the golf course. We did have dead fish and birds on the course and the crew did a fantastic job of cleaning up. The hurricane hit on Thursday and we were open for business on Sunday. One thing we did have to do was give away all the food in our freezers because we didn't have electricity."

Signal Hill currently has 31 employees, with 10 of them working in maintenance. Like most golf courses, the family spends a lot of time consistently rebuilding tee boxes and greens and the course is in excellent shape.

New Clubhouse today at Signal Hill Golf Course.

MIRACLE STRIP PARK—SHIPWRECK ISLAND

t would surely please Jimmy Lark if he could see Miracle Strip Park and Shipwreck Island Waterpark today.

The visionary Lark built a roller coaster on Panama City Beach in 1963, at a time when everyone said there would never be anyone there to enjoy it.

The roller coaster, all 2403 feet of it, still is the anchor of the park today. It was built by Philadelphia Toboggan Co. and John Allen, who was responsible for the construction, did not have the first blueprint. Yet he knew exactly what pieces had to be fabricated and where they must go to make the roller coaster the exciting ride it is.

Buddy Wilkes, the general manager of the park, is in awe of the way the wooden roller coaster was built. "It was a daring invention," he says. "There weren't many around the country."

"Roller coasters work by gravity," Wilkes says, "and when they were ready to test this one, they ran one car on it, knowing that it would go much faster with two, later. Well, the one car couldn't make it up one of the inclines. Everyone thought it was a failure, but Allen went

Jimmy Lark Started A Great Park!

Jimmy Lark's original roller coaster.

to one particular spot, tapped it with a hammer, and the thing worked!"

The price of admission has gone from 25cents a ride on the roller coaster, to a $15 armband for a day at the entire park, including the waterpark which was developed just before Jimmy Lark died in 1983.

There is live entertainment and the thirty rides and attractions include indoor theme rides, live cabaret style shows, a ride through a dark house, and a walk through one that is haunted. Thousands of dollars have been spent on lavish landscaping.

Wilkes, presides over the entire operation, as General Manager.

The Lark family has worked hard to continue the legacy begun by Jimmy Lark. Billy Lark's children Will and Mary Elaine are now officers and shareholders and now participating in the day-to-day operations. The Lark philosophy is to continue to develop a quality family entertainment facility operated by a family. Family

run facilities have a closer bond with the needs and values of family customers.

Rides that have been added in recent years have been targeted toward families. The Copter Command helicopter ride, The Free Whale ride, and The Bumble Bee ride all allow parents to ride with their children at the Miracle Strip Park. The same concept applies at the Shipwreck Island with the new one million dollar addition known as, "White Knuckle River." This new ride can accommodate up to five family members in the same inner tube.

Jimmy Lark wanted to provide a facility that would not only entertain families, but one that would help compel them to Panama City Beach when making a vacation selection. The James I. Lark Visitor's Center is now gone, but the "Starliner" roller coaster will always surge up from the sand below to serve as a fitting monument to the man that did the most to make Panama City Beach a top family vacation destination.

Peyton Scott enjoys one of the rides.

CHAPTER VII

EDUCATION, QUALITY OF LIFE & HEALTH CARE

*Gulf Coast
Medical Center*

185

Stephen Myers,
DMD

187

*Gulf Coast
Community College*

188

*Florida State
University*

189

GULF COAST MEDICAL CENTER

The Beginning of Gulf Coast Medical Center

n the 1960's there were two hospitals in Panama City, Bay Memorial and Lisenby Hospital, a private 40-bed facility built in the late 1930s and owned by Dr. Horton Lisenby. Both facilities were aging; and, according to a group of local physicians, not meeting the needs of the community. The doctors were overworked due to the lack of physician specialties, non-existing emergency departments and working conditions that were less than desirable.

By the late sixties, Dr. Lisenby decided to sell Lisenby Hospital, and Dr. Tim Smith and Dr. James Poyner worked with a group of 19 physicians and bought Lisenby with the intent to build a new facility. "The only purpose for building another hospital was to increase medical care for the community," pointed out Dr. Dixon McCloy, one of the 19 physicians.

After receiving the Certificate of Need from the state for a 150-bed hospital, the group began meeting to discuss the project. The 19 doctors met every two weeks for about nine years, encountering obstacles such as financing, building plans and a location for the proposed new facility. They felt the community needed a hospital on the north side of town and purchased 150 acres on

23rd Street near Jenks Avenue. According to Poyner, "These 19 doctors were totally responsible for the initial growth and development of this side of town by the hospital. There was nothing here but forest land."

The group, along with an architect, designed the floor plans for the hospital, allowing each physician specialty to have a say in designing the departments. The plans were drawn and financing arranged.

After realizing the project was more involved than they had anticipated, the doctors voted on whether to keep the responsibility of operating and owning the hospital or to call on an outside organization. Due to increased interest rates during this time, and other concerns the physicians had, they decided to contact several hospital organizations about purchasing their project. The negotiating between HCA

(Healthcare Corporation of America) and the doctors was done by Dr. Tommy Frist, Jr., President of HCA at that time, and the physician group. The result ended with HCA as the ultimate choice to complete the project.

In 1976, the groundbreaking began for the new facility and, in 1977, Gulf Coast Community Hospital opened its doors and the Lisenby Hospital closed. Most of the inpatients at Lisenby had been discharged and the 12 remaining patients were transferred to Gulf Coast.

Dr. Smith played a major role in upgrading the medical services offered to the community. "I am proud of my role in helping increase the grade of medical care in the community and I believe competitive business is good because it makes one work harder," he said. Dr. Byron McCormick also played a prominent role in the hospital

Original Gulf Coast Community Hospital.

and said he believes both hospitals (Gulf Coast and Bay Medical Center) have a definite place in town. "I am proud to be a part of this hospital," he added.

Since opening in 1977, Gulf Coast Medical Center's highest priority has been to serve the healthcare needs of the community. The 176-bed, acute care hospital has expanded its services to include a Level II Neonatal Intensive Care Unit and a Neonatal Transport Team; a Cancer Program, which received the highest approval awarded by the American College of Surgeons Commission on Cancer; a Free Standing Diagnostic Center; Rehabilitation Center; and a Wound Care Center. The

Grand Opening of Gulf Coast Community Hospital in 1977.

facility provides a full range of services, including inpatient, outpatient and 24-hour emergency care.

Gulf Coast's medical team is comprised of almost 200 physicians and more than 700 nurses, healthcare specialists and support staff. Most recently, the Cherry Street Senior

Health Center of Gulf Coast Medical Center has added the services of a Geriatric physician who specializes in the needs of seniors. This specialty is the only one of its kind in the area.

Twenty years ago, 19 doctors had a vision of how to enhance healthcare availability to the people of Bay County. Today, Gulf Coast Medical Center provides accessible health care to everyone. Down through the years, the hospital has gone through several name changes to the most recent Gulf Coast Medical Center. In the meantime, it has continued to support the community in every aspect of the health care delivery system.

DR. STEPHEN C. MYERS
Dentist was Inspired by Kindness

r. Stephen C. Myers, who in 1981 became the first dentist to establish a practice on Panama City Beach, is delighted about his decision to return to his home town.

The son of Mr. and Mrs. A. F. (Sonny) Myers, he graduated from Bay High School, Gulf Coast Community College, and the University of Florida, where he earned the International College of Dentists Award for Outstanding Student.

He credits the kindly manner of Dr. Louis Leo with interesting him in the profession when he was 5. His practice today is primarily in the field of cosmetic and restorative dentistry.

He is married to his high school sweetheart, Mary Jo Nowlin. They have two sons, Stephen and Jordan.

Dr. Myers and his staff concentrate on their philosophy of meeting the individual needs of each patient on a personal and quality-oriented basis. "Getting to know each patient and meeting their needs and desires for their health is what we strive for daily," he says.

Dr. Myers attended an extensive continuing education program at the L.D. Panley Institute for Advanced Dental Education and was subsequently voted to become a member of their Board of Directors.

He served as a board member of the Bay Medical

Center Hospice and currently serves on the Gulf Coast Community College Dental Assisting and Hygiene Advisory Board. He is past president of the local dental society.

Dr. Myers believes that dentistry is an exciting and rewarding profession because of the constant changes in technology and the personal rewards of helping others.

Dr. Myers and Staff.

Internet-based courses, and interactive video courses.

Partners in Higher Education

 Gulf Coast Community College and Florida State University Panama City are committed to serving the higher education needs of Bay County.

GULF COAST COMMUNITY COLLEGE

 ince it was founded in 1957, Gulf Coast Community College has continued to provide a first class education to the citizens of Bay, Gulf, and Franklin counties. With its strong emphasis on student success, regardless of students' academic background, age, or educational goals, Gulf Coast prides itself on the success of its graduates who transfer to state universities and its vocational students who have extremely high placement rates in the careers they have chosen.

Programs. At its main campus on the bay in Panama City, Gulf Coast offers university-trans-

fer Associate in Arts programs, Associate in Science and certificate programs in a number of career fields, adult basic education and GED preparation, workforce training, economic development, citizen leadership, and cultural enrichment.

Sites. For the first two years, Gulf Coast held classes in the Wainwright Shipyard Building across from the current 74-acre campus on U.S. Hwy. 98. Gulf Coast provides a warm, friendly atmosphere for learning, not only at its main campus but also at Tyndall Air Force Base, the Gulf/Franklin Center in Port St. Joe, and the North Bay Center, north of Southport.

Scheduling. Because 75 percent of its students work, the college offers classes at convenient times...morning, afternoon, evenings, and weekends. Gulf Coast also has extensive offerings through distance learning, which provides courses on video tape that students can view at their own pace in their own homes,

GCCC Foundation. The Gulf Coast Community College Foundation, Inc., was established in 1967 to provide scholarships to deserving students. With initial assets of $21,000, the Foundation has grown to more than $14 million. The strength of the Foundation's endowment will provide both scholarships and state-of-the-art instructional technology training into the foreseeable future.

In addition to the excellence of the teaching faculty and support staff, the college also prides itself on its internationally recognized Citizen Leadership Institute and its public radio station, WKGC-FM.

Partnership with FSU. Most Gulf Coast graduates transfer to the Panama City Campus of Florida State University. The close partnership between these two institutions means that local students can receive a seamless bachelor's degree without relocating. Because both institutions are in such proximity, they are able to share a library, classrooms, and other facilities.

As a learning centered enterprise, Gulf Coast Community College strives to maintain the excellence of its academic ratings and its success in training students for careers.

THE FLORIDA STATE UNIVERSITY
PANAMA CITY

ith all the advantages of a major university campus, FSU Panama City offers students a unique bayside atmosphere and classroom setting. In cooperation with Gulf Coast Community College, students can achieve their higher education goals while still working and living in Bay and surrounding counties.

Campus History. The University of West Florida founded a university center in Panama City in 1972 which was acquired by The Florida State University in 1982. The branch campus, was relocated from the old shipyard buildings to the modern brick facility bordering North Bay in 1987. Since its inception, the campus has graduated over 4,000 students.

Programs. The Panama City Campus offers upper division courses and programs (junior/senior and graduate level), while Gulf Coast Community College provides the first two years of coursework. Presently, nearly 900 students are enrolled in over 31 undergraduate and graduate degree programs.

Classes at FSU PC are small with many opportunities for personalized instruction and student interaction. Full-time faculty, both resident and those commuting from Tallahassee, teach 83% of courses for degree programs and elective options from other departments. All faculty meet the same high standards for teaching, research, and service as those on the main campus.

Location. Located just 100 miles from FSU's main campus in Tallahassee, the waterfront setting is one the campus' most striking attributes. Nestled among oaks along the sparkling waters of North Bay and only three miles from the Gulf of Mexico, the Panama City Campus provides students a serene learning environment. The environment is also a perfect setting for a lecture in nature's classroom. With an outdoor amphitheater overlooking North Bay, it isn't unusual for professors to conduct a class or two outdoors.

While the location is not only visually pleasing, access to the water also serves as an educational tool. Complementing its coastal location, the Advanced Science Diving Program, which has been in existence at FSU for 25 years, has been relocated to the Panama City Campus.

Looking to the Future. In response to the growth of Bay and surrounding counties, the Panama City Campus is in the process of adding additional degree programs and resident faculty. In addition, a conference center facility was completed in January of 2000. The master plan for the development of the campus over the next decade includes the construction of two new classroom buildings.

With a firm commitment to the needs of the community, fall 2000 marked the debut of full-time daytime programs offered at the Panama City Campus. This new scheduling, coupled with programs already offered in the evenings, serves to accommodate the needs of the diverse student population. In addition, new resident faculty have been hired to meet these new program demands.

Continuing its pledge to academic excellence, FSU Panama City is committed to providing area students with a quality education from a nationally recognized university.

CHAPTER VIII

LOCAL GOVERNMENT & COMMUNITY SERVICE

*City of Panama
City Beach*

191

*Bay County
Sheriff's Office*

193

*City of Cedar
Grove*

194

*Panama City Beaches
Chamber of Commerce*

196

*Panama City Beach
Convention and Visitors
Bureau, Inc.*

198

CITY OF PANAMA CITY BEACH

Fast Growing Area

ew municipalities in Florida have a greater growth potential than Panama City Beach, not excluding neighboring communities along the beaches in Northwest Florida, more commonly referred to as the Panhandle.

The estimated population in 1998 for the Bay County area west of the Hathaway Bridge (the dividing line between Panama City and the beaches) was 25,000, but that has been expanding almost daily. And although the population of Panama City Beach within the city limits is approximately 5,300, the city serves hundreds of people who are officially in the county. With people moving to the area in record

numbers —and annexation a familiar term—the population could approach 10,000 within five years.

And, with development proceeding at an incredible pace, Panama City Beach appears on the verge of an economic boom that could entirely change the image of the beaches and Bay County as a whole. The St. Joe Company, through subsidiary Arvida, is working on a development that could become the downtown area of Panama City Beach. The Pier Park Project, so named because of its close proximity to the Dan Russell (City) Pier on the Gulf of Mexico, will include many new projects and should be a multi-million dollar plus for the economy.

However, the city, with a new Mayor and a revamped

City Council, is not putting all of its eggs in the Pier Park basket, and is not waiting for St. Joe developers to fill up its coffers.

Philip W. Griffitts

The progressive attitude of Panama City Beach can be placed directly at the feet of Philip W. Griffitts, who served the city for a record-setting 18 years as Mayor, and longtime City Manager Richard Jackson. When Griffitts, a lifetime

Greetings—The new Panama City Beach Visitors Center, which houses the Convention and Visitors Bureau and the Tourist Development Council, is one of the many projects that have been completed in Panama City Beach during the past few months.

Lee Sullivan

resident of Panama City Beach, became Mayor in 1982, the city had less than 2,500 people. When he departed after losing the Mayor's race to former Police Chief, Lee Sullivan by seven votes in May, the city's population was more than 5,300.

Since four communities merged to create what is now Panama City Beach in 1970, the city has had only four Mayors and Griffitts served more years than all the rest combined. Dan Russell was Mayor for

Dan Russell

ten years after serving as Mayor of what was then known as West Panama City Beach for one year. Aaron Z. Bessent, founder of the prestigious Indian Summer Seafood Festival, served as Mayor for two years before losing to Griffitts, a political newcomer at the time, in 1982.

Griffitts was seeking an

Aaron Z. Bessent

unprecedented eighth straight term before losing to Sullivan in a run-off May 9, 2000.

Many projects have been completed and many more are still in progress as the city heads into a new era, with a new mayor and two new City Council members. The city already has invested $4.5 million dollars in renovations and new facilities at a recreational complex called Frank Brown Park, located on the shrub inhabited Panama City Beach Parkway, a half-mile east of Highway 79, the main artery heading north from the beaches.

The park features seven 300-foot softball fields and two full-sized baseball diamonds. These fields are built for tournament-level play with seating for 180 people at each. The park also features several lighted soccer fields, with the latest consisting of three full-sized NCAA soccer fields. There are two lighted tennis courts, a lighted outdoor basketball court and a large picnic shelter for up to 100 people. In addition, the ultra-modern Under-The-Palms playground, a $200,000-plus facility, is now open in Frank Brown Park and will enhance not only the beauty of the park, but also the versatility of its use. Also, located in the park is the Philip W. Griffitts Community Center, named for the long-time Mayor. Recreation and meeting rooms are a part of the community center and the park features a 1-¼ mile lighted walking and jogging track and paved sidewalk throughout.

State Highway 79 is a different matter altogether. The Department of Transportation has already announced that the road, along with westbound US 98 to Sandestin, will be four-laned in the future. The two highways represent the major

evacuation routes in case of a hurricane, or some other catastrophe. DOT is also providing funds to replace Hathaway Bridge with two bridges that will have four-lanes each going east and west. Also, in the works is building interchanges at several spots, including Thomas Drive, the most congested intersection in the county.

City officials are studying plans to construct a Boys and Girls Club building and are hoping to renovate and expand the current Senior Center, recently purchased form the Optimist Club. The first high school on Panama City Beach, J.R. Arnold, is scheduled to open this fall and eventually all students from the beaches will be relieved of the burden of crossing the big bridge to attend schools in the metropolitan area of Panama City.

Sun, surf, sand-nowhere are they more prevalent, more perfect and more popular than on Panama City Beach, known to thousands as "The World's Most Beautiful beaches." While Panama City Beach is noted as a haven for Spring Breakers in March and April and for Snowbirds when the cold comes to Canada and northern states, the image of the area has changed drastically since four cities merged to create what is now the current City of Panama City Beach 30 years ago. The Four Cities/Towns incorporated into the current City of Panama City Beach were; The City of Panama City Beach, The City of Long Beach, The Town of Edgewater Beach and the City of West Panama City Beach.

BAY COUNTY SHERIFF'S OFFICE

ay County Sheriff's Office has come a long way since the first jail was built in 1913.

The wooden structure was built on a boat dock and had to be replaced when prisoners found they could pry up the floorboards and swim to freedom in the bay below!

After many expansions and moves, the Sheriff's Office Operations Center is now located on Highway 77 in Panama City, in a facility completed in 1995.

Sheriff Guy M. Tunnell has been in office since 1989. Born in Bay County in 1951, he has worked in law enforcement most of his adult life, and is past president of the Florida Sheriff's Association.

Working for the Sheriff's Office doesn't just mean wearing a uniform and patrolling the streets, although these aspects are important. There are many other specialized groups who work together to safeguard the citizens of Bay County.

Deputies in the Community Services Division provide leadership for *Neighborhood Watch* and *Church Watch* programs to promote education on safety and crime prevention. The *D.A.R.E.* program teaches kids to make good life choices. School Resource Officers work in middle and high schools for security and guidance, and a 12-week *Citizens Police Academy* gives adults insight into law enforcement operations.

Offers Service, Education

The Field Services Division, which includes patrol deputies, also oversees such special services as the *Dive Team* (underwater rescue and recovery); the *K-9 Unit* with bloodhounds and drug and bomb detection dogs; and the *Air Unit* (helicopters for search and rescue). *The Sheriff's Posse* includes mounted volunteers, and the *S.W.A.T. Team* is trained for response to high-risk incidents, such as hostage situations or barricades.

The Criminal Investigations Division is one of two investigative divisions. This division is tasked with solving crimes, and contains the Crime Scene Unit, which collects evidence and presents it in court.

The Special Investigations Division is manned by undercover officers working on drug and narcotic crimes and vice.

Every case, large or small, involves records which are stored and maintained within the Support Services Division.

The Court Services Division provides bailiffs to circuit and county courts and serves warrants and other legal documents.

The Boot Camp Program provides guidance and physical and educational training for juvenile offenders, and is one of the most successful in the state.

The Bay County Sheriff's Office employs nearly 300 people. An emphasis on community service and education has helped build a reputation of dedication to the task. The Bay County Sheriff's Office will continue to maintain this level of excellence in the twenty-first century.

The modern Sheriff's Office complex from the air.

THE CITY OF CEDAR GROVE

CEDAR GROVE CITY HALL…A place where the business of the city and the people are conducted.

Cedar Grove Seventh Fastest-Growing City

rom one of the smallest municipalities nestled in a two-square-mile area, as described by local historian, Tommy Smith in 1993, Cedar Grove has blossomed into the seventh-fastest growing city in the State of Florida.

Cedar Grove currently measures approximately 12 square miles with a population of 3,500 and was recently called the "Gateway to the World's Most Beautiful Beaches." Cedar Grove, a thriving community, has more than ten percent of Bay County's manufacturing industry.

In 1993, Hildrie O. Peel became mayor and has maintained this position to present. The members of the City Commission, Jean Andrews, Jerry Walsh, Rickey McNeil and Eddie Curti, have remained in their seats since 1994. The

Board has gone through four elections unopposed, demonstrating the harmony, stability and trust the citizens of Cedar Grove have in the accomplishments of their city government.

The management of the city's Police Department is directed by Chief John Ferrick, with the Water Department supervised by City Clerk Ruth Fuqua and the Planning and Administration Department headed by City Manager James A. Woods.

Mayor Peel has assumed the lead role in changing the face of the city and Bay County. He has done so by establishing a "Vision for the City," creating a government to serve the people with the motivation and commitment to "make a difference" his overall mission to improve the quality of life for the citizens of Cedar Grove and Bay County. The mayor is well known for his contention that "We're all Bay Countians first."

The foundation for Cedar

Grove's vision is economic development with managed growth coupled with strong infrastructure. By means of cooperation with various federal, state and county agencies, Cedar Grove has been able to engage in the development of extremely needed public infrastructure. The city has embarked upon the pursuit of providing water and sewer to all its residents through community development block grants and U.S. Department of Agriculture low-interest grants and loans. The maintenance of roads and streets and the collaboration with the Department of Transportation has allowed the city to provide safe means of travel for those living and passing through Cedar Grove.

The city has worked very effectively with the Florida Department of Environmental Protection, Florida Department of Community Affairs and the Bay County Commission to construct recreational facilities throughout Cedar Grove through their use of FRDAP and P2000 grant programs. Cedar Grove Recreational Park, located on Spring Avenue, is a 13-acre nature park with a half-mile hike and bike path. Hildrie O. Peel Park is a first-class recreational complex with a four-field facility that hosted the 2000 Florida Junior Major Little League Tournament.

At that time, the Florida Little League Commissioner stated, "this is the finest facility I have ever seen."

Presently, the city is working on a conservation park on Baldwin Avenue, preserving the diverse and unique ecosystems of Florida.

Cedar Grove is committed to its investment in the community and is lending a hand to those in need. The Police Department annually sponsors a "Toys for Tots" motorcycle run for the children of Bay County and the Cedar Grove Posse holds an annual Christmas "Trots for Tots" horseback ride to gather gifts for the children. The Posse is a volunteer search-and-rescue outfit offering its services to all of Bay and surrounding counties. Cedar Grove also participated in the annual "Food Drive," sponsored by the National Letter Carriers and held at the main post office on Sherman Avenue in Cedar Grove.

Each October, coinciding with the state's "City Government Week," Cedar Grove holds one of its most important events, "Citizen Appreciation Day." At this time, the city has a community-wide barbecue and the citizens come out for a day of socializing and enjoyment. It allows citizens the opportunity to interact with their elected officials in a relaxed atmosphere and to clear up issues before they become a serious problem.

This single event contributes to making Cedar Grove the best community it can be. The people in Cedar Grove consider their city Florida's greatest place to live, work and do business.

PANAMA CITY BEACHES
CHAMBER OF COMMERCE

The year was 1987. The tourism industry was just starting to pick up momentum in Bay County and the Panama City Beaches Chamber of Commerce held its first meeting.

Over seventy businesses paid an initiation fee with Hank Swicord as the first president. The group rented office space and a new organization was born.

Since that meeting, the Panama City Beaches Chamber of Commerce has compiled a long record of working to attract industry and recognizing local businesses for their achievements. It has lobbied to expand and improve roads, utilities services, landscape and sign ordinances and has been a strong supporter of education.

In recent years, the Chamber has extended its role in the community. Debi Parish took over as Executive Director in 1992 and began an aggressive campaign to increase membership and establish new programs. Since then, with an aggressive, supportive Board of Directors and a dedicated, hardworking staff, membership has grown from 300 to 900 members.

The Chamber created an "Award-Winning Web Page," offered quarterly tours at the Coastal System Station, Small Business of the Year Award, Outstanding Citizen of the Year Award, Pioneer of the Year Award and started a New Members Welcome Day.

In 1998, the Chamber was proud to win "Chamber of the Year," competing with Chambers across the state. The criteria were based on the past three years accomplishments, increase in dues, and increase in membership, new programs, services and technology that stands above the rest.

The Chamber sponsors a wide range of activities, including monthly Business After Hours programs, Small Business Seminars, Hospitality Appreciation Party, Annual Business Expo and Holiday Auction. The Chamber held its first Business Expo in 1992, which allowed local firms to showcase their products and services to the business community. At that time, 30 businesses participated. Today, over 100 exhibitors and 2,000 in attendance, make the Business Expo the largest Chamber event of the year.

PCB Chamber of Commerce Business Expo 98.

PHOTO COURTESY OF PICTURE PERFECT

PCB Chamber of Commerce – Grand Opening & Ribbon Cutting at Seawind Medical Clinic
with John Gheesling III and Dr. John England

Another important part of the Chamber's mission is promoting education. The education committee sponsors various schools with a number of events and projects, has given thousands of dollars in scholarships and builds a partnership between businesses and schools.

The Chamber produces eight publications each year. The Circuit Newsletter, Official Visitor Guide, Membership/Business Directory, Calendar of Events, Referral Brochure, Demographic Profile, City Map and Program of Work.

The Chamber raised over $68,000 with a matching grant to landscape three gateways on Panama City Beach Parkway. Today, the beautiful gateways lead people to the "World's Most Beautiful Beaches."

In 1997, the Chamber created a "Beach Vision Group" to focus on the needs and growth of Bay County. The first meeting was held in September of '97. The City of Panama City Beach, Tourist Development Council, County Commissioners and Chamber Board members attended. The group started planning for future growth on Panama City Beach. The meeting was open to the public and plans were made. The group still meets regularly and a better understanding of roles, tasks and ordinances have been approved or accomplished.

The Chamber moved its office from the visitor center on Front Beach Road to the Peoples First Building on Hutchinson Boulevard in 1995 due to lack of space and parking.

Today the Chamber continues to be the leader in business development, planned growth and quality of life.

PCB Chamber of Commerce Appreciation Party.

197

PANAMA CITY BEACH CONVENTION & VISITORS BEAUREAU/BAY COUNTY TOURIST DEVELOPMENT COUNCIL

he mission of the Bay County Tourist Development Council and the Panama City Beach Convention & Visitors Bureau is to promote a positive image for Panama City Beach, increase tourism, and coordinate the marketing efforts of the total tourism community.

According to Visit Florida, the state's public/private promotional agency, over 7 million visitors a year are attracted to Northwest Florida.

Of those 7 million visitors, 4 million select Panama City Beach as their destination. Legendary worldwide for its 27 miles of beautiful beaches and emerald-green waters, Panama City Beach is a natural draw for vacationers seeking warmth and sunshine.

Tourism is the largest industry in Bay County and the number one employer, creating over 14,000 jobs. Tourism's impact on the area is $547 million in

Tourist Council Helps Promote Area, Restore and Develop Beach

direct expenditures with a total economic impact of $1.5 billion.

The Bay County Tourist Development Council was created by the Board of County Commissioners. In February, 1986, the local option tourist tax was placed on a referendum, which voters passed to allow the county to levy a tourist development tax on lodging facilities only and spearhead a

unified marketing program to enhance economic growth on behalf of Bay County.

The Tourist Development Council is comprised of nine members: the Bay County Board of County Commissioners Liaison (appointed by the Chairman of that Board), two elected municipal officials, three owners or operators of hotels, motels or other tourist accommodations subject to tax, and three individuals who have demonstrated an interest in the industry, but who are not owners or operators of hotels, motels or other tourist accommodations.

The Tourist Development Council contracts with the Panama City Beach Convention & Visitors Bureau to perform the destination marketing efforts.

Reggie Lancaster

Mr. Reggie Lancaster, Chairman of the Bay County Tourist Development Council, expresses the enthusiasm and dedication which has brought worldwide recognition to the area.

"I love the tradition of Panama City Beach," he says. "You begin coming here as a child and before you know it, you are bringing your own children and eventually your grandchildren.

"I believe the initial attraction to our area is the beach. I also believe the repeat factor is due to the friendliness and affordability of our destination.

"There is something for everyone on Panama City Beach!"

#1 Beach in America .....

Tourist tax collected in the Panama City Beach tourist tax district is used to market Panama City Beach with a $1,200,000 advertising budget, support ten major special events annually, maintain street landscapes, maintain storm-water drainage outfalls, clean the beaches, support the "Beach and Surf" patrol safety program, and fund the "Turtle Watch" environmental protection program.

One of the most significant uses of the tourist tax has been the funding of the $25 million beach preservation program.

Because of the tax, Panama City Beach was able to complete the largest renourishment project in Florida's history. With the addition of 8.32 million cubic yards of sand, the beaches were extended to a new width of 100 feet and dune systems were created. The

project included the planting of 600,000 sea oats and modification of 60 drainage outfalls.

Panama City Beach has become the recipient of numerous prestigious awards for its stunning, white sand beaches and wide variety of activities. Coastal Authority Dr. Stephen P. Leatherman recognized the beach's world-famous shoreline in 1995 as the #1 beach in America and in 1998 as the #1 sports beach on the Gulf Coast.

For 2000, the Travel Channel featured Panama City Beach as the #4 beach in America and the Surfrider Foundation identified Panama City Beach the #3 beach in America due to its beautiful beaches and environmental leadership.

TDC programs helped enlarge, restore storm-damaged beach

CHAPTER IX

NETWORKS

Utilities, Transportation and Communications

*Bay Lincoln-
Mercury-Dodge*

201

*Comcast Cable
Vision*

202

Cellular One

204

Beach TV

205

*Clear Channel
Radio*

207

Waitt Radio

208

Gulf Power

209

BAY LINCOLN MERCURY DODGE

George Gainer, an unusual man with a lust for life, has been around, so to speak. In 1968, Gainer, a then Bay County commissioner, purchased the local Lincoln-Mercury store. He sold it in 1972 and then bought it back in 1998.

In between, Gainer, who has been in the automobile business

for 34 years, owned Magic City Dodge in Birmingham. He also ran a big metro Ford dealership in Atlanta, did consultant work for Bill Heard, who has Chevrolet dealerships in several locations in the south, and ran Freeway Ford in Columbus, Georgia from 1994-97.

"I sold my first car in that little building on the corner," Gainer said, pointing to a small office on the corner surrounded by used cars. "I have always loved cars."

Gainer also loves fire engines. At least, he was traveling up U.S. Highway 231 the other day when he saw these fire engines and decided he might buy them. What for? "They were there and I just thought it sounded like a good idea," he said, and it was difficult to know if he was kidding

or being dead serious. He dialed another phone number between words and then nodded for an interviewer to continue while he talked.

Gainer, who said his great great grandfather was the first settler in Bay County, grew up here. He attended Bay High School, graduating in 1960, and also attended Gulf Coast Community College.

In front of Gainer's office in the big showroom on 15th Street was a luxury Lincoln with a price of almost $50,000. Is that the most expensive car the dealership has? "We sell cars from $12,000 ranging all the way up to the Lincoln Navigator at $60,000," he explained.

The Lincoln Mercury dealership, combined with the Dodge dealership, is the Number 1 volume dealership, selling more vehicles than anybody in town. Although Gainer has two silent partners, he is the man who makes the wheels go around.

"We are enjoying one of the highest customer satisfaction rates in the country," Gainer pointed out. "We are a five-star dealer and that's top of the line for Chrysler in advanced training and advanced equipment."

Gainer's dealership retails about 3,000 cars a year and wholesales another 1,000, and employs approximately 100 people.

Heavily involved in the community, Gainer said he is "a member of everything that meets after dark." Actually, he spends most of his spare time at the local Shrine Club and does a lot of charity work. He also is a member of the First Baptist Church of Panama City. He donated a 2000 model Cougar to the Shrine Club to raffle off. His company has donated over $200,000 in the past two years to various charitable organizations. He is proud of his antique cars and is an active member in several antique auto clubs.

When a student at Bay High School, Gainer worked on fishing boats as a deck hand. He is traveling a little bit more in first class these days.

COMCAST CABLE

On April 7, 1999, Comcast Cable acquired controlling interest in one of the leading cable companies for Panama City Beach, Jones Intercable. Since the acquisition of Jones Spacelink, Comcast has made significant upgrades in programming resulting in increased programming choice including Comcast Digital Cable and Comcast @ Home high-speed Internet service. Comcast added 11 networks to the Panama City Beach channel line-up such as the Food Network, Game Show Network, Outdoor Life, Weather Channel Local Edition and Speedvision. Comcast has spent in excess of one million dollars for a rebuild to a new state-of-the-art fiber optic system that will enable us to provide customers on Panama City Beach with the most up-to-date technology possible through the deployment of digital compression technology.

Comcast Digital Cable offers over 150 digital channels including 33 channels of digital basic channels, 43 screens of premium channels, 37 pay-per-view channels, and 45 commercial-free music channels, which encompass a variety of music genres, for approximately $15 more each month. In addition, Comcast Digital Cable features an interactive program guide, which allows the customer to search for programs by title, time, channel or category to find the programming they want, when they want it. The IPG also provides easy-to-use parental lockouts for mature programming, as well as programming reminders. Comcast Digital Cable will provide the platform necessary to make future interactive services possible for Comcast Customers, such as Internet TV and e-mail, e-commerce, banking and games. Comcast @Home is a high-speed Internet Service which features a cable connection with downloads up to 100 times faster than a regular 28.8 phone modem. Comcast@ Home provides our customers with a constant Internet connection, unlimited Internet surfing, multiple e-mail accounts and personal Web space for a flat monthly fee.

Comcast provides over 550 hours of the local programming and news coverage that customers find valuable, such as Comcast Around Town and Panama City Beach City Council meetings. Comcast airs over 300 public service announcements for a variety of non-profit organizations in the community. In

addition, over 15,000 commercials are aired on 14 local networks for various organizations. Comcast Cable further supports the community through sponsorship and participation in local projects and charities such as March of Dimes, American Cancer Society, Muscular Dystrophy Association, Gulf Coast Community College and the Boys and Girls Club.

Comcast Cable provides free-of-charge over 540 hours of commercial-free, educational programming for K-12 public and private schools in our area, as well as other learning institutions like our community college and vocational programs.

In addition, Comcast provides free-of-charge a monthly magazine to all educational facilities in our county for whom we provide complimentary service. Comcast hosts workshops during the year to keep educators updated and abreast of changes in cable programming.

As competition for voice, video, and data grows throughout the telecommunications marketplace, Comcast understands how important it is to offer our customers the best possible service at the best possible price. Comcast truly values its customers and believes that they, in return, receive great value from its services.

Comcast of Panama City leads the local cable television industry in professional expertise with over 350 years of combined cable television experience. All Comcast Cable technicians are encouraged to complete all of the National Cable Television Institute's training programs on the latest technological advancements, a program which all technicians employed over 3 months have successfully mastered. Customer Service Representatives are continuously updated and trained through internal programs, such as Comcast University, and external programs with program vendors.

CELLULAR ONE *Keeping Pace With the Times*

ellular One in Panama City has kept pace with a changing world since opening in 1988 and now employs more than 20 people, including Melinda Clements who moved here from Montgomery recently to assume the duties of General Manager. Everything is in-house now and the company offers local customer service, technical service and also has a complete sales department.

"Competition is pretty fierce," pointed out Trish Griffith, who has been with the local store since 1990, longer than any other employee. "But, the one thing we don't do is put down the competition. We just try to give our customers the very best service possible and I believe we are doing that."

With a specified plan, Cellular One offers local service to four states – Florida, Georgia, Alabama and South Carolina. As a matter of fact, the cellular phone company has a plan for just about everybody. Rates start at $15 a month and go up, depending on how many minutes you need. With other plans, toll free services to all states are offered and the company also has international dialing.

The local cellular company started out in a much smaller office in the Biddle Communications Building, located at 11th Street and Beck Avenue in Panama City, and then moved into another building on 15th Street. The move to the current location, in what is commonly referred to as the Wal-Mart shopping center, was made in 1995.

Jeanne Eddins, who was born and raised in Bay County and has been with the company since 1993, said there definitely has been a lot of growth and a lot of changes, particularly in the technical field. "We now have digital service and that gives you a much clearer sound, voice privacy and far superior equipment. We have a plan for just about everybody in the Panhandle."

Cellular One offices are independently owned and the local company belongs to Price Wireless, which also owns operations in Alabama cities Montgomery, Dothan, Auburn and Eufaula and Columbus, Georgia, and altogether has 36 offices.

Cellular One has long been involved in local charity and community work. "We are real heavy in the Relay of Life," Trish pointed out, "and everybody is involved. We also deliver food baskets during Thanksgiving. Customers can bring in canned food and get a discount on their accessories. In particular, the Relay of Life is a real fun time, because we are so involved."

BEACH TV

Beach TV A Network Pioneer

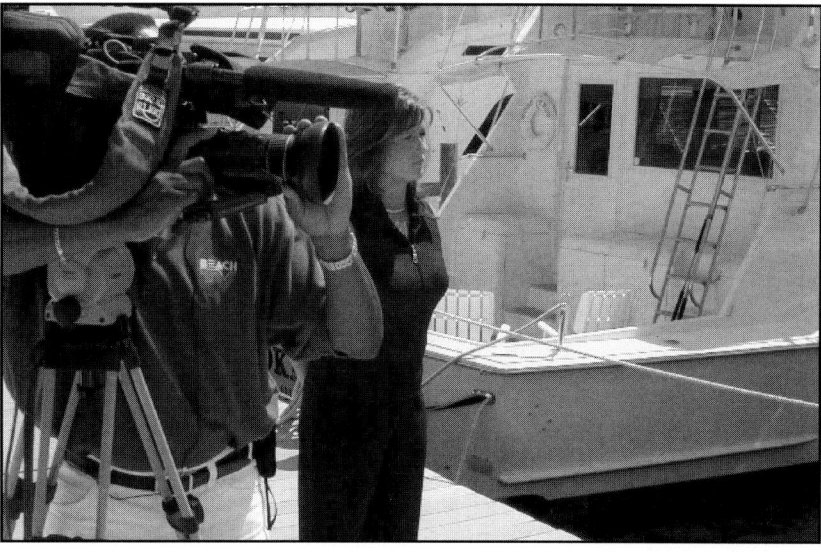

Beach TV means different things to different people—to most people in this area, it means mouthwatering restaurant reviews, a video library of the area's history and culture—and those famous Alvin's bikini videos! Few people realize that Beach TV is considered a true pioneer in the television broadcast business...one of the first of its kind, and the founding station of The Tourist Network.

Beach TV was founded in Panama City Beach, in 1987. Jud Colley and Toni Davis, along with partner, Myron Hines, created a whole new kind of television station—from scratch! In the beginning, it was basically just the three of them. Colley, with a real estate development background, provided the financing and business expertise; Hines, with over 17 years of television broadcasting experience, provided the operation and production expertise; Davis, with an advertising agency background, did all the script-writing, marketing and selling. Due in large part to the prepaid advertising support of several advertisers who had the foresight to understand this "new" form of programming, the station was an instant suc-

cess on Panama City Beach! (Historical Note: Original advertisers for Beach TV included Alvin's Island Tropical Department Stores, Boar's Head Restaurant, Montego Bay Restaurants and Spinnaker Beach Club.)

In 1990, the Tourist Network acquired Key TV in Key West and Beach TV in Destin. In June of 1991, the Tourist Network added NOTV (New Orleans Television) in New Orleans, Louisiana. The New Orleans market was the first to target conventioneers and business travelers as the

primary audience. August of 1992 saw the addition of Beach TV in Myrtle Beach, South Carolina. In July of 1993, a second travel market was added, The Atlanta Channel in Atlanta, Georgia (the #10 television market in America). In 1999, Beach TV expanded to include Fort Walton Beach, and, in 2000, the Pensacola market was added.

The Tourist Network is a specialized broadcast television network serving a vital "tuned-in" audience with programming which targets their specific interests: tourist, business travelers, conventioneers, relocating families—the "Out-of home viewer" seeking information about their environs. Tourist Network stations provide a wonderful array of live and pre-produced programming. 100 percent local programming in each market— carefully segmented dayparts designed to entertain, educate, persuade the visitor with imagination, variety, color and an ever-changing array of fascinating subjects and spell-binding stories, combined with essential up-to-the-minute information: hourly weather reports and special event updates. This is a proven format that allows advertisers the flexibility of traditional "spot" buys or highly persuasive "Advertorials" of varying lengths.

National network affiliate research proved that, for 75 percent of all travelers, out-of-home viewing averages three hours per day. Lodging Hospitality reveals that, "next to the bed, the television is the most important amenity in the room, with most visitors leaving it on constantly except when they leave the room or go to sleep." The privacy of a hotel room creates an ideal environment; the visitor is tuning in to see and hear the advertisers' messages— actively seeking the information; there are no distractions and no competition for the attention of the viewer.

When the World came to Atlanta for the 1996 Centennial Olympic Games, a Tourist Network station welcomed, entertained, and educated them, in multiple languages, with award-winning style and with state-of-the-art digital technology! The Tourist Network was one of the first broadcasters in America to use a 100 percent digital program origination source. When 10,000 Olympic athletes checked into their rooms at the Olympic Village, a very special closed circuit Tourist Network station greeted them. When the Super Bowl came to New Orleans and Atlanta, Tourist Network stations were chosen as the official NFL Super Bowl stations and

welcomed football fans from around the globe.

1999 witnessed the formation of Tourist Network Interactive and the beginning of a two year web development project. In the Spring of 2000, with Tourist Network Interactive's New Media partner, Will Barnes, at the helm, another historic achievement was recorded: the Tourist Network was the first broadcast television network to offer 24 hour live broadband broadcast of their television stations on the internet! In late October of 2000, the web site was unveiled. www.tripsmarter.com was a hit from the start! Today, internet users across the globe can watch Beach TV and other Tourist Network television stations on the web. They can go behind the scenes of local restaurants and attractions; they can make their hotel, airline and car rental reservations on-line, and they can access the information they need to make their vacation and buying deci-

sions before they ever leave home. The streaming television technology and video clips available on demand at www.tripsmarter.com add an element of entertainment and excitement that is not available on other travel sites.

From historic Olympic success, to Mardi Gras and Fantasy Fest—from Super Bowl to Spring Break—golf vacations at the Grand Strand to tropical escapes on America's only Caribbean island, Tourist Network stations and Tripsmarter.com reaches and influences the most sought-after consumers in the world.

www.tripsmarter.com
850-234-2773
P.O. Box 9556 P.C. Beach,
FL. 32417

CLEAR CHANNEL RADIO

Offers a Variety of Entertainment

he Panama City Clear Channel Radio Stations began serving the Bay County area more than 50 years ago with 590 AM. Today, the Clear Channel family in the county consists of six top-rated stations that are listened to by more than 175,000 people each week.

Whatever your musical preference, you can probably find it on a Clear Channel station and officials are proud their "family" is the Primary Emergency Alert System radio outlet for the Bay County Operational area.

The stations work very closely with the Emergency Operations Center to make sure residents are fully informed in times of emergency; they have a fully redundant series of back-up emergency generators to make sure it will be there when the public needs it.

Although headquarters for the stations are located at 19th Street and Lisenby Avenue in Panama City, the towers for WPAP, one of the most-listened-to country stations in the Southeast, and WFSY-FM "Sunny 98.5" are located off Highway 231 in the Fountain area. The two stations are equipped with generators, in case of a hurricane or some other emergency, and will always be on the air.

"We team with Channel 13 (WMBB-TV) on our weather coverage," pointed out Charlie Wooten, Director of Engineering for the stations and a lifetime resident of Bay County. "Since they

Serving you then......... and NOW!

have full-time weather people, they do our forecasts and we have a link to the TV station so we can know what weather conditions are like at all times."

"We are proud to serve our listener area and we provide well over a quarter of a million dollars of public service advertising while raising hundreds of thousands of dollars for charity," pointed out Jeanie Hufford, who is Market Manager for Clear Channel Radio stations in both Panama City and Pensacola. In addition to the six Clear Channel stations here, there are two in Pensacola.

Peter Norden is Station Manager and Director of Sales for the local Clear Channel Stations and Pat Quirk and Kelly Tutt serve as local Sales Managers.

Tom Hanrahan is Program Director for WPAP-FM, WSFY-FM "Sunny 98.5", WPBH-FM "Beach 99.3", and WEBZ "93.5 The Beat." Woody Tidwell is program Director for WPPT "94.5 Pirate Radio."

Tom Lewis, News Anchor for WMBB-TV, teams with Dr. Shane

Collins on the WPAP Morning Show. Eric Steiner and Meg Grimes are hosts for the Morning Show on Sunny 98.5; Jim Dooley, who has been in the radio business here for many years, is Morning Show host for Beach 99.3, and BC and Woody are Morning Show hosts for Pirate Radio.

Clear Channel Communications, Inc. (www.clearchannel.com) is a global leader in the out-of-home advertising industry with radio and television stations and outdoor displays in 37 countries around the world. Clear Channel operates more than 700,000 outdoor advertising displays including billboards, street furniture and transit panels.

Including announced transactions, Clear Channel also operates 1,200 radio and 19 television stations in the United States and has equity interest in more than 240 radio stations internationally. Along Florida's Emerald Coast, Clear Channel owns and operates more than 20 radio stations and one television station.

WAITT RADIO   *Well Known For its Variety of Entertainment*

aitt Radio made its debut in the Panama City market in February of 1999 by purchasing four stations; WRBA Arrow 95.9, WAKT Kat Kountry 105.1, WMPX Lite Rock 103.5 and WLHR Hot 107.9; operating them as a cluster. The acquisition was a complement to another Waitt property, WPGX Fox 28 television.

Waitt Radio is owned by Norman Waitt, Jr., who along with his brother, Ted founded Gateway 2000, the computer company.

Norm has always had a passion for music, which led to his desire to get into the broadcasting business. The company has grown fast by purchasing broadcasting properties in Florida, Alabama, Georgia, Iowa, Nebraska, South Dakota and Minnesota.

Kat Kountry 105.1 (WAKT-FM) is a spirited blend of modern country music and traditional favorites. The station is very personality oriented, kicking off every morning with The Banana Joe Show. Banana Joe and his wife Krissy are very active in local happenings and regularly feature guests from the community on their show. Kat Kountry personalities make numerous public appearances throughout the area and are known for their "off the wall" contests that create an enormous amount of interest for their audience.

Arrow 95.9 (WRBA-FM) has been a solid leader in the market with its unique classic rock format. The morning show fea-

tures John Boy and Billy. These two popular personalities have a very special brand of rural humor that has made them a sensation all over the Southeastern United States. Contesting is an important element in the station's programming and Arrow 95.9 regularly features deep libraries of music on the weekends, showcasing classic artists of the seventies and eighties.

Hot 107.9 (WLHR-FM) is a legendary frequency that shines with the younger generation. The station's format features "Today's Hottest Hits" and is anchored by a sensational morning team. Hot 107.9 has a unique partnership with Club La Vela that enables the station to broadcast "live" from a "state of the art" studio poolside at the club, the largest nightclub in

the United States.

Lite Rock 103.5 (WMPX-FM) starts each day with the talented morning team Steve and Linda. The show is referred to as being completely "kid safe," meaning that moms can be assured that the program content is safe for children's listening. The music is a bright blend of contemporary favorites that has a firm stronghold in office listenership throughout the day.

Randy Wahlberg, who is heavily involved in community activities, is General Manager of Waitt Radio.

GULF POWER COMPANY

ulf Power Company's story begins on the doorstep of the Depression in 1925 when it was organized as a subsidiary of Southeastern Power and Light Company, now Southern Company.

Its objectives were simple: to increase efficiency, to make electricity available to more people, and to encourage appreciation and utilization of electricity.

Serving only Pensacola and Chipley, most homes consumed an average of 287 kilowatt-hours per year and paid 13 cents per kilowatt-hour. Today, residential customers pay about 6.6 cents per kilowatt-hour and consume an average of about 14,000 kilo-watt-hours per year.

A weak, post-World War I economy made Northwest Floridians slow to embrace the untried magic of electricity.

Only after a hurricane devastated Gulf Power's facilities in late 1926 did things change as the company rebuilt and constructed new transmission lines, bringing in cheaper, more reliable power.

Its distribution network began reaching out to farms and small communities throughout the Panhandle.

At the same time, a military presence was beginning to take hold in Northwest Florida. It would eventually employ thousands in Fort Walton Beach, Milton, Panama City and Pensacola.

In the 1940s, Gulf Power began building its own generating plants to meet the new demand.

The post World War II days of the 40's and 50's saw housing developments spring up everywhere. Suddenly, Fort Walton Beach was a modern city and Panama City and Pensacola were more metropolitan.

Theaters and retail stores started using air conditioning, and as electricity prices fell, consumption soared.

Construction methods changed, attitudes shifted and summer was more to be enjoyed than endured. Recruiting workers from the north became easier as hot temperatures and humidity were controlled, at least indoors.

The history of any organization is essentially a history of the communities it serves. On the threshold of its 75th birthday, Gulf Power looks at its history.

This REO "Speedwagon" line truck held the entire Gulf Power Company line crew for the Panama City area. (December, 1926)

During the 1950s, as Gulf Power's customer base doubled, its electricity sales increased six-fold.

The need for new generating facilities resulted in Gulf Power's newest generating plant on North Bay in Bay County being put in service in 1965. The second unit began serving the area in 1967.

In the 1970s, at the height of the energy crisis and inflation, The GoodCents Home program was created by Gulf Power. Now marketed by more than 270 electric utilities nationwide, it is the energy efficiency standard for the housing industry.

Throughout the 1980s and 1990s, Gulf Power has continued to emphasize efficiency by lowering costs while improving reliability and customer service.

Approaching 75 years in Northwest Florida, Gulf Power has achieved the objectives it set back in 1925.

Operating today with 1,300 employees, the company delivers electricity to more than 360,000 customers with a reliability of 99.9 percent.

Gulf Power continues to plan wisely for the future by meeting the energy needs of Northwest Florida, offering among the lowest prices for electricity in Florida and across the nation. Coupling low prices with an unmatched level of service makes for an unbeatable value. It's a relationship that goes back to 1925 and one that Gulf Power Company is committed to through the 21st century and beyond.

CHAPTER X

BUILDING PANAMA CITY BEACH & BAY COUNTY

Real Estate Sales-Development, Property Management and Construction

Condo World

212

Aquatic Realty

213

JRA Architects

214

Century 21 Ryan Realty

215

The St. Joe Company

216

Carr Engineering

217

Carillon Beach

218

CONDO WORLD *Helps Build The Area*

Sylvia Harrison

robably no one on Panama City Beach knows more about condos than Sylvia Harrison.

In the business since 1974, Sylvia has played a part in fourteen different projects ranging from Moondrifter to her newest venture, Ebb Tide.

She started her own business—"Condo World"—with condominiums her forte from sales, management, rentals, decorating and what became her real love—development. She had a personal part in the development and marketing of Moondrifter, Pelican Walk, Sunbird, Aqua Vista and Watercrest.

Her reputation and success attracted other developers and her company played a major role in marketing, sales and management for them, including Sea Chase, Sea Side Villas, Sugar Beach, Continental, Windward and Leeward and Mariner East and West.

To many she is known as "The Condo Queen"—a title

which makes her smile. But if it is apt, she has two Crown Princesses also involved in Panama City Beach condos. One, Helen, has been involved with the company for over 16 years, and runs the rentals and management aspect of the business.

The other, Ann, a licensed Community Association Manager and a licensed Real Estate Salesperson, is active in condominium sales, as well as general real estate. Both have been involved in the business over the years and followed in Sylvia's footsteps.

Coming here from the Adirondack Mountains of New York in 1958, the beach was an abrupt change of scene with which Sylvia Harrison immediately fell in love. She has lived on the white sand and enjoyed the blue-green Gulf waters for many years, embracing with enthusiasm the laid-back beach lifestyle.

Condo world has been part of the astonishing growth of Panama City Beach and Sylvia has clearly established it as the

last word in condo sales and management.

She is a former Chairman of the Resort Council, which she credits with having a most important input in beach development. She diligently pursued the passing of a Bed Tax for the beach, and served on the first Tourist Development Council. She is a member of the PC Beach Chamber of Commerce.

Although her business occupies most of her energies, she is keen to help efforts to beautify and improve the area—like the present work on Thomas Drive—but still finds plenty of time to enjoy her six grandchildren (especially when they visit her at her beach condominium.)

Running a business which caters to vacationers, Snowbirds and would-be residents, Sylvia Harrison has been an important part of this growing community. As condos grow in numbers and popularity, maybe the title "Condo Queen" for her is not too far-fetched!

AQUATIC REALTY, INC.

Aquatic Realty Offers Services for Condos

quatic Realty, Inc. was formed and chartered in 1984 with the specific intent of providing a full range of real estate services for condominium associations and owners.

In spite of a soft declining real estate market in the early years, the company prospered. In 1987, the company contracted with the Aquavista of Panama City Beach Owners Association, Inc. to manage the association and provide an onsite rental program, with continued services into the new millennium.

In 1993, the corporation was sold to new stockholders. The new owners, Jim Holsombake and Gary P. Witham, longtime residents of Panama City, began setting new goals, which included expanding the company.

Holsombake, a native of Birmingham, AL, moved to Panama City with his parents in 1965 and grew up in and around the hospitality and construction industries. He attended Bay High and graduated from Louisiana State University in Baton Rouge. Holsombake is currently involved in construction, hospitality and real estate business on Panama City Beach. He and wife, Marsha have three children, Kristy, Katy and Jamey.

Witham, a graduate of Florida State University where he earned a Bachelor of Science and a degree in Business Administration with a major in real estate, worked in the real estate industry for several years before moving to Panama City in 1983 to accept a position with Nolan & Associates, Inc., as a property appraiser. He started his own appraisal business in 1995. Witham holds a State of Florida Certified General Appraiser license as well as a Broker/Salesperson license. The corporation's broker from 1994 to 1998, he and wife, Suzanne have two children, Gary Paul and Melanie.

On October 4, 1993, the corporation contracted with Charles R. Briard to become the general manager.

Briard moved to Panama City Beach from Union City, GA, a suburb of Atlanta. He retired from commercial construction supervision in 1983 and spent the next ten years as the onsite manager for one of Georgia's largest condominium associations, consisting of 424 units on 38 acres.

Briard is a licensed Community Association Manager (CAM) and has a Broker/Salesperson license in Florida. In 1995, Briard became an equal stockholder in the corporation. He and wife Betty have two children, Richard E. and Malcolm (A Licensed Salesperson with the corporation), and two living grandchildren, Morgan and Devon.

In 1998, the corporation restructured and Betty A. Briard became the Broker and Corporation President.

In 1999, the company purchased new additional office space at Panama City Plaza on Panama City Beach Parkway and opened a new office in mid-April 2000.

**ONCE IN A LIFETIME
HAVE A "SUN" DAY**

PHOTO: CORY CHASE BRIARD

J.R. Arnold High School, only high school on Panama City Beach, opened in August of 2000.

JRA ARCHITECTS, INC.

It was the Spring of 1975—April 1, to be exact—that JRA Architects made its debut. Serving clients in Florida, Georgia, and Alabama, JRA is responsible for projects ranging from schools and public libraries to university buildings, airports, recreation centers, office buildings, state parks, courthouses and correctional facilities. Altogether, JRA has designed 450 projects since 1975 with a combined value of over $1.1 billion dollars.

JRA designed J.R. Arnold High School, which opened for classes the Fall of 2000. The school has a total of 330,000 square feet, consisting of three two-story classroom buildings, a gymnasium, performing arts auditorium, and a food service building that houses the school's hotel/restaurant vocational program. There are offices, athletic facilities, and a media center.

For the Bay County Tourist Development Council, JRA designed a headquarters building that houses the council's tourist information center. The building totals 5,000 square feet and contains the council's administrative offices, conference room, and welcome center. JRA renovated the facade of the adjacent Panama City Beach City Hall Annex to match the architecture of the TDC building.

Over the years, it has been JRA's commitment to education that has been particularly noteworthy. The firm has successfully completed more than 80 projects for public schools, colleges and universities, representing more than 1,600 classrooms. JRA's first middle school, Deerlake in Tallahassee, won an award for innovative design from the National School Boards Association and was featured in *The New York Times*. The Bobby E. Leach Student Recreation Center at Florida State University was honored by *Athletic Business magazine*.

Panama City Beach Visitor Information Center adjacent to City Hall, opened in February of 2000.

The firm worked with Bay District Schools on the renovation and expansion of Mowat Middle School, a project that resulted in the addition of new science labs and renovations to seven buildings on campus. JRA also designed renovations and improvements to Oscar Patterson Elementary School and to Lynn Haven Elementary School. JRA designed the Robert Young Transportation Center for the school system. That facility has garage space, parts storage and offices for staff in charge of the district's bus and vehicle fleet.

For Bay County, the firm designed the Mosquito Control Facility building.

Company President Jim Roberson, AIA, started JRA Architects in Tallahassee, but it wasn't long before the firm's business growth called for a branch office in Columbus, Georgia, then a third location in Panama City. The total staff numbers 30.

Just as the firm has done professionally through architecture, JRA has made it a priority to have a positive impact on the Panama City Beach community. The firm supports the Bay Education Foundation, the local chapter of the American Red Cross and the Gulf Coast Council of the Boy Scouts of America. JRA has helped sponsor various charity events, and

has devoted time and energy to such organizations as the Economics Club of Florida, Future Farmers of America and the Chamber of Commerce.

Jim Roberson attributes JRA's growth to a similar commitment to provide the best professional services possible to clients, whether the project they're planning is $50,000 or $50 million. Clients know best what they want, so in that sense, they are the true architects on a project, he believes.

CENTURY 21 RYAN REALTY

Tribute to an Unforgettable Lady

elissa Ryan, President of Century 21 Ryan Realty says she was inspired to open a real estate company on the beach by a very special lady.

"When Mary Sue Brock suggested that I open an office on the beach, and then said she would work with me, there was no doubt in my mind," Melissa recalls.

Mary Sue Brock

"Mary Sue was a lady who, as a realtor, was admired and respected by all who knew her. She was the most noble and gracious, pure and lovely individual and friend a person could possibly have," Melissa says. "She inspired everyone to give their very best. Quality Service was her personal motto. The lessons she taught and the traditions she passed along will continue to inspire us and live in our hearts. She was blessed with many talents, one being a messenger of God."

Century 21 Ryan Realty has grown from a small office to a very large real estate company located at 8212 Thomas Drive. "Having my daughter Katie in the business has been a blessing to me," says Melissa.

Melissa and Katie Ryan

Other members of the family, notably Melissa's husband, Mike, son Michael and daughter Natalie offer support and advice along with the team of caring, quality individuals within the company. "We are fortunate to have some of the best associates and staff in the business," stated Melissa. "We give thanks to God for all we have accomplished"

THE ST. JOE COMPANY *in Northwest Florida*

he roaring twenties conjure up images of flappers and bathtub gin, gangsters and industrial robber barons. It was also a frenzied period of real estate speculation and land deals, with moneyed investors looking for new frontiers.

While the rest of his family was building 50-room summer "cottages" in chic watering holes like Saratoga and Newport, Rhode Island, one well-known multimillionaire, Alfred Irenee duPont had his sights set on the virginal Gulf Coast of Florida, a vast, undiscovered wilderness far from the gilded palaces of his peers.

Considered a maverick by his Wilmington, Delaware family, Alfred duPont was originally the head of the famed DuPont Chemical Manufacturing Company. In 1921 he wed the former Jessie Ball and soon employed his brother-in-law, Edward Ball, as manager of his many enterprises.

Two years later, as the duPonts—in white linen and straw hats—cruised in a yacht down Florida's Atlantic coast, Ball was sent on a mission. "Mr. DuPont had been watching the development of the Florida real estate boom," Ball recalled, "and it was partly as a result of his suggestion and partly my curiosity that made me want to see Northwest Florida."

At the time, the paved highway ended at Lake City, 60 miles west of Jacksonville and resumed at Milton, 20 miles from Pensacola. DuPont and Ball had two goals: buy land and build roads to make the land accessible. Ball's first purchase was St. James Island in Franklin County and East Peninsula on St. Andrews Bay, in Bay County, followed by the acquisition of 40,000 acres in Walton County. To open up the region, the men backed the Gulf Coast Highway Association, which led to construction of, among other projects, U.S. 98 through Panama City.

In 1933—having escaped the Wall Street financial crash, which bankrupted many of his peers, and sent investors scurrying—duPont bought the town of Port St. Joe. He already owned 280,000 acres in Northwest Florida, making him one of the largest private landowners in the state.

DuPont died in 1935. A year later the duPont estate founded The St. Joe Paper Company. By the late 1970's, St. Joe Paper Company owned one million acres of timberland in Florida and 50,000 acres in southern Georgia.

The same unwavering love of the land and commitment to the economic potential of Northwest Florida remains. The St. Joe Company is a direct descendant of St. Joe Paper and the living legacy of duPont and Ball's vision.

Development of the land holdings assembled by their partnership is now the core mission of the company, which reorganized in 1997 and no longer owns its paper manufacturing operations. St. Joe projects—new communities of vacation and second homes like WaterColor in south Walton County, and recreation and entertainment venues like Pier Park in Panama City Beach—are opening the northwest to newcomers as surely as Ed Ball did,

traveling those dusty roads in the 1920's.

At the turn of another century, the migration of retiring baby boomers will write a new chapter in the history of this region of Florida, beyond what Ball imagined.

The St. Joe Company is playing a key role in this economic boom by unlocking the intrinsic value of the Northwest Florida landscape. From Pier Park to WaterColor, St. Joe developments are evidence of the area's emerging era of popularity and prosperity. Northwest Florida's huge remaining tracts of unspoiled land—held off the real estate market for more than half a century by St. Joe—guarantee that the environmentally protected region will become an alternative to palm trees and crowded beaches.

Just as one multimillionaire had in mind.

CARR ENGINEERING & CONSTRUCTION, INC.

Michael V. Carr

Carr Offers Many Services

 ichael V. Carr, a certified general contractor and registered professional engineer, founded Carr Engineering & Construction, Inc., in June 1991. Carr is a West Point graduate who holds a Master's degree in facilities engineering. He has worked as a project engineer for the Corps of Engineers and as the project engineer for the Germany and Italy Pavilions at Epcot Center.

Carr came to Panama City from Jacksonville where he managed a $13-million expansion of the Gator Bowl that was completed in a 10-month period. Locally, he was appointed as project manager for Phoenix Construction Services in Lynn Haven and managed multiple projects throughout the Southeast.

In 1991, he opened Carr Engineering & Construction, Inc., in Panama City and then, in 1994, built a new 3,000-square-foot office complex in Panama City Beach on Panama City Beach Parkway. Services offered by Carr Engineering & Construction, Inc., include civil and structural engineering for projects of all sizes and complexity, which focus on site design and structural integrity of buildings located in a Coastal Hurricane Zone and general construction of residential, commercial and industrial facilities.

Carr Engineering & Construction, Inc., also offers complete design-build services, including feasibility and planning, design, permitting and construction. The design-build concept is geared to saving the client time and money by eliminating the need to deal with the numerous professionals traditionally involved in completing a project, facilitating transition of the project from phase to phase, and allowing the earliest possible occupancy.

Construction services include construction of custom homes, condominiums, commercial buildings and grounds, structural repairs and waterproofing system installation. Carr Engineering & Construction, Inc. was instrumental in rebuilding coastal structures across the Panhandle following Hurricane Opal in 1995.

Construction projects have been completed for Bay and Okaloosa County School Boards; U.S. Postal Service; Coastal Systems Station; Pensacola Naval Air Station; Tyndall Air Force Base; Eglin Air Force Base; U.S. Coast Guard; Hurlburt Field; Gulf Coast Community College; Bay, Santa Rosa, Washington and Calhoun Counties; City of Port St. Joe; Panama City; and Panama City Beach, as well as numerous commercial projects throughout Northwest Florida.

The skilled craftsmen of Carr's Construction team are experts in concrete structural repairs and waterproofing systems. The harsh climate of Northwest Florida wreaks havoc on concrete structures within a few miles of the Gulf of Mexico. Sea salts (chlorides) and water penetration into concrete rusts the reinforcing steel embedded in the concrete and eventually causes cracking of the concrete.

Carr's specialists can expertly repair the steel and concrete and apply a specially designed waterproofing system to protect structures from water and chloride penetration in the future.

The success of Carr Engineering & Construction, Inc. can be attributed to its personnel's dedication to quality and customer satisfaction and is exemplified by the number of repeat clients and multiple contracts awarded to the firm. The company has been instrumental in the growth of the area and has definitely become an integral part of the community.

CARILLON BEACH
Truly A World Apart

n Europe, a properly maintained carillon (French for bell tower) is considered the reflection of a vibrant community. That tradition is carried on at Carillon Beach. Located along the Gulf Coast on U.S. Highway 98 at Phillips Inlet on the western edge of Bay County, Carillon Beach contains 104 acres with 3,800 feet of crystal white beach.

The William D. Biggs family has carefully planned the entire gated community.

So cautiously, in fact, the land lay dormant for years until the family was certain their creation would serve as an ideal village for its residents and guests.

To blend the relaxed and elegant atmosphere with numerous amenities including seven dune walks, a 12-acre fresh water lake, three swim-

ming pools, a town hall and meetinghouse and a commercial market area, the Biggs turned to noted New Orleans architect, Lloyd Vogt. An expert in neo-traditional communities, Vogt's master plan envisioned an environment that featured spacious verandas, porch swings, gazebos and picket fences, all to recapture the small town feeling from years gone by.

"Carillon Beach is a unique development designed with people instead of the automobile as the primary element," said Vogt. "This provides the perfect balance of home, community, environment and culture while living by the sea." Streets in Carillon connect residents with strategically located themed pavilions, which honor the environment, children, wellness and the arts. Neighbors visit on front porches or relax in the solitude

found at the environmental pavilion while their children play on the beach and swim in the pools.

Meticulous details are found in the community's strict code governing everything from building materials to landscaping. Homeowners are able to design a home with flourishing touches that express individual taste yet blends into the fabric of the neighborhood.

Set on Lake Carillon is approximately 40,000 square feet of retail shops, offices and a gourmet restaurant. Condominiums above all of the retail establishments further create a sense of community while offering breathtaking vistas of the Lake and Gulf of Mexico. These, together with spacious green areas provide residents and visitors alike with the excitement and comfort of a working village.

For cuisine never before enjoyed on the Gulf Coast, Chef Paul's at Carillon Beach, owned and operated by Chef Paul Albrecht (formerly of Pano's and Paul's in Atlanta), provides a casual, yet sophisticated dining experience featuring eclectic gourmet and seafood cuisine.

The natural elements of the beautiful Gulf of Mexico inspired the interior design of the restaurant and food shop. Limestone, mahogany, tumbled marble and exotic granites were used as a rich background for the intense palette of colors found in the furnishings, carpet and artwork.

For those wishing a casual picnic on the beach, a catered dinner in their home, or an elegant reception to conclude the wedding of their dreams, Chef Paul's can provide the perfect solution.

Carillon Beach...tranquil and serene...beautiful and intimate...exciting and fun...is truly a world apart.

CARILLON BEACH: A World Apart

Before the days of back porch barbeques and privacy fences, old-fashioned homes were built to encourage neighbor interaction. Large verandas, porch swings, gazebos and picket fences served as welcome mats for all visitors.

Today, Carillon Beach, a 104-acre community along U.S. Highway 98 in Panama City Beach, next to Phillips inlet, has been carefully designed to recapture that sense of social togetherness.

Carillon Market

Mix the style of New Orleans, the merchandise of an upscale boutique and world-famous cuisine, and you have the makings of a phenomenal market-Carillon Market. The first phase of Carillon Market is complete and now houses Carillon Beach's real estate office and four shops. Including Beachwalk Birkenstock, Gidgets, Bungalows and Sterling Shores.

Surrounded by cobblestone streets and gas lights, Carillon Market will offer visitors a tranquil setting in keeping with the style at Carillon Beach. As with similar developments, the shops in Carillon Market will be a focal point in the community. Each of the buildings will have townhouse-style residences above the shops, which offer views of Lake Carillon and the Gulf.

Chef Paul Albrecht

Chef Paul Albrecht, formerly of Pano's and Paul's of Atlanta, brings casual, yet sophisticated dining to the Florida panhandle with the opening of Chef Paul's at Carillon Beach. For an exquisite dining experience, the restaurant, located on the second floor at Carillon Beach, offers a menu featuring the finest seasonal fish, shellfish, rack of lamb, fowls and those famous fried lobster tails. The Chef's very special attention and high standards, for which he is famous, are given to each detail. The restaurant will, indeed, add an important culinary touch to the Carillon Beach lifestyle.

Architect

To create Carillon Beach's master plan, developers William Biggs, Sr. and his son, William, Jr. turned to noted New Orleans architect Lloyd Vogt, who governed each home's site placement, as well as materials, proportions, colors, fences, roof pitches and outbuildings. Having been in the business for over 22 years, Vogt has thoroughly researched the vernacular traditions of the Gulf Coast environment.

Vogt's award-winning work has been featured in several national publications. Trained at the Fontainebleau School of Art and Architecture in France and Louisiana State University, he oversees the Vogt Group/Architects in New Orleans. Vogt has taught at Tulane University and at the Louisiana Design Institute. In addition, he has lectured throughout the Southeast on a variety of architectural topics.

Vogt's master plan creates an aesthetically pleasing place that is convenient and functional. The development also features a Meeting House; a bell tower, where a carillonneur performs concerts; a beach clubhouse and many other features.

Carillon Beach is nine miles east of Seaside on U.S. Highway 98 and six miles west of Highway 79 in Panama City Beach. Gulf, lake and interior home sites are available. Currently over 100 homes are in the community. Visit the real estate office, open daily from 10:00 a.m. to 5:00 p.m. in Carillon Market. For additional information on Carillon Beach, call 850-234-5600 or visit the web site at www.carillon-beach.com.

HISTORICAL INDEX